Professional Accountability in Social Care and Health

Creating Integrated Services – titles in the series

Professional Accountability in Social Care and Health

Challenging Unacceptable Practice and its Management

ROGER KLINE
and
MICHAEL PRESTON-SHOOT

Los Angeles | London | New Delhi
Singapore | Washington DC

www.learningmatters.co.uk

Los Angeles | London | New Delhi
Singapore | Washington DC

www.learningmatters.co.uk

Learning Matters
An imprint of SAGE Publications Ltd
1 Oliver's Yard
55 City Road
London EC1Y 1SP

SAGE Publications Inc.
2455 Teller Road
Thousand Oaks, California 91320

SAGE Publications India Pvt Ltd
B 1/I 1 Mohan Cooperative Industrial Area
Mathura Road
New Delhi 110 044

SAGE Asia-Pacific Pte Ltd
3 Church Street
#10–04 Samsung Hub
Singapore 049483

Editor: Luke Block
Production controller: Chris Marke
Project management: Swales & Willis Ltd,
Exeter, Devon
Marketing manager: Tamara Navaratnam
Cover design: Code 5 Design
Typeset by: Swales & Willis Ltd, Exeter, Devon
Printed by: TJ International Ltd, Padstow,
Cornwall

Library of Congress Control Number:
2011945610

British Library Cataloguing in Publication data

A catalogue record for this book is available
from the British Library

ISBN 978 0 85725 847 2
ISBN 978 0 85725 689 8 (pbk)

MIX
Paper from
responsible sources
FSC
www.fsc.org   FSC® C013056

Contents

About the authors

Roger Kline has been a trade union official for 24 years working for eight unions in health, social care, education, airlines, the voluntary and private sectors. He has represented staff at every level on many of the issues discussed in this book and written extensive guidance and developed training on professional accountability, how to raise concerns, organising at work, health and safety, and how to challenge discrimination and bullying at work. He has represented whistle blowers from students to very senior managers. He is currently a member of the Social Work Reform Board, and has recently become a special adviser to Public Concern at Work.

Michael Preston-Shoot is Professor of Social Work and Dean of the Faculty of Health and Social Sciences at the University of Bedfordshire. He is an Independent Chair of a Local Safeguarding Children Board and a Local Safeguarding Adults Board. He is one of the founding editors of the journal *Ethics and Social Welfare*, having previously been editor of *Social Work Education* and Managing Editor of the *European Journal of Social Work*. He has specialised as a social work academic in researching and teaching social work law. His most recent research and writing also spans the governance of safeguarding adults and children, and adults who self-neglect. He is an elected Academician of the Academy of Social Sciences and a past chair of the Joint University Council Social Work Education Committee.

Acknowledgements

We would like to thank a group of critical friends with whom we met or corresponded on several occasions to ensure the book addressed and adequately responded to issues faced by practitioners, managers and their advocates. They are: Tina Mackay, Sarah Carpenter, Gerard Looker, Robert Carter, Claire Dent, Russ Escritt, John Bamford and Yvonne Cleary. Sadly Tina Mackay died whilst this book was being completed.

We acknowledge the anonymous contributions of individual practitioners and managers who have shared their lived experience of work with us and sometimes relied on our advocacy, support and advice. Many of their experiences have helped to shape the motivation behind this book and the examples used within it.

We remain grateful for the support of our work colleagues, particularly Lesley Baillie, Sharon Black, Judith Chappell and Amanda Thorpe at the University of Bedfordshire, who commented on drafts of several chapters.

Finally we express our continued thanks to our families: Naledi, Laura and Leah, and Suzy, Hannah and Sebastian.

Introduction

All of us will depend, at some points in our lives, on the services of health and social care professionals. How health and social care professionals respond will be crucial to our health and well-being. How we respond will depend, partly, on the degree to which we feel confident in relying upon their knowledge and skills, in trusting that they will behave ethically and lawfully, and in sensing that the environment in which they are working is open, accountable, safe and supportive. All of us will have images of what characterises a sound professional encounter, in which the relationship is personalised and shaped by respect, dignity and concern.

All of us who work in the social and healthcare professions will have come to appreciate what differentiates valued as opposed to unsettling places of work. It may revolve around the degree to which workloads feel manageable and the support received to develop our preparedness to meet challenges. It may centre on the degree to which we feel our advocacy for those with whom we work is valued, enabling us to make a real difference in terms of service development and the provision of quality care and support. We may be exercised by how to raise concerns, for example about an organisation's attention to equality, human rights and respect, or by whether to request or share information that might otherwise remain confidential. Essentially, how we experience particular places of work may depend on the degree to which it is possible to profess the values, knowledge and skills for which we have trained and been employed, and to exercise in full our duty of care towards those with whom we work.

Many of us who work in and around the social and healthcare professions had personal and professional motivations for engaging with a particular career choice. Particular ethical commitments may well have been important, coupled with building relationships through which valued outcomes, centred on health and well-being, might be achieved. The degree to which these original and ongoing motivations and inspirations have proved compatible with how regulatory authorities and employing organisations envisage professional accountability is a theme that runs through the book. You will be invited to consider the complexities and contrasts between expressions of professional values, knowledge and skills, employer requirements and expectations, and the outcomes of practice and its management. This is why the book's title not only draws readers into thinking about how to conceptualise, assert and maintain professional accountability for their work, but also alerts them to the unacceptable face of some practice, and its management, and the importance of thinking through how to conceive and advocate for quality standards.

Many social workers, social care and healthcare practitioners, doctors, youth workers and staff from other professional backgrounds, maintain high standards of professionalism, often in stressful, demanding, challenging and sometimes frightening circumstances. Drawing on their values and ethical commitments, the legal rules, their knowledge and their practice skills, they navigate through difficult dilemmas, concerns and issues that comprise their daily lived experience of work. The conscientious approach of many social workers, frequently when overworked and lacking the resources to practise as they would like, has attracted positive judicial comment (*Re F* [2008]), as has the fact that many departments with social services responsibilities perform valuable work that demonstrates dedication, skill and care in meeting people's complex needs (*Re X (Emergency Protection Orders)* [2006]; *Re B* [2007]; *Re D* [2008]).

The independent inquiry into events at the Mid Staffordshire NHS Foundation Trust (Francis, 2010) reported that many staff did express concerns about the standard of care being provided, and that a substantial minority of members of the public who contacted the inquiry team offered positive comments about the care they or their relatives had received.

An investigation into a mental health NHS trust found that service users had mixed views about the care they received, with some reporting positive experiences (Care Quality Commission (CQC), 2009a).

The Social Work Task Force (2009a, b) noted that some service users and carers had reported having received outstanding support, although others had described more mixed experiences, and that examples had been found of excellent practice, innovative work and strong management in action.

The CQC (2011) reported examples of older people being treated with respect and given excellent care, although it also criticised situations where care needs had not been assessed, where tissue viability had not been properly treated, where dignity had not been shown, and where older people had been discharged inappropriately.

In her review of child protection, Munro (2011) commented positively on how the receptiveness of some managers and practitioners to feedback from the front line and about the experiences of some children and families was helping to improve practice. Some social work practice, the review found, was excellent, with practitioners from various professions having a positive impact on young people's lives by spending time with them and focusing clearly on their needs.

A serious case review into the death of a woman with physical disabilities (Flynn, 2011) noted the determined and considerable efforts that health and social care practitioners had made to agree and deliver a care plan that she would accept. The coroner in this case is reported as having expressed satisfaction that the right questions were asked and available options considered by senior managers.

In another serious case review, concerned with abuse and neglect in a residential care home (Sheather, 2011), the investigation that eventually concluded with a successful criminal prosecution was triggered by staff who raised concerns. The report identifies occasions when different professionals, including district nurses, GPs and community pharmacists, took responsibility and shared their concerns.

Research, inquiry and practitioner evidence, which this book explores in detail, also reveals a different side to professional practice, however, namely instances where individual practitioners and managers, and indeed organisations, have failed to take professional action in response to concerns, or have failed to act lawfully, ethically and/or care-fully.

Sometimes this disregard, arguably of people's humanity, has been found in the relationship between employers and employees, or in the interface between registered practitioners and the regulatory or licensing authority.

Walker v *Northumberland County Council* [1995] is one example where employers failed to act when a social work team leader was experiencing psychiatric and physical ill-health as a result of how work was being managed.

Social workers have been reinstated onto their professional register when the relevant care council has been found to have acted disproportionately because employers failed to provide adequate management support, which is essential to prevent good practice from breaking down (*LA* v *General Social Care Council* [2007]; *Forbes* v *General Social Care Council* [2008]). Similarly, Margaret Haywood was reinstated by the Nursing and Midwifery Council, which had originally struck her name from the professional register, following high court intervention. She received instead a one-year caution from the regulator in response to how she had raised concerns about poor care standards.

Sometimes disregard, or absence of dignity and evidence of abuse or neglect, has focused on the care given to patients, service users and their carers.

The Mid Staffordshire inquiry found an appalling catalogue of clinical errors and failures in basic nursing care, resulting in denials of dignity and unnecessary suffering. Staff who raised concerns about care standards had been ignored. Hospital senior managers and the board had given insufficient attention to the maintenance of professional standards, and had failed to support staff adequately through appraisals, supervision and continuing professional development.

In one mental health NHS trust, an investigation found staff working in difficult conditions, compounded by competing priorities and nationally set performance targets (CQC, 2009a). This investigation concluded that the trust had tolerated mediocre and sometimes low care standards. People, it observed, deserved better, namely safe care that promoted their health and well-being and protected them from harm.

An inquiry into incidents at another NHS trust (Cantrill et al., 2010) was concerned that evidence of verbal hostility towards and unacceptable treatment of patients and staff was not followed up. Here too there were incidences where patients' requests for help were delayed or ignored, clinical supervision and staff appraisal systems were lacking, there was a shortage of staff, and the available skill mixes on wards were not meeting the needs that patients were presenting.

A serious case review into the care and treatment of older people in a care home (Sheather, 2011) found that the registered manager, who was also a registered nurse, broke the law and failed to uphold her code of professional conduct. Some staff and relatives did not appear well-informed about how to raise concerns about professional conduct and care failures. Respectful uncertainty (Laming, 2003), the inquiring and challenging curiosity that should characterise interactions between professionals entering an organisation and its staff, in this instance a care home, had also been lost.

Sometimes abuse and neglect is exposed by the media, as in television documentaries about the care and treatment of learning disabled people.

Public Concern at Work (2011) reported that the highest number of calls to its helpline came from the care sector, with around one-third of callers stating that their initial attempts to raise concerns around practice standards within their employing organisations had been ignored, mishandled or denied. In one adult protection research inquiry (Manthorpe et al, 2007), incidents of neglect and mistreatment by residential care staff were uncovered, together with a lack of attention to people's basic needs, and a negative, even hostile, attitude towards complainants. Flynn (2006) concludes that there has been insufficient attention towards inhumane treatment and the endurance of inflexible and ineffective procedures, and that some managers have failed to appreciate just how damaging or impoverished their organisations' services have become.

In two reports, Laming (2003, 2009) found that social work personnel were frequently working under immense pressure in a context characterised by poor supervision, high caseloads, insufficient resources and low morale. We add, additionally, that managers often demonstrated unrealistic expectations towards staff, especially newly qualified or early career practitioners. The Social Work Task Force (2009a) also found that some services were experiencing severe pressures that were threatening high-quality work. These included staff shortages, high workloads and high eligibility thresholds for services, together with performance management priorities and targets which were unhelpfully emphasising quantity and processes over quality and outcomes. The Social Work Task Force's final report (2009b) urged employers to hold frank and open discussions with frontline practitioners and managers about the reality of practice and how to improve services. Munro's review (2011) also found that the bureaucratic aspects of child protection work had become too dominant, and that too often organisational cultures had stifled professional expertise. We argue, additionally, that the dominance of expected compliance with procedures has undermined practitioners' and managers' legal and ethical literacy.

This evidence is disturbing. These experiences and the structures which produce and maintain them are quite simply wrong (Sercombe, 2010). However, how should practitioners, managers and those responsible for governance through council committees, local safeguarding children boards, local safeguarding adults boards and NHS trust boards begin when seeking to uphold the highest standards of care? How should they respond when it emerges that individuals or the organisations of which they are a part are neglecting their duty of care?

This book is concerned with providing guidance for practitioners and managers across the health and social professions on how to maintain accountable professionalism and ethical and legal literacy in the face of tricky 'what if?' situations. Its focus is on daily practice, with its challenges, realities, dilemmas and uncertainties. This book has been triggered by a shared sense of outrage in response to breakdowns in the standards of care provided to patients, service users and their families, and to how some practitioners and managers have been treated by the organisations that have employed them, ostensibly for the values that shape their professional behaviour, the knowledge that informs their practice, and the skills with which they interact with those they are asked to serve.

We share a mutual interest in the interface between law, ethics and practice. One of us (Roger Kline) has had a trade union career which has often involved representing practitioners in health and social care organisations. Roger Kline has supported staff who have blown the whistle on poor practice and/or who have found themselves in conflict with their employers. He has published practical guides for healthcare and social care professionals on upholding their duty of care (Kline, 2003, 2009). One of us (Michael Preston-Shoot) has researched and written widely on the interface between law and professional practice, and on how qualifying education for professional practice may or may not prepare students for the legal and ethical challenges they will encounter, both as students and once qualified. This has included an exploration of how social workers might uphold their practice values and standards in the face of an employer's expectations, and whether recent inquiries into social work practice have adequately addressed the organisational context in which that practice takes place (Preston-Shoot, 2000, 2010a). As an independent chair of both a local safeguarding children board and a safeguarding adults board, Michael Preston-Shoot has commissioned serious case reviews and engaged directly with how individual organisations and multi-agency partnerships might deliver quality standards.

Our parallel professional preoccupations initially came together in evidence to a House of Commons Select Committee inquiry into social work training (Preston-Shoot and Kline, 2009). That submission highlighted research evidence across social and healthcare services that organisations were attaching greater importance to agency procedures and targets than to legal and moral duties. It demonstrated how resource pressures could undermine legislative requirements, neglect service users' needs, and distort compliance with ethical and practice codes. It charted the experiences of some whistle blowers and made recommendations for how a duty of care could be better underpinned by a training and regulatory framework. The concerns and proposals within that submission reappear and have been considerably expanded here, in a shared concern that the workforce across the health and social professions should know what they have a right to expect and be supported to recognise and deliver good practice.

Chapters 1–4 are quite theoretical in tone, and explore research, practitioner and service user evidence to understand how high standards of professional practice are maintained but also sometimes undermined. The book begins with a presentation of the research, inquiry and practitioner evidence that reveals occasions when practitioners and/or their employing organisations have departed from best practice and failed to uphold the highest professional standards. Chapters 2 and 3 then explore the nature and meaning of accountability, and lay out relevant legal rules and details from codes of practice and conduct for health and social care staff. Chapter 4 concludes with a review of the knowledge and skills that should help practitioners and managers address challenging dilemmas and issues within organisational life and maintain their duty of care in respect of those with whom they work.

Chapters 5–10 are essentially practical, offering advice and guidance to practitioners and managers in the social and healthcare professions. These chapters explore tricky 'what if?' issues. They provide guidance for readers, both as individual practitioners and, where appropriate, as a collective team or department.

The book will appeal to, and has been written for, students and newly qualified practitioners in healthcare (including medicine) and in the social professions, including but not restricted to youth work, social work and social care. It is also relevant to experienced and expert practitioners and managers, particularly those with supervisory responsibilities, who wish to refresh their knowledge and skill set. Staff teaching on qualifying and post-registration courses should find the book's content informative when planning modules concerned with law, ethics, working in and understanding organisations, supervision and practice teaching. The book's importance derives from evidence of practice falling short of appropriately high professional standards, coupled with a challenging political and economic environment. Indeed, the current political and economic context makes the book's theme and contribution both timely and highly topical, whilst continuing disclosures of abuse in residential and nursing care highlight the ongoing importance of finding ways to help staff maintain their duty of care. Moreover, there are no books currently that link the theory of accountable professionalism with evidence of the erosion of ethical, lawful and good practice and with skills for addressing scenarios which challenge best practice.

Each chapter begins with a set of objectives and a short introduction identifying how the chapter is laid out. Exercises and research tasks are used so that readers can engage actively with the book's contents and so that we, as authors, advocates and educators, can communicate directly with those who are interested in working through the ideas being presented. Bullet points summarise key points for learning and for practice. Where appropriate, chapters conclude with pointers to further reading.

This book considers health and social care together because, whilst they are distinct services, they also share many common characteristics, particularly when considering the duty of care and professional accountability. They have many challenges in common, services and their regulation increasingly overlap, and the architecture of professional registration and accountability is similar. Each example may be specific to a particular profession or service, but the lessons to be drawn should have resonance across both sectors and all professions.

Chapters consider the responsibilities of all those working in social care and health, from students to senior managers. Although the book primarily considers the position of those employed by health and social care organisations, attention is also given to the position of students, trainees, agency staff and contractors.

On terminology, the word 'patient' is used when referring to services provided by health-care practitioners, and the phrase 'service user' is employed when the discussion covers the social professions. The latter phrase is also used when a general reference is made to anyone in receipt of services from either health or social care professionals, as below in the discussion of ethical and legal literacy. The conceptual analysis, including discussion of legal and ethical frameworks, covers all four nations within the UK, except where specifically stated.

Finally, reference has already been made to the idea of ethical and legal literacy, and it reappears in subsequent chapters as a co-ordinating theme. In essence, ethical and legal literacy refers to a distillation of knowledge, understanding, skills and values that enables practitioners and their managers to connect relevant legal rules with the professional priorities and objectives of ethical practice (Preston-Shoot and McKimm, 2011b). It entails being able to navigate the complexities of doing things right (knowledgeable use of legal rules), doing right things (law's interface with values), and right thinking (engaging with human rights) (Braye and Preston-Shoot, 2006), and being able to communicate and apply an emerging understanding of any situation to colleagues, other professionals and service users and carers.

Website materials

You can find useful practical materials linked to this book on the Sage/Learning Matters website. Point your browser to **www.uk.sagepub.com/books/Book238690** (please note that this is case sensitive), and click on the 'sample materials' tab. Available on the site are:

- some of the practical resources referred to in the book, such as model letters and a sample staff survey;

- links to useful organisations and references;

- occasional updates on statutory changes and important case law;

- occasional updates on relevant policy developments.

Table of cases

Chapter 1
Cause for concern?

> **OBJECTIVES**
>
> By the end of this chapter, you should have an understanding of:
>
> - Findings from various types of inquiry into unethical and/or unlawful practice in health and social care organisations, and into the management and regulation of that practice.
>
> - Ways in which practitioners, managers and their organisations have failed to uphold their duty of care towards service users.
>
> - Ways in which practice has departed significantly from standards on how values, knowledge and skills should contribute to decision making and intervention.
>
> - Obstacles which might have prevented the learning from such incidents becoming embedded in practice.

Introduction

Why should we be concerned with questions of professional accountability? Can we not rely on social and healthcare practitioners and managers, and the organisations that employ them, to uphold professional values and standards, and to provide services with care and skill, founded upon up-to-date knowledge? Not always, apparently.

People appear concerned about the quality and safety of local health services (NHS Future Forum, 2011). Phair and Heath (2010) remark that 10 per cent of referrals to the Nursing and Midwifery Council (NMC) professional conduct committee in 2007–08 were for neglect of basic care of older people, including failures in respect of medication management, appropriate discharge procedures, assistance after falls and meeting core needs.

Sercombe (2010) indicates the type of problems which may occur in youth work, including sexual exploitation of young people, misuse of agency resources, and buying or selling of drugs. He also cautions that the organisational and political environment may be unsympathetic towards youth work practice, managers may prefer conformity to advocacy from youth workers, and agencies can become susceptible to corruption, rationalisation and self-deception. Preston-Shoot (2000) gives examples from social workers where organisations have acted unlawfully and/or unethically.

Preston-Shoot and Kline (2009) highlight the pressure on managers and how provision is adjusted to inadequate funding, often at the expense of considering legal rules and accountability. Across the social and healthcare professions, greater importance may have been attached to meeting financial and other targets, and adhering to agency procedures and customs, than to legal and moral duties (Braye et al., 2007; Healthcare Commission, 2007a; Preston-Shoot, 2010a).

ACTIVITY 1.1

Access the Commission for Local Administration (Local Government Ombudsman; LGO) web pages (www.lgo.org.uk) and read the latest social services summaries. Alternatively or additionally, access the Health Service Ombudsman website (www.ombudsman.org.uk) and explore the latest investigations into complaints about NHS provision. List what you consider to be the key findings and themes, and consider their implications for professional practice.

ACTIVITY 1.2

Take an organisation with which you are familiar. Ask yourself:

- *What might it be like to be a service user or patient there?*

- *How effective might be the systems for ensuring that patients or service users receive quality care and are appropriately safeguarded?*

- *What are the strengths and weaknesses of the organisation?*

Investigations into standards in healthcare settings

The Patients Association (2011) has reported examples of exemplary care given with genuine compassion. However, it has also detailed distressing accounts of poor nursing and medical care, which were not isolated incidents but indicators of a systemic problem in the NHS.

The government (Department of Health (DH), 2011a) has recognised that people using NHS provision have had variable experiences. Inquiries into serious breakdowns in patient care consistently report a range of organisational, cultural and systemic factors, which together impact on the ability of services to ensure that provision is safe and patients are protected from harm (Care Quality Commission (CQC), 2009a; Cantrill et al., 2010).

A review of standards of midwifery practice (Healthcare Commission, 2008) uncovered concerns about inadequate staffing levels, poor team work, and poor communication by staff with women. It pointed to wide variations between trusts concerning women's reported levels of satisfaction with the care they received. One-fifth of trusts were not performing well, with criticism of doctors and midwives for not engaging in continuing professional development, for inadequate continuity of care, not adhering to recommendations regarding antenatal care practice, and poor communication and support post delivery.

Equally, referrals about individual practitioners' fitness for practice have risen. The NMC (2011a) has reported double the number of cases considered by its investigating committee in 2011 compared with 2010, and almost an equivalent rise in cases referred to a conduct and competence committee for hearing.

Standards of patient care

Inquiries have found examples of poor patient care. Patients' requests for help have been ignored or responses delayed, communication with patients and their relatives has been poor, doctors have not questioned the treatments being given, and the skills, for instance assessment skills, to inform clinical interventions have been lacking. Attitudes have been experienced as uncaring, basic care has been neglected and discharges have been inappropriate. Patients have been left in soiled sheets, medication has not been given on time, medical reviews of patients have been insufficiently frequent, and infection-control practices have been insufficiently promoted and monitored (Kennedy, 2001; Healthcare Commission, 2007a; Cantrill et al., 2010; Francis, 2010).

One inquiry – that by Francis (2010) – is not unusual in the list of areas where practice standards had become unacceptably low. The Francis report details failings in respect of continence care, falls, hygiene, nutrition and hydration, pressure area care, cleanliness and infection control, patient privacy and dignity, delayed and inaccurate diagnosis, patient involvement in decision making and information sharing, and discharge management. Assessment and communication practices were inconsistent and poor. People were left in pain and distress.

Lack of management oversight and action

Systems to monitor the supply and administration of drugs, the management of pain, the adequacy of ward areas, and staffing in terms of available skill mix and numbers of doctors and nurses on duty have been insufficiently robust to prevent malpractice or risks to patients. Changes in key personnel have also meant that action plans to secure improvements have drifted (Kennedy, 2001; Healthcare Commission, 2007a; CQC, 2009a; Cantrill et al., 2010; Francis, 2010).

Organisational culture

Inquiries often criticise organisations for being isolated, reactive, closed, and unwilling to acknowledge that there might have been errors (Kennedy, 2001; Healthcare Commission, 2007a; Francis, 2010). One review, for example, by Marsden and Mechen (2008), found no evidence that doctors and nurses were sufficiently concerned to escalate issues within the hospital, including to the board, and that the trust was not predisposed to seek help with its problems. Another inquiry (Francis, 2010) found evidence of denial rather than self-criticism, and an organisation that had accepted poor standards of conduct and been unwilling to use governance and disciplinary procedures to tackle poor performance. The pressure to meet externally imposed performance targets, including for financial savings, is seen to have diverted attention from clinical issues and delayed recognition of breakdowns in patient care (Healthcare Commission, 2007a; Marsden and Mechen, 2008; Francis, 2010).

Research has demonstrated the significant improvements to patient health outcomes, service quality and satisfaction, and to staff health and well-being, from a supportive collegial working environment (Borrill et al., 2001). However, too many organisations persist with hierarchical and authoritarian leadership. Here staff may believe that employers do not value their health and well-being. High levels of bullying and harassment prevent the questioning of practices and challenging of decisions, and impact negatively on stress and mental health (Boorman, 2009; Santry, 2009; Peters et al., 2011; *Bowen* v *Hywel Dda NHS Trust*, 2010).

Training and support

Low attendance at mandatory training, and the scarcity of advice, for instance from pharmacists, have been noted (Healthcare Commission, 2007a; CQC, 2009a). Staff may also not have been trained to keep records appropriately or been given sufficient time for continuing professional development, clinical supervision and appraisal (Kennedy, 2001; Cantrill et al., 2010).

Clinical governance and audit

Inquiries have found that clinical governance has been insufficiently embedded, and that monitoring and audit systems have failed to identify problems and risks or to follow through with constructing, implementing and then reviewing the outcomes of risk management and action plans (Healthcare Commission, 2007a; Cantrill et al., 2010). Action plans may have been developed without the involvement of key staff, and systems for disseminating lessons to be learned may be obscure (CQC, 2009a; Cantrill et al., 2010). Clinical supervision and staff induction and appraisal systems may also have been insufficiently embedded (CQC, 2009a; Cantrill et al., 2010). There may not have been any agreed standards for, and means of, assessing the quality of patient care (Kennedy, 2001).

Legal literacy

There have been examples where the implementation of legal requirements to safeguard adults (DH, 2000a) has been delayed (Cantrill et al., 2010). Record keeping has also not conformed to legal requirements or best practice (Cantrill et al., 2010). Junior doctors have reported feeling inadequately prepared for some tasks such as certifying deaths (Cantrill et al., 2010), echoing research that has criticised medical education for giving insufficient prominence to law, and that has found medical students to be insufficiently confident in their knowledge of, and skills for implementing, legal rules (Preston-Shoot and McKimm, 2011).

Lines of accountability

Inquiries have reported ambiguity concerning who might be responsible for patient safety, the delivery of quality service standards, and the implementation of action plans. Doctors and nurses have been unclear about the arrangements and allocation of responsibility for reporting incidents (Kennedy, 2001; Healthcare Commission, 2007a; CQC, 2009a; Cantrill et al., 2010).

Settings

Buildings have been old and unfit, not conducive to high quality care (Kennedy, 2001; Healthcare Commission, 2007a; CQC, 2009a). Risks derived from having insufficient beds have not been addressed (Healthcare Commission, 2007a; CQC, 2009a).

Record keeping

The absence of signatures, legible notes, care plans and detail such as the timings of medication reviews, coupled with inattention to the patient's history, has made it difficult to track the care given to patients, as has the practice of doctors and nurses maintaining separate records (Cantrill et al., 2010; Francis, 2010). Equally, the recording of adverse incidents has sometimes been insufficient to inform organisational learning about patient safety and the performance of systems and procedures, or available data has not been analysed (Marsden and Mechen, 2008; Cantrill et al., 2010).

Handling complaints

Concerns and complaints expressed by patients and their relatives have not been adequately recorded or responded to, conveying the impression that people's experiences have not been taken seriously (Marsden and Mechen, 2008; Cantrill et al., 2010). Communication with and support for patients and relatives in such situations has been poor, characterised by delays in providing information, conveying the outcomes of investigations, and apologising.

Handling staff concerns

Inquiries note the presence of an informal culture where issues of concern, if discussed at all, are not documented and not addressed via organisational management structures (Kennedy, 2001; Cantrill et al., 2010). Staff frequently comment about being unclear with whom and how to raise concerns of patient care, and have also referred to organisational and management cultures involving bullying and harassment (CQC, 2009a; Francis, 2010), conveying the perception that critical comments are not welcome and will be ignored. Consequently, staff have been reluctant to raise issues of concern.

There is a perception, supported by evidence (Kennedy, 2001; House of Commons Health Committee, 2009a), that raising concerns may have adverse consequences for staff members' careers and health. One study (Peters et al., 2011), for example, has reported the long-term serious impact on nurses' emotional well-being of whistle blowing, including intense and long-lasting distress, aggravated by bullying, ostracism and a hostile working environment. This has led the Health Committee to call for better protection for whistle blowers and for NHS employers to banish a blame culture and give patient safety the highest priority. Greater protection for whistle blowers may follow by strengthening the right and duty in the NHS Constitution to raise concerns in response to neglect of patients' needs (Santry, 2011).

Serious incident management

Not all unexplained deaths or other types of serious incident have been reviewed effectively, and some evidence about patient outcomes has either not been analysed sufficiently to identify concerns and/or has not been reported to regulatory authorities and hospital governing bodies. Practitioners and managers have been confused about what procedures to follow for different types of serious incident reporting and follow-up action, sometimes resulting in significant delays in reporting and investigation (Kennedy, 2001; CQC, 2009a; Cantrill et al., 2010; Francis, 2010).

Concerns have been expressed about the priority given by managers and boards to safeguarding and patient safety (Healthcare Commission, 2007c; CQC, 2009b; House of Commons Health Committee, 2009a), with serious case reviews having shown some failures to take responsibility for raising safeguarding concerns regarding children, and to act decisively. The CQC (2009b) has criticised primary care trusts for giving insufficient oversight to safeguarding when commissioning services, and for failing to ensure that doctors engage with training on child protection and are clear about their roles and the leadership expected of them.

Organisational change

Inquiries frequently highlight reorganisation within NHS trusts and within the architecture surrounding them (strategic health authorities, primary care trusts and regulatory authorities) as contributing to the failure to recognise and/or respond effectively to breakdowns in patient care. Organisational reconfigurations may contribute to a lack of clarity about roles and responsibilities, and may have resulted in commissioners of services exercising inadequate reviews of performance (CQC, 2009a; Cantrill et al., 2010).

Governance

Inquiries have found that NHS trust governing bodies have not always been adequately appraised of serious incidents and/or have not exercised sufficient oversight of senior executives' responses to risk management and to breakdowns of patient safety. NHS trust governing bodies may have been too slow in pressing senior managers for action or challenging executive reports (Healthcare Commission, 2007a; CQC, 2009a; Cantrill et al., 2010). Regulatory authorities have also been criticised for failing to identify and address serious shortcomings, even when drawn to their attention by whistle blowers, as in the case of Winterbourne View, where some staff have now been charged with the abuse and neglect of vulnerable learning disabled patients (Morris, 2011).

This evidence has led one committee (House of Commons Health Committee, 2009a) to criticise NHS managers and board members for having too little grounding in patient safety, and to recommend more effective use of data and of specialist training so that NHS managers and board members are better able to measure and scrutinise performance and hold trusts accountable for patient well-being. Government has consulted on proposals to develop a more transparent and safer NHS for patients by introducing a duty of candour as a contractual requirement (DH, 2011c). This duty would require NHS providers to be open with patients and communities when things go wrong, and to demonstrate how incidents have been investigated and learned from.

Human rights and equality

An understanding and implementation of human rights and equality ought to be at the heart of institutional planning and good professional practice. Failure to ensure this is so erodes the ability of organisations to plan services appropriately and of professionals to provide good care, treatment and support. Guidance has been issued on the interface between equality, human rights and health and social care outcomes, for example involvement, personalised care, suitability of staff and management, training, and record keeping (Care Quality Commission and Equality and Human Rights Commission (CQC and EHRC), 2011).

Investigations into standards in learning disability services

Significant failings and distressing breakdowns in provision have been uncovered by investigations into services for people with learning disabilities, although some examples of good practice relating to service quality are also reported. Inquiries have found poor standards of care, unacceptable variations in quality, prolonged suffering, and institutional failings in hospital, residential care and day care settings that have deprived learning disabled people of their human rights and dignity (for example, LGO and Parliamentary and Health Service Ombudsman (PHSO), 2009).

Fyson and Kitson (2010) note the history of poor practice, including individual and institutional abuse, in residential care, NHS hospitals and supported living provision. They suggest that patterns of service provision and organisational structures have failed to respond adequately to learning disabled people's needs. They argue that their human rights have been breached routinely.

Other analyses of abuse in institutional settings have suggested that signs have been missed, warnings have not been acted upon, and guidance has been inadequate for identifying the range of causes of abuse and the circumstances in which it can occur (White et al., 2003; Marsland et al., 2007). These analyses suggest that relatives and staff have been deterred from raising concerns by uncertainty about whether the concerns are reasonable, a lack of hard evidence or clear sense of what might be wrong, disbelief that care standards could be so poor, and an unclear sense of what the outcome might be. The analyses argue that poor care cultures increase people's vulnerability and also impact on the practice of well-intentioned staff. The authors caution that community settings may not be immune from the type of problems encountered in institutional settings, including management failings, organisational isolation and negative environments. They warn against simply searching out 'bad apples' and believing that regulations on screening and barring particular individuals from entering or remaining in the workforce will sufficiently safeguard children and adults at risk.

The significance of environments and their cultures should not be overlooked, and studies draw attention to factors that might influence staff behaviour and practice. Management competence and leadership styles, the culture of accountability, poor training and frameworks for measuring the performance of services, the quality of supervision, staff engagement with people's lived experiences, willingness to monitor and challenge attitudes and practices, levels of staff confidence and experience in relation to the demands faced – all these factors can impact on whether abusive practice is recognised, how it is responded to, and how professionals practise.

Using similar headings to those derived from the picture painted above from inquiries into standards in healthcare settings, a mosaic of issues emerge (Box 1.1).

BOX 1.1

A synthesis of concerns

A thematic analysis of inquiries into services for learning disabled people (Commission for Social Care Inspection (CSCI) and Healthcare Commission, 2006; CSCI, 2007; Healthcare Commission, 2007b; LGO, 2008; LGO and PHSO, 2009) uncovers concerns relating to:

Standards of patient care: *inconsistent reviews of care plans; poor quality and outdated service provision, often focused on what people cannot do rather than oriented around a strengths perspective, and geared to the convenience of the institution rather than people's individual needs; inter-agency and multi-professional partnership working patchy, including inadequate planning of service development designed to promote people's independence, choice, well-being and inclusion. Learning disabled people and their family carers are insufficiently engaged in decision-making about services, and their voices are seldom heard. Poor communication, care planning and inter-agency coordination, linked to unacceptable standards of care. Inappropriate and illegal use of restraint and restriction of people's movements, with evidence too of institutional, physical, emotional, financial and sexual abuse.*

Lack of management oversight and action: *inadequate scrutiny of frontline practice, including a failure to consider and address the skill mix available in teams, and the staffing ratio necessary to achieve high quality care, deal with challenging behaviour, and engage service users in community activities. Poor leadership of services for learning disabled people.*

Organisational culture: *improvements are required in how disciplinary investigations are conducted. Isolation of services and limited staff engagement with external organisations. Poor practice ingrained in the provision of care and the management of services.*

Training and support: *inadequate support for staff, including failures to train them in appropriate use of restraint. Poor attendance at mandatory training, coupled with ineffective supervision and appraisal.*

Clinical governance and audit: *warning signs and concerns not picked up or addressed, with inadequate action to address identified risks. Absence of independent outside investigation of adult protection referrals. Insufficient scrutiny given to service quality when control of services transferred between NHS trusts and local government.*

Legal literacy: *safeguarding procedures not followed, equality and diversity standards not consistently achieved, and duties under disability discrimination legislation not met. Practice found that fails to conform to the requirements of the legal rules within the Human Rights Act 1998, with particular reference to principles of respect, dignity and fairness, and*

BOX *1.1* *continued*

within the Mental Capacity Act 2005 with respect to best interests decision making. Staff lack awareness of adult protection procedures and therefore fail to communicate and follow through on concerns effectively. Local authority failure to coordinate adult protection work, for example by ensuring effective systems for managing inter-agency referrals, and to ensure that community care assessments are undertaken (NHS and Community Care Act 1990; Disabled Persons Act 1986), leading to doubts about the appropriateness of placements and the provision of services.

Lines of accountability: *staffing roles unclear, aggravated by a failure to effectively disseminate policies to staff, and to review procedures routinely.*

Settings: *unsuitable houses in which people live.*

Record keeping: *ineffective care resulting from poor recording.*

Handling complaints: *insensitive and unsatisfactory responses to complainants.*

Handling staff concerns: *healthcare practitioners report an authoritarian culture where they feel powerless and unsupported in respect of raising issues.*

Serious incident management: *failure to record and report all incidents where patient care was compromised.*

Governance: *Primary care trust and strategic health authority failure to monitor commissioned provision for quality and safety, aggravated by frequent changes in senior staff and in the organisations responsible for oversight, leading to a lack of continuity and ineffective follow-up. Boards of governors not given the full picture by managers, and failing to investigate identified risks.*

Investigations into standards in services for older people

A similar picture of good practice being undermined by serious concerns emerges when investigating the standards of care experienced by older people. One particularly damning ombudsman report (PHSO, 2011) used ten cases to illustrate personal and institutional attitudes and practices that failed to recognise people's humanity and individuality, and to respond with sensitivity, compassion and professionalism. The report notes the gulf between NHS principles, the values of healthcare professions, and the reality experienced by patients and their relatives. This reality includes shambolic and inappropriate discharges, misdiagnosis, loss of dignity, lack of nutrition, and a failure to review medication. The ombudsman criticises the failure to provide even basic care standards and the disregard of people's needs and wishes, depressingly cautioning that these case examples are neither exceptional nor isolated.

To underline this conclusion, serious concerns continue to be raised about the care of older people in hospitals (CQC, 2011a), with a few hospitals failing to meet legal standards on dignified treatment, provision of food and drink, and monitoring of tissue viability and weight. Patients are not being engaged by staff, for example when assisted to eat, or being involved in their own care. Explanations for treatment are not given, and consent, as required by law, is not requested. Provision of information can be poor, for instance about continuing care funding at the point of discharge from hospital to care homes (Health Service Ombudsman, 2003).

Adult safeguarding

Serious case reviews and research studies have also uncovered instances of institutional neglect and mistreatment of adults at risk in care homes, supported living services and day centres. One inquiry (EHRC, 2011a) found that older people's human rights were overlooked in the provision of care at home. Staff were failing to deliver adequate home care, resulting in neglect of people's personal and nutritional needs. Dignity and privacy were not respected, with staff lacking awareness and training. Systems were not enabling staff to spend sufficient time with service users, with the consequence that basic essential tasks were being neglected. Social workers have also voiced concerns about abuse in care homes, coupled with criticism of staffing levels, lack of leadership and training, and poorly thought-through placements (British Association of Social Workers, 2011).

In addition, some staff lacked awareness of adult safeguarding procedures and whistle blowing policies, in a context where a substantial number of perpetrators of abuse are care staff. There has been marked variation between areas in the effective implementation of the statutory guidance (DH, 2000a; Mansell et al., 2009; Manthorpe and Martineau, 2011). This suggests again a low level of legal literacy. Organisational culture is again implicated, with findings that services need to be more open and transparent so that abuse may be more likely to be detected. Neglect and mistreatment by care staff has been found in settings that lacked attention to people's basic needs, and which were unwelcoming towards complainants (Manthorpe et al., 2007; Mansell et al., 2009). Penhale (2002) has drawn attention to the need for support and supervision in order to enable staff to manage ethical dilemmas presented by their work.

Flynn (2006) found that policies and procedures were out of date, again profiling an organisation's levels of legal literacy, and that there was inattention to inhumane treatment and the proper investigation of complaints. Other researchers, whilst stressing the existence of some positive practice founded on personalisation and empowerment, also note the existence of institutional practices where neglectful behaviour becomes the norm and overrides patients' needs, where levels of physical and psychological abuse observed by staff are high, and where psychological and emotional needs are often ignored in favour of physical and practical concerns (Richardson et al., 2002; Furness, 2006; Dwyer, 2009; Phair and Heath, 2010). These practices parallel many of the themes already identified in this chapter (Box 1.2).

BOX 1.2

Adult safeguarding findings

Standards of patient care: *lack of privacy, poor nutrition, inappropriate use of restraint, denial of individuality, and impersonal interactions.*

Lack of management oversight and action: *low staffing levels and weak leadership overall, rendering staff and residents vulnerable.*

Organisational culture: *closed and defensive institutions.*

Training and support: *low levels of training and continuing professional development.*

Clinical governance and audit: *a focus on finances and targets distorts the organisation's culture.*

Legal literacy: *lack of understanding of adult safeguarding and serious incident reporting procedures, leading to inconsistencies in how good practice is conceptualised, and inconsistencies in when abuse or neglect is identified.*

Lines of accountability: *a lack of acceptance of responsibility for the care of adults at risk, and uncertainty about how to respond when abusive practice is observed.*

Settings: *insufficient recognition of a sense of place, routines and relationships when people are transferred between home and hospital, or between residential and nursing homes.*

Record keeping: *inconsistent identifying, documenting and reporting of abuse.*

Handling complaints: *not all care home residents feel able to speak out.*

Handling staff concerns: *practitioners experience difficulty in raising issues about practice standards, and are unsure what to do, who to tell and how to proceed if managers fail to act when abuse is reported.*

Serious incident management: *practitioners and managers may not document abuse or report it to regulatory bodies because of the powers that organisations like the CQC can exercise or because of anticipated responses from home owners and senior NHS executives. Practitioners and managers may also lack confidence in dealing with cases of abuse or neglect.*

Investigations into standards in social work

Excellent social work practice exists (Social Work Task Force, 2009a, 2009b; Welsh Assembly Government, 2011a), but it is insufficiently widespread (Munro, 2011). There is evidence of improvement across services – including in the assessment of need, and the commissioning and delivery of care plans – with people receiving services they value and which safeguard them from harm (Munro, 2011; Welsh Assembly Government, 2011a). Nonetheless, disconcerting evidence has emerged from inquiries into social work and social care, the themes of which parallel those uncovered within healthcare settings.

The General Social Care Council (GSCC) (2011a) has reported its first successful prosecution of an unqualified person deceiving service users by claiming to be a social worker. It has also revealed a marked rise in conduct hearings, many of which have resulted in admonishments, suspensions or removals from the register. The Care Council for Wales (2011) and the Scottish Social Services Council (SSSC) (2010) have also reported growth in the numbers of registered social workers and social care workers referred for misconduct. In Wales, referrals have particularly highlighted the use of restraint in residential child care, and practice with older people. In Scotland, referrals have led the SSSC to be concerned about the need to enhance the development of professionalism in qualifying training. Interestingly, all the reports are silent on how, if at all, the care councils have monitored the employer's code of conduct (Care Council for Wales, 2002; GSCC, 2002; Northern Ireland Social Care Council, 2002; SSSC, 2009), and yet the context which councils with social services responsibilities provide in order to maintain quality standards is highly variable, and each care council should be enforcing care standards.

Major reviews have found that the amount and quality of supervision is insufficient for social workers to act confidently and safely, partly because, when provided, supervision is seen as having focused on organisational performance requirements rather than the emotions and dilemmas triggered by the work and offering a containing space in which practitioners can avoid burn-out. Social workers have reported that they have not been supportively managed and do not feel valued by employers. Staff shortages, high caseloads and inexperienced practitioners carrying responsibility for work beyond their level of experience and therefore competence have undermined high quality work (Laming, 2009; Social Work Task Force, 2009a, 2009b; Munro, 2011). Reviews have also suggested that employers have shown erratic support for continuing professional development.

The orientation of frontline practice has also been criticised. For example, Munro (2011) stresses the need to restate the importance of reliability, honesty and continuity for children, with practitioners spending time with them and focusing on their needs. She emphasises the importance of respectful treatment and of involving children and parents in decision-making. The Welsh Assembly Government (2011a), mindful of the real and unsustainable increases in demand, envisages the reshaping of social services based on principles which include professionalism, safety and respect, and on values enshrined in United Nations conventions and in the Children Act 1989.

The governance of social services has not escaped criticism either, with reviews finding that inspection has measured standards quantitatively and focused too much on performance targets rather than privileging the quality of provision, such as the degree to which children feel that their wishes and feelings are espected (Social Work Task Force, 2009a, 2009b; Munro, 2011). Indeed, Munro (2011) concludes that the volume and type of performance indicators have undermined professional responsibility for practice. The governance of social work has become over-bureaucratised in the mistaken belief that greater prescription and procedural regulation will guarantee quality practice. Parallel criticisms emerge from Wales (Welsh Assembly Government, 2011a), with proposals to reshape social services around a workforce that is confident and supported in applying its own professional judgement and, as professionals, in using evidence of what works instead of over-reliance on government guidance.

Similarly, questions have been asked about how staff concerns are handled by employers. Laming (2009) felt it necessary to stress the importance of recognising social work's stressful content, and of therefore creating an environment where social workers can share feelings and anxieties without being labelled inadequate. Munro (2011) stresses that managers should listen to frontline staff and enable them to advise how features of the work, and the context in which it occurs, affect actual practice. The Social Work Task Force (2009b), in its description of a healthy workplace, includes employers openly discussing the realities of practice with frontline staff, listening, and foregrounding an employee welfare system that includes risk assessments of roles and tasks, monitors stress levels, manages workloads effectively, and contains an accessible whistle-blowing procedure.

To a lesser extent reviews also question the legal literacy of social services organisations and their employees. Laming (2009) found mixed evidence for the degree to which processes for safeguarding children are understood. He suggests that some departments are ill-equipped with regard to their knowledge of the legal rules. Munro (2011) felt it necessary to remind councils with social services responsibilities that there must be sound links between services for children and provision for adults at risk, given that the latter include parents with learning disabilities or mental distress, and others living in situations of domestic violence or where drug and alcohol issues feature strongly. Equally, she found that staff across agencies involved with young people may need greater understanding of when and how to share information about families and how to differentiate between children in need and children requiring protection. The Welsh Assembly Government (2011a) criticises services for being built around the convenience of organisations rather than people's needs, and found that safeguarding is yet to become a shared responsibility across all statutory partners.

Thus reviews find it necessary to recommend improved working conditions for social services staff (Social Work Task Force, 2009b; Munro, 2011). Recommended improvements include binding standards and requirements for supervision, formal induction programmes, promotion of continuing professional development and of research in practice, stronger leadership, and a career structure and systems approach that enables social workers to develop their expertise and to introduce new learning into practice.

The government response has been to recognise the importance of securing work environments which enable practitioners to exercise the skills and judgements needed to safeguard and promote the welfare of children and of adults at risk (HM Government, 2010). Such a work environment includes effective workload management and skill development through supervision, training, career development standards for employers and balanced caseloads.

There is, however, evidence about social work that the major reviews have not considered; it may be found in reports by the Local Government Ombudsman (LGO, 2002, 2007) and in the judgements delivered in judicial reviews of practice and the management of practice. This evidence (Preston-Shoot, 2010b), examples of which follow (Box 1.3), spans services for children and provision for adults at risk, and its existence raises questions about whether the recommendations from the major reviews have gone far enough in addressing this inside story of practice.

BOX **1.3**

Judicial review and ombudsman reports

A thematic analysis of judicial review cases and ombudsman reports uncovers criticism of:

Flawed assessment and service provision: *in* Pierce *v* Doncaster MBC *[2007] a looked-after young person was returned to abusive parents without adequate safeguards; in* R (LH and MH) *v* Lambeth LBC *[2006] a care plan for a disabled child and family was unlawful, because needs had not been properly assessed; in* R *v* Avon CC, ex parte Hazell *[1995] the local authority failed to include psychological need in an assessment of a learning disabled young man; in* London Borough of Hillingdon *v* Neary and Another *[2011] assessment was flawed because an independent mental capacity advocate was not appointed early enough, a best interest assessment was not balanced, and the disadvantages for the young man living away from home and the significance of the father–son relationship were not acknowledged. Ombudsman reports have criticised local authorities for failing to assess the needs of parents as carers, omitting to review and update care plans, neglecting to assess disabled children's needs and make proper arrangements, and failing to monitor the care that they commission for older people.*

Unlawful practice: *in* R (G) *v* Nottingham CC *[2008] a child was removed from parents without the lawful authority required by the Children Act 1989;* R (Kaur and Shah) *v* Ealing LBC *[2008] was one of several cases where a local authority failed to give due consideration to equality legislation; in* London Borough of Hillingdon *v* Neary and Another *[2011] a learning disabled young man was unlawfully detained in a respite care unit contrary to his own and his father's wishes, with the local authority misunderstanding its obligations in the Mental Capacity Act 2005 and Mental Health Act 2007, and acting in breach of Article 5 (the right to liberty) and Article 8 (the right to private and family life) of the European Convention on Human Rights.*

Failure to follow statutory guidance: *in* R (AB and SB) *v* Nottingham CC *[2001] assessment of children's needs did not accord with policy guidance (DH, 2000b); in* R *v* Avon CC, ex parte Hazell *[1995] the local authority failed to follow policy guidance on choice; in* R *v* Sefton MBC, ex parte Help the Aged and Others *[1997] the local authority failed to follow guidance on charges for residential care. Ombudsman reports have criticised local authorities for failing to prevent neglect and ill-treatment of children whose welfare should have been safeguarded, and for breaching the statutory guidance on charging for Section 117 services (Mental Health Act 1983).*

Avoidance of legal duties: *in* R (Behre and Others) *v* Hillingdon LBC *[2003] asylum-seeking young people were not given the level of support required in law; in* R (S) *v* Sutton LBC *[2007] young people leaving young offender institutions did not receive the support required through Section 17 of the Children Act 1989 and the provisions of the Children (Leaving Care) Act 2000.*

Organisational culture: *in* Bath and North East Somerset Council *v* A Mother and Others *[2008] the local authority failed to complete core assessments of the children, and, additionally, newly qualified social workers reported being required to take on too much work, to accept responsibility for cases beyond their level of competence, and to practise*

BOX *1.3* *continued*

*in a management culture where they felt pressurised and placed within vulnerable situations without adequate support or supervision. Inadequate supervision, the absence of support and the lack of effective management action have been used as mitigating factors by social workers facing possible removal from the professional register because of concerns about their practice (*Forbes *v* GSCC *[2008];* Cordingley *v* Care Council for Wales *[2009]).*

Attitudes and values: *in* Re F *[2008] a local authority did not respond to a birth father's late request to be considered as his child's carer, instead of the child being adopted; in* R (L and Others) *v* Manchester CC *[2002] a policy of paying kinship carers less than other foster parents was ruled unlawful because it failed to meet a child's needs and was arbitrary and discriminatory; in* R (Goldsmith) *v* Wandsworth LBC *[2004] the authority was criticised for behaving insensitively and unreasonably towards an older woman in residential care and her daughter; in* London Borough of Hillingdon *v* Neary and Another *[2011] the local authority tried to prevent proper scrutiny of its intervention and attempted to break down the father's opposition to its approach. Ombudsman reports have criticised local authorities for failing to respond adequately to complaints and for negative attitudes towards complainants.*

Resource-driven decisions: *in* R (M) *v* Hammersmith and Fulham LBC *[2008] there was no evidence of commitment to ensure that the needs of a young person leaving care were properly identified and the most appropriate services made available; in* R (Goldsmith) *v* Wandsworth LBC *[2004] the authority unlawfully chose a cheaper care option, failing to consider the older person's Article 8 right to private and family life, and failing to consider an assessment indicating that a move from residential into nursing care was unnecessary. Ombudsman reports have criticised local authorities for failing to provide support workers for disabled children on grounds of insufficient resources.*

Poor practice standards: *in* R (CD and VD) *v* Isle of Anglesey CC *[2004] a review of a care package failed to meet the requirements of the Children Act 1989 in ascertaining and giving due consideration to the expressed wishes and needs of a disabled young woman and her mother; in* R *v* Birmingham CC ex parte Killigrew *[2000] the local authority failed to adequately analyse how much care was needed, and gave an inadequate statement of needs and the objectives of community care provision; in* R (Bernard) *v* Enfield LBC *[2002] sufficient assistance was not provided to disabled people in a reasonable time, in breach of their Article 8 rights to private and family life (European Convention on Human Rights). Ombudsman reports have criticised local authorities for failing to identify alternative forms of respite care despite recognising that the service being provided was inadequate.*

Ofsted (2009) has also found lack of compliance with statutory requirements, for instance regarding assessment of needs of disabled children, care planning and foster placements. Inspections have raised concerns about practice standards (Chief Inspectors, 2008), for instance with respect to the use of restraint in secure settings, lines of accountability, priority and responsibility for child protection in some settings, conformity with statutory duties, and the adequacy of provision for young people with specific needs. Braye and Preston-Shoot (2009) reviewed the research evidence that shows variable awareness of, and attitudes towards, human rights provision, inconsistent responses with respect to legal rules on direct payments and adult protection, insufficient attention to what service users say, and unmet needs experienced by carers and disabled parents. Some service users have also raised concerns about poor practice standards, including exclusion from decision-making, poor practitioner attitudes, and the impact of performance targets and resources on how service users' needs are perceived (Braye and Preston-Shoot, 2007).

This failure to comply with the legal rules raises questions about the legal and ethical literacy of councils with social services responsibilities, and of the practitioners and managers who work within them. It also asks questions about the relationship between organisations and their social work and social care employees. Research evidence suggests that agency procedures rather than legal rules or ethical standards may come to dominate decision-making (Braye et al., 2007; Preston-Shoot, 2010a). Individual practitioners and managers may also be uncertain about their legal knowledge or find its provisions difficult to understand and use (Drury-Hudson, 1999; Perkins et al., 2007; McDonald et al., 2008; Pinkney et al., 2008; Preston-Shoot and McKimm, 2011a, 2011b).

Research evidence also draws attention to organisational culture. Practitioners and managers may collude with the misuse of power and authority, and with the erosion of service users' legal entitlements (Horwath, 2000; Preston-Shoot, 2000). Some newly qualified social workers appear to lose confidence when confronted by the reality of practice and organisational life, expressing concerns that employers fail to recognise the person within the developing professional (Jack and Donnellan, 2010). Newly qualified social workers may also lack confidence in using their legal knowledge and ethical awareness to challenge their own agency or other professionals (Preston-Shoot and McKimm, 2011b). They may be deterred from raising concerns also because of how organisations have responded previously to whistle blowers (Preston-Shoot and Kline, 2009). Heavy workloads, rigid performance timescales, variability of induction into new roles, erratic availability of continuing professional development, harsh management styles, and inadequate supervision in terms of frequency and its preoccupation with agency targets (Coffey et al., 2009; Bates et al., 2010; Jack and Donnellan, 2010) contribute to low morale and demotivation. Managers too can feel inadequately supported and uncertain or uninformed about aspects of their work, including legal knowledge (Skinner and Whyte, 2004; Jack and Donnellan, 2010).

In such a context, it is doubtful whether proposals in England to reinforce standards for employers, which will nonetheless remain voluntary, will alone provide the transformation in the workplace which the Social Work Task Force (2009b) thought essential. In part, this scepticism derives from recognition that current preoccupations with the effectiveness of regulation, the availability of supervision, and the loss of social work's 'heart' (Munro, 2011) have been expressed before – for example by Preston-Shoot (2001) writing about the impact of regulation on practice, Stevenson (1974) on the importance of supervision, and Drakeford (1996) on the challenge for social work to maintain its humanity.

A hidden inside story

Return to the findings you compiled when exploring the ombudsmen websites.

• *What do you think might explain the situations where inquiries were critical of practice?*

In one judicial review, a judge compared a council with social services responsibilities to a computer system. The judge suggested that the council's systems had become infected and corrupted by a virus.

• *What viruses do you think might corrupt healthcare or social care systems?*

• *Who or what might protect organisational systems and individual practitioners and managers from such viruses?*

A 'hidden' or 'silent' curriculum is reported in medical and healthcare research. These terms refer to how legal and ethical teaching can be undermined, if not eroded, in settings where there are pressures to conform to organisational cultures. A hidden curriculum might emerge in pressure to act unethically and/or unlawfully, in encouragement to overlook personal or colleagues' errors, in derogatory attitudes towards patients and bullying of staff, and in misleading patients, for example around consent to treatment and confidentiality (Cordingley et al., 2007; Kroll et al., 2008). Two questions then arise, namely the degree to which ethics and law teaching in medical and healthcare education is sufficient (Preston-Shoot and McKimm, 2010), and furthermore whether it is effective in the development of professionalism when juxtaposed with observed practice.

Practice may be generated by organisational policies, resource allocation decisions, use of positional power and interpersonal interactions, and a negative attitude towards critical questioning, as revealed in the subsequent careers of whistle blowers (Goldie et al., 2003, 2004). Flynn (2006) suggests that in healthcare contexts, abuse and neglect may thrive where wards, teams and organisations are inward-looking, isolated and impoverished, where there is minimal understanding of indicators of risk to patient safety coupled with a fear of retribution if concerns are raised. One inquiry (Francis, 2010) refers to systemic failings; another (Kennedy, 2001) attributes less to individual failures than to general shortcomings in the NHS. Flynn (2006) also refers to system-wide failings and structural lethargy that amount to inhumanity in some healthcare organisations and emptiness in their authority and legitimacy.

Much less emphasis has been placed on exploring the organisational environment in the social professions, with no comparable recognition of this hidden or silent curriculum (Preston-Shoot, 2012). This omission is betrayed, for example, in Munro's observation (2011) that serious case reviews have contained less emphasis than might be expected on supervision and such staff resources as experience and knowledge. Yet it is known that staff are routinely asked to do work for which they are insufficiently experienced (Laming, 2009). Put another way, there has been insufficient attention on what might make it difficult for staff to comply with professional standards.

Sercombe (2010) warns youth workers of the dangers of corruption, which he links partly to the dependence of agencies on state funding. Wardhaugh and Wilding (1993), exploring serious abuses in the provision of social services, implicate an absence of accountability, the complexity of the work exacerbated by resource constraint, the use of power in closed or isolated organisations, and a neutralisation of moral concerns for service users. Munro (2011) foregrounds inadequate systems. Writing about organisations more generally, Adams and Balfour (1998) warn that administrative evil might result from conformity to agency procedures when coupled with an erosion of personal judgement and independent critical thought. They illustrate the fragility of the ethical foundations of organisational life, and the human consequences for staff and service users of administrative action.

In Box 1.4, some features which establish and maintain the hidden curriculum across the health and social professions are described, with indicative references. The challenge for practitioners, managers and, indeed, policy makers is how then to respond.

BOX *1.4*

The hidden curriculum

Procedures and training in health, medicine and social care may only have a modest effect on professional practice, increasing knowledge of good practice, and developing staff attitudes and values (Richardson et al., 2002; Preston-Shoot, 2012). Managers and practitioners face additional barriers to implementing new learning in their organisations, because of lack of confidence and supervision, time and workload constraints, and resistance from colleagues (Karban and Frost, 1998; Brooker, 2001; Skinner and Whyte, 2004).

Underlying negative attitudes generate and maintain individual and organisational poor practice. There is also a failure to be morally active in scrutinising tasks and procedures through an ethical and legal lens (McDonald et al., 2008; Galpin, 2010).

The impact of bureaucracy and managerialism – reflected in the prominence given to agency procedures and to instrumental goals which demonstrate institutional 'success' – marginalises other values and ethical considerations, relegates codes of practice to the sidelines, distances staff from service users' humanity, priorities and needs, and obscures the perceived need for research, reflection, use of theory and supervision (Skinner and Whyte, 2004; Bilson, 2007; Dwyer, 2009; Sullivan, 2009; Ayre and Preston-Shoot, 2010; Francis, 2010; Jack and Donnellan, 2010).

Strong pressure to remain silent and perceived powerlessness to act undermine individuals' moral responsibility and human agency, risking their professional self-respect (Bilson, 2007; Green, 2009).

Practitioners are insecure in their ethical and legal knowledge with which to challenge organisational decision making. This is coupled with (perceived) lack of clarity in legal rules and statutory guidance (Preston-Shoot, 2010a; Preston-Shoot et al., 2011b).

Practitioners cope with unrealistic expectations and conflicting directives, for instance to maintain care quality but within available resources and pre-determined performance targets, or to maintain people's private life and to foreground empowerment, choice and personalisation whilst also guaranteeing protection from harm (Newton and Browne, 2008; Galpin, 2010).

C H A P T E R　　S U M M A R Y

Service users have a right to expect that social and healthcare professionals will be confident when challenging decisions, credible when presenting their assessments, critical when analysing and managing the complexities and dilemmas they encounter in practice, and creative in responding to people's needs. In some contexts, as this chapter has shown, service users have been seriously let down, sometimes by individual practitioners and managers, more often by a complex web of organisational dynamics. In such contexts practitioners and managers have to make choices, especially about how to navigate between the interests, expectations and demands of service users, regulatory bodies, professional associations and employers, and how to express their professionalism.

Qualifying education and post-registration training should enable professionals to develop and retain the resilience, understanding, attitudes and capability to manage within such environments. Subsequent chapters in this book are designed to assist social and healthcare professionals to develop relevant knowledge, values and skills, and to retain rather than lose morally responsible personhood (Dombeck and Olsan, 2007), realigning what is taught and written with the realities of practice.

Chapter 2
Accountable professionalism

OBJECTIVES

By the end of this chapter, you should have an understanding of:

- The meaning and nature of professional accountability:

  - What does it mean to be a professional?

  - What does it mean to be accountable?

Introduction

ACTIVITY 2.1

- *To whom or what do you believe yourself to be accountable, and why?*

- *If you have identified that you may be accountable to more than one person or body, how would you determine between them?*

- *What might influence the priority you give to different sources or expectations of accountability?*

Chapter 1 offered insights into the accumulating evidence of significant organisational short-comings in health and social care, where professional standards and values have become compromised, and where ethical and legal requirements have been eroded. This evidence stands in marked contrast to pronouncements from the professions themselves. For example, both social work and medicine assert that they are moral professions, working within ethical and legal frameworks, demonstrating appropriate attitudes and adherence to professional standards (Branch, 2000; Quality Assurance Agency (QAA), 2002, 2008). Both the nursing (Nursing and Midwifery Council (NMC), 2008a) and medical professions (QAA, 2002) assert that their overriding duty is to patients. Sercombe (2010) similarly argues that youth work has ethics at its core, and that this ethical orientation is what distinguishes a professional person.

As this chapter's opening exercise might have highlighted, however, accountability may appear as a complex web of obligations to different stakeholders, whose demands may not necessarily be compatible (Braye and Preston-Shoot, 1999). Immediately on qualifying as a health or social care practitioner, the registered professional may be expected by an employer to be fully prepared for the roles required within that organisation, whilst the regulatory authority may regard the qualification as having provided evidence of a more general fitness for practice. Individual practitioners themselves may feel more prepared for some tasks than others.

Apparently straightforward pronouncements, then, of what it means to be a nurse, doctor, midwife or social worker may appear more complicated when professionals seek to express these commitments in practice. How, for instance, should health or social care professionals respond when the organisational context in which they find themselves – perhaps one with serious resource shortages – has a negative impact on their ability to use their knowledge and to demonstrate their values.

In Scotland, good social work outcomes have been seen as dependent on clarity about responsibilities and accountabilities (Changing Lives Practice Governance Group, 2011), which provides a framework to guide professional judgement and discretion when making decisions about rights and risks. Munro (2011) argues that social work practitioners and managers in England need to be very clear about their accountability. Indeed, she urges government to clarify roles, values, responsibilities and accountabilities in respect of child protection, but only makes specific recommendations in relation to directors of children's services and lead elected members. She identifies the damage that may be done when procedural compliance and performance targets dominate practice, but she does not assist practitioners and managers with how they might express their duty of care in such circumstances. For nursing and midwifery, government (Department of Health (DH), 2011a) has stressed that accountability must be clear, embedded within an acceptance by NHS organisations of a corporate responsibility for care. However, the increasing emphasis on accountability may also create anxiety (Marsh and Triseliotis, 1996; Preston-Shoot, 2000), with practitioners and managers concerned about being found wanting when their actions are held up for detailed scrutiny against professional benchmarks.

Moreover, professional accountability may sometimes appear muddled in writings about health and social care. Taylor (2008), for instance, suggests that professionals may owe a moral obligation to service users but a legal obligation to their employers. Boylan and Dalrymple (2011) argue that social workers are compromised as advocates for service users by their role as service providers, allocating scarce resources within a particular target and performance culture. Researchers have found that care staff struggle with determining whether and how to exercise professional discretion and judgement in order to meet service users' needs when working with agency policies and procedures, concluding that the concept of a duty of care probably needs greater exploration (Penhale, 2002; Dunworth and Kirwan, 2009). Ethical codes may offer little guidance about when and how to prioritise competing claims of service users and employers (Preston-Shoot, 2010b).

Members of the health and social care professions may work in organisational environments where the legal rules and values that should underpin practice are implicit, and where individual commitment to provide the best possible care is challenged by limited openings to discuss and question the ethical and lawful basis for decisions. The purpose of this chapter (and the next) is to explore professional accountability in terms of the ethical, legal and regulatory framework, addressing specifically questions of accountability which professional bodies through their codes, employers through their appointment and induction procedures, and qualifying education programmes through modules on ethics and law either fudge or fail even to acknowledge. If the health and social care professions are forms of moral activity, as articulated in codes of ethics and practice, then this chapter (and the next) focuses on the compass that may help practitioners to profess their values and knowledge, and to demonstrate their skills in settings where other magnetic fields may seek to distort its readings.

ACTIVITY 2.2

- *What do you understand by the concept of a duty of care?*

- *How do you believe you should and would respond when your accountability to your employer and your agency challenges how you understand your obligations to codes of ethics and practice?*

Defining accountability

Understanding and demonstrating accountability is important because social and healthcare professionals exercise statutory authority, hold positional power, and draw on substantial bodies of knowledge (Welbourne, 2010).

There are proactive and responsive forms of accountability (Braye and Preston-Shoot, 1999). Proactive accountability includes benchmark statements (QAA, 2002, 2008) and codes of practice and conduct (National Youth Agency (NYA), 2004; Health Professions Council (HPC), 2008; NMC, 2008a; General Medical Council (GMC), 2009; Scottish Social Services Council, 2009). Responsive accountability comprises complaints procedures and scrutiny by courts and non-judicial bodies (the Local Government Ombudsman and Health Service Ombudsman).

Similarly, different forms of accountability may be described (Braye and Preston-Shoot, 1999; Audit Commission, 2005; Welbourne, 2010); see Box 2.1.

BOX 2.1

Types of accountability

Explanatory accountability – *giving an account to an individual or organisation that gives a professional legitimacy, reporting and perhaps justifying decisions, including how legal duties have been used, dignity and respect shown, and conclusions about treatment or intervention reached.*

Being held to account – *accountability for practice and the management of practice, through audit, inspection and scrutiny, against benchmarks focused on targets, standards and use of recognised professional knowledge and skills.*

Taking into account – *involvement of patients and service users in decision making, consulting where possible before deciding whether and how to act, with such practice often underpinned by legal rules that require professional decision-takers to ascertain the wishes and feelings of those with whom they are working.*

Redress – *systems for making representations and complaints, with legal rules underpinning how they are constructed and managed.*

One example of explanatory accountability is when social workers must be able to make and defend complex judgements, especially when using legal powers to ensure that people are safe (HM Government, 2010). Nurses and midwives, similarly, must be able to demonstrate how they have made the care of people their first concern, respecting people's dignity and supporting their rights to accept or decline treatment and care (NMC, 2008a; Jones, 2011). Care workers, as part of their duty of care, should be able to articulate the ethical assumptions or principles behind their decision-making, whether these are based on reference to moral rules (deontotology), meeting needs (ethics of care) or the best overall consequences (consequentialism) (Dunworth and Kirwan, 2009).

Doctors, other healthcare professionals and social workers may be held personally accountable for their practice, in specific cases and more generally in how they have maintained their knowledge and skills. Negative judgements from a registration body may lead to sanctions such as admonishment, suspension or removal from the register. Critical judgements from a court may hold that practice has been negligent and find not just an employer vicariously liable but also, where a person's practice has significantly departed from accepted norms, the individual practitioner (*W and Others* v *Essex County Council and Another* [2000]).

Accountability to and for practice may, however, only really be meaningful if referrals are made for investigation by a regulatory authority, if inspection and audit is effective in detecting and rectifying concerns, and if those organisations to whom reports must be given can exercise meaningful influence in response, perhaps through the use of sanctions (Braye and Preston-Shoot, 1999; Horwath, 2010). It speaks volumes that the Welsh Assembly Government (2011a), for example, has concluded that it is necessary to reinforce the corporate parenting role of local authorities and to simplify accountability by making it clearer, so that those using services may experience that quality and safety is held firmly by providers and commissioners. Similarly, the opportunity to have views taken into account and to seek redress will only prove meaningful forms of accountability if patients and service users know about their rights, feel able to exercise them and are respected when they do. Sadly, on all counts, the evidence is often disappointing (Braye and Preston-Shoot, 2009).

Duty of care

Healthcare professionals owe a duty of care to their patients; social professionals owe one to service users. Professionals owe a duty of care to each other also. What, however, might this mean in practice?

The test against which to measure practice is what a responsible body of fellow professionals would define as competent practice (Preston-Shoot, 2000). A duty of care will have been met where a professional has provided a service of a quality that would be expected from someone with the skills and knowledge of a competent member of that profession (*Bolam* v *Friern Hospital Management Committee* [1957]). Thus, a healthcare assistant or family support worker must work to the standards of a reasonable person who has appropriate training, and to take that level of care which would be reasonable in all the circumstances of a particular incident or case (*Penney, Palmer and Cannon* v *East Kent HA* [2000]). However, even if responsible professional opinion supports a practitioner and/or their organisation, courts may determine the standard of care required in particular cases and may disregard expert analysis when it is considered unreasonable or to have failed to balance the risks and benefits of different options (*Bolitho* v *City and Hackney Health Authority* [1997]).

Codes of practice, ethics and conduct (for example, General Social Care Council (GSCC), 2002; NMC, 2008a; GMC, 2009), together with benchmark statements (QAA, 2002, 2008), National Service Frameworks (Braye and Preston-Shoot, 2009) and quality standards (for example, Care Quality Commission (CQC), 2010) populate this duty of care. Statutory guidance, issued by government departments in the four countries of the United Kingdom, will add standards or requirements for particular roles and tasks, which should be followed.

Thus, Jones (2011), writing about midwifery practice, argues that the duty of care includes a duty of:

- fidelity – to avoid deception, to tell the truth and to act in good faith;
- beneficence – an obligation to help;
- non-maleficence – to avoid harm;
- justice – to avoid discrimination.

Actual practice, to meet this standard, will need to draw upon values and knowledge from all the sources identified above, the use of which will be carefully and skilfully done.

BOX **2.2**

Duty of care

A duty of care means:

- *Using best evidence and current knowledge to inform practice, drawn from research, policy documents, professional statements of theory and methods, practice experience, and service user perspectives.*

- *Keeping knowledge and skills updated.*

- *Understanding and weighing up the legal options, powers and duties that might apply to a specific case (such as those in the Children Act 1989; Mental Health Act 1983; Mental Capacity Act 2005).*

- *Promoting human rights and counteracting discrimination (Human Rights Act 1998; Equality Act 2010) in order to meet professional obligations to promote people's dignity and autonomy.*

- *Understanding and balancing what different ethical approaches might offer.*

- *Knowing and following an organisation's procedures where, on critical reflection, these are consistent with responsible professional opinion.*

- *As a practitioner or manager, not accepting work that is beyond your competence and capacity to undertake adequately, and not delegating work to others whose competence or capacity to perform the tasks safely and skilfully is in doubt.*

BOX **2.2** *continued*

- *Using this legal and ethical literacy, and these other sources of knowledge, to ensure that services are provided safely.*

- *Keeping accurate records which clearly indicate with whom a situation was discussed and on what basis decisions were taken.*

- *Taking action when services are inadequate, notifying appropriate managers and/or regulatory bodies of concerns that these standards are not able to be met.*

Thus, in one case (*D* v *East Berkshire Community Health NHS Trust and Others* [2005]), a duty of care was judged to have been met when practitioners acted in good faith, interfered with people's human rights only with cogent justification and according to the legal rules, involved service users in decision-making, shared information and concerns unless this would place someone at risk of harm, and followed decision-making principles when reaching sound professional judgements.

Interfaces between accountabilities

Practitioners may be held to account by both their employer and a regulatory authority. How should professionals manage the interface between accountability to an employer and that to a professional organisation or register?

Registered professionals, including managers, should follow lawful and reasonable instructions, and exercise skills and care in their work, as would be expected of a professional. However, at all times they should comply with their registration code. Put another way, where an employer's interpretation of a role or task is defensible in terms of the law, code of conduct and/or ethics, and definitions of good practice, then this should be followed (Preston-Shoot, 2000). Compliance with professional codes is an implied term of a contract of employment, but may additionally be articulated explicitly. If instructed to act in a manner which might breach the code or place the worker in circumstances where they are unable to uphold it, the worker should question the instruction as unreasonable and, if necessary, refuse to comply.

For professionals who are not registered, such as youth workers, as indeed for registered practitioners and managers, an employer should not ask an employee to do anything that would conflict with professional ethics, values and knowledge, often identified in a person specification for a particular role. A relationship of confidence and trust must exist between employers and employees, and could be undermined if an organisation implies that staff should, or explicitly expects staff to, breach their duty of fidelity to standards as articulated in professional values, ethics and knowledge (Preston-Shoot, 2000; Kline, 2003, 2009).

A key task, then, for individual workers, whether or not licensed to practise through membership of a professional register, is to give personal meaning to the codes that surround their practice.

If you are a registered practitioner or manager, take the code that comprises the standards for conduct in practice.

- *What do the statements about performance mean to you?*
- *How has your professional community of practice understood the requirements?*

Understanding the codes that relate to practice is important because it may prove insufficient, if workers are called to account by a registration authority, to argue that there were insufficient resources (skilled staff, equipment, supervision) to perform work safely, or that an instruction was being followed, or that work delegated required experience, skills and training which the registrant did not possess.

The NMC (2008a), for instance, requires that registrants provide a high standard of practice at all times, which includes monitoring the quality of care being offered and acting without delay if anyone is put at risk. Practitioners must understand relevant legal rules, for example concerning mental capacity and consent to treatment. They must monitor the quality of their work, delegate effectively and work within the limits of their competence. Practitioners should keep accurate records and uphold the reputation of their profession. They should demonstrate a commitment to equality and to the avoidance of discrimination.

Medical practitioners must understand and accept the legal responsibilities involved in protecting and promoting the health of patients (GMC, 2009). This includes skills in managing the legal and ethical issues which arise in practice, working within the limits of their competence, protecting patients from harm, and raising concerns about the performance of colleagues.

The Health Professions Council (2008) expects its registrants to act in the best interests of service users, to demonstrate respect and dignity, and to be capable of justifying their decisions. They must keep their knowledge and skills up to date and act within the limits of their competence. Registrants with the Health Professions Council should keep accurate records and ensure they have obtained informed consent. They must behave with integrity and honesty, seeking advice when necessary, reporting concerns about their personal conduct and competence, and effectively supervising tasks that they delegate to others.

The duty of care for youth workers includes demonstrating commitment to promoting equality and counteracting discrimination, and acting with integrity. This means practice that is based on principles of respect, human rights, safety and accountability, that involves young people in learning and decision-making, that reports concerns about young people at risk of harm, and that builds trust between services and families. It includes an ethical literacy, reflecting on and discussing issues, taking and being able to justify decisions, and seeking advice when accountabilities to different groups conflict. The duty of care requires youth workers to maintain and develop their skills and knowledge, and only to undertake work at which they are competent (NYA, 2004).

The Care Council for Wales (2002) expects registrants to examine their own practice, adhere to relevant standards, maintain people's trust and confidence in social services, and seek assistance when feeling unable or unprepared for particular tasks. In England the social work professional capabilities framework helps to populate the duty of care and to clarify practitioners' accountability (Social Work Reform Board, 2010). Social workers must be knowledgeable about the profession's value base, its ethical standards and relevant law, and the obligation to promote human rights and equality. They must demonstrate reflection and analytic skills when taking decisions. In Scotland (Changing Lives Practice Governance Group, 2011), similar emphasis is given to upholding social work values and ethics in practice. Compliance with codes and with legislation should be prominent when taking decisions. Practitioners should work within the limits of their competence whilst also developing their knowledge and skills.

Upholding codes is an individual responsibility. Codes should be upheld even where other registrants in a particular location are not making representations. Registrants are personally accountable for their actions or omissions (NMC, 2008a). That said, if a person has a good record, an admission of misconduct and personal stress (Hussein et al., 2009a), coupled with evidence of mismanagement within the organisational environment (see, for example, *Forbes v General Social Care Council* [2008]), might be accepted as mitigation.

Thus codes of conduct, ethics or practice provide a set of national, organisational and individual standards (Welbourne, 2010), which are promises to service users about service delivery or an expression of expectations. Potentially they can act as a countervailing force against how organisations and government might want on occasions to drive health and social care (van Heugten, 2011). Codes name good and suspect practice, and offer guidance through challenging situations (Sercombe, 2010). However, filling them with meaning, discussing them in organisational settings, and publicising their existence is necessary if their potential for promoting ethical behaviour is to be fulfilled. Codes may not be well known amongst patients and service users. Their general wording, without additional reflection, may limit their usefulness in complex situations where different principles or perspectives compete, or promote defensive practice, or render it difficult to prove a breach (Orme and Rennie, 2006; Dunworth and Kirwan, 2009; Preston-Shoot, 2010b; Welbourne, 2010).

ACTIVITY 2.4

Take a recent task that presented particular dilemmas.

- *Using this discussion of accountability, describe how you resolved the dilemmas that arose.*

- *Reflect on what the components of a duty of care would offer to the process of resolving this dilemma, so that, if held to account, you could offer an explanation.*

Employer and organisational accountability

Employers have reciprocal obligations in this accountability and duty of care mosaic. This is important for two reasons. Firstly, the working environment has been implicated in allegations of misconduct with vulnerable adults (Hussein et al., 2009a), in child protection tragedies (*LA v General Social Care Council* [2007]), in failures to safeguard and protect children from professional abuse (Estyn and Care and Social Services Inspectorate Wales (CSSIW), 2011), and in breakdowns in patient care (Cantrill et al., 2010; Francis, 2010). Criticisms about organisational environments have included staff shortages, racism, victimisation, lack of supervision, delegation of work beyond the competence and capacity of practitioners to undertake it safely, inadequate management of checks on staff records and of disciplinary procedures, minimisation of safeguarding concerns, and poor strategic and operational leadership.

Secondly, if the way in which employing agencies deploy their resources and meet their statutory and ethical responsibilities is not included in the frame of analysis, the risks will be seen as located within, and the burdens will be carried by, individual professionals alone when, in fact, systems failings feature significantly (Marsland et al., 2007; Estyn and CSSIW, 2011; van Heugten, 2011).

Case law has established various requirements so that whatever professional work is undertaken can be performed safely and to the Bolam standard of what would be expected of an ordinarily competent professional. Employers should provide appropriate training and support (*Lancaster* v *Birmingham City Council* [1999]; *Fraser* v *Winchester Health Authority* [1999]). They must ensure a safe place of work, one which protects staff from the unreasonable behaviour of service users (*R* v *Kensington and Chelsea RLBC, ex parte Kujtim* [1999]) and which considers their own mental as well as physical health (*Johnstone* v *Bloomsbury Health Authority* [1991]; *Walker* v *Northumberland County Council* [1995]).

Employers are responsible for providing proper standards of care and decision-making. They may be found negligent for failing to provide staff with sufficient skills and experience (*Wilsher* v *Essex Area Health Authority* [1986]) or for failing to ensure adequate facilities (*Knight* v *Home Office* [1990]). Councils with social services responsibilities have been found negligent, for instance, for failing to provide correct information (*W and Others* v *Essex County Council and Another* [2000]), for carelessness in decision-making, and in monitoring and review of looked-after children (*Barrett* v *Enfield LBC* [1999]; *Pierce* v *Doncaster MBC* [2007]). Aftercare providers might be liable for negligent failure to discharge their duties (*AK* v *Central and North West London Mental Health NHS Trust and Kensington and Chelsea LBC* [2008]).

Employers must not discriminate against employees on grounds of race, gender, disability, age, sexuality, religion or belief (Equality Act 2010), and must not do anything that could undermine the confidence and trust which must characterise the employment relationship (Preston-Shoot, 2000). For instance, an employee's grievances should be properly investigated, and work should not be delegated which a staff member cannot undertake safely. Similarly, registration bodies must not unlawfully discriminate, for example around fitness-for-practice decisions.

Finally, employers should inform registration authorities about the misconduct of registrants where acts or omissions leading to complaints, dismissal or resignation before disciplinary investigations have been concluded question the person's suitability for practice. However, practice here has been inconsistent (Social Work Task Force, 2009a; Estyn and CSSIW, 2011).

Social work is unusual in the emphasis given in codes of practice (Care Council for Wales, 2002; GSCC, 2002; Northern Ireland Social Care Council, 2002; Scottish Social Services Council, 2009) to employers' responsibilities. Employers must adhere to the standards therein and support staff to meet their obligations. This includes ensuring that supervision is effective, the work environment does not place social workers at risk of losing their registration and licence to practise, information about relevant legislation is available, and commitment to social work values and knowledge is evident. Crucially it includes having systems whereby staff may report operational difficulties that impact on safe working.

The Social Work Reform Board (2010) in England expects employers to have transparent systems to manage social workers' workloads and to guarantee their capacity and competence to manage the demands of practice. This includes ensuring that risks are assessed and managed, supervision, advice and continuing professional development are provided, and contingency plans are in place to respond when demand exceeds workforce capability. Employers must enable practitioners and managers to raise concerns without fear of recrimination.

The Changing Lives Practice Governance Group (2011) in Scotland has followed a similar trajectory to the Social Work Reform Board in England. It too has articulated employers' responsibility for developing and sustaining a competent and confident workforce, and for providing an environment that takes ownership of the need to deliver safe and effective practice. Accountability here means supporting staff to exercise professional judgement, providing clear guidelines about how to balance risks, needs and autonomy, auditing and reviewing in order to learn from practice, ensuring staff have appropriate skills, supervision, workload management and training, and overseeing compliance with codes of practice and other standards, including legislation.

The employers' code of practice does not have statutory force, however, although Laming (2009) recommended this to ensure clear lines of accountability for the requirements necessary to facilitate quality service provision. The absence of a statutory basis for the employers' responsibilities articulated in codes of practice leaves social workers exposed when negotiating ethical issues in practice and confronting conflicts between professional values and organisational expectations (Braye and Preston-Shoot, 2009), especially but not just in the types of situations described in Chapter 1.

Health trusts have similar challenges. They too must demonstrate that appropriate priorities are chosen within available resources, and they must comply with statutory duties regarding equality, human rights, and health and safety. Health trusts must ensure that those providing care are able to practise safely and competently perform their duty of care to each patient.

Delivering an organisation's duty of care to staff and to service users requires determined and skilled leadership from managers who know their organisations well (Munro, 2011). There needs to be clarity about who is responsible for securing the different components of a healthy and safe working environment (Cantrill et al., 2010).

ACTIVITY **2.5**

- *Using work settings with which you are familiar, how well do you judge that employers have met their duty of care to staff and to service users? What is your evidence?*

- *Using the health check for organisations (Social Work Task Force, 2009b), how well is your organisational setting performing in relation to:*

ACTIVITY 2.5 *continued*

- – Unfilled posts?

- – Sickness absence?

- – Provision of supervision, training and staff appraisal?

- – Allocation of work?

- – Staff working hours?

- – Access to advice, for example from lawyers?

- – Employee welfare systems?

- – Staff surveys?

- – Mechanisms to raise concerns?

- • Have any concerns been raised within the agency?

Whistle blowing – a form of accountability

One responsive form of accountability is whistle blowing. Good whistle blowing procedures can save lives and prevent abuse (Public Concern at Work (PCaW), 2008). Evidence indicates that fewer patients are harmed, concerns are handled well and staff are not penalised when organisations promote the raising of issues. A healthy workplace includes support for whistle blowing (Social Work Task Force, 2009b).

The NMC (2008a) expects nurses and midwives to act without delay and report in writing if workers and/or the care environment are placing people at risk. Registrants are expected to inform someone in authority if there are problems with implementing professional standards. The NMC (2010a) has issued guidance on raising and escalating concerns, which covers health and safety violations and issues relating to staff conduct and behaviour, care delivery and the organisational environment and culture. The guidance should be used by qualified staff and students alongside local whistle blowing, clinical governance, safeguarding and risk management procedures. Registrants are advised to seek advice from a professional association, trade union or voluntary organisation (such as Public Concern at Work) if they are unsure about how to respond to a situation and/or need support in what can be a stressful time. Where safe to do so, concerns should be raised internally first prior to contacting an appropriate external agency such as the professional regulator.

The General Medical Council (2009) expects doctors and medical students to raise concerns about the behaviour and/or performance of colleagues where patients are being placed at risk. The Health Professions Council (2008) requires its registrants, such as physiotherapists, to place the safety of service users always ahead of personal and professional loyalties. Registrants must discuss with senior colleagues and, where necessary, other appropriate people, situations where service users are in danger.

Social workers and social care staff are also expected to identify for an employer or regulatory authority situations where resource or operational difficulties affect or might impact on the delivery of safe services (Care Council for Wales, 2002; GSCC, 2002; Northern Ireland Social Care Council, 2002; Scottish Social Services Council, 2009). The Social Work Reform Board (2010) has advised employers to have robust whistle blowing policies and to provide an environment where concerns can be raised about staff performance, workload issues and resource shortages without fear of recrimination.

Youth workers are not governed by registration, so their code is explanatory rather than disciplinary (Sercombe, 2010). However, youth workers too are required to promote respect, human rights, safety and accountability in their employing organisations, and to be prepared to challenge colleagues and agencies when their actions are contrary to these principles (NYA, 2004). Youth workers must warn employers and take action if there are risks and dangers attached to their work, and draw attention to ways in which organisational activities or policies may seriously harm children and young people. If their employers respond ineffectively, youth workers should disclose to other organisations and/or the general public (NYA, 2004).

Such official pronouncements about this aspect of professional accountability are not reflected in the picture consistently emerging from practice. The result is that perpetrators of abuse and neglect may be working undetected (Richardson et al., 2002). Equally, professional regulators seem reluctant to produce proposals designed to counteract the difficulties which professionals have in raising concerns. Surprisingly, the Health Professions Council (2011a), in its consultation on future social work standards, omits any mention of whistle blowing and any obligation to hold employers to account by raising concerns about the resources they provide and the degree to which they protect service users and staff from the consequences of excessive workloads, unsafe instructions or inappropriate delegation of work.

Research, inquiries and the lived experience of whistle blowers themselves identify the reasons why staff may decide to remain silent (see Box 2.3).

BOX **2.3**

Possible reasons why poor practice is not reported

Research identifies that, across different professions and organisational settings, workers are apprehensive about speaking out, encounter difficulties when attempting to do so, including serious levels of distress and/or career detriment, and therefore may not respond to poor practice (Goldie et al., 2003; Banks, 2005; Marsland et al., 2007; Preston-Shoot and Kline, 2009; Peters et al., 2011; Preston-Shoot, 2012).

One report on a whistle blowing advice service advised that the care sector generated the largest number of concerns, and the health sector the second largest (PCaW, 2011). Half of all concerns were about abuses or poor practices in care settings. In many cases a whistle blower's concerns had been ignored or disputed by managers.

Staff may be frightened to speak up for a number of possible reasons:

- *The anticipated and possible negative consequences and reactions from colleagues, managers and regulatory bodies. This might include victimisation, bullying, reprisals and labelling (Skinner and Whyte, 2004; PCaW, 2008; GSCC, 2009).*

BOX **2.3** *continued*

- *The possibility of substantial detriment, including loss of employment despite successfully proving unfair dismissal before industrial tribunals.*

- *Threats of retaliation, including disciplinary action, and pressure to comply with institutional performance targets and procedures, with conformity bringing organisational rewards (Pemberton and Tombs, 2008; Green, 2009; Peters et al., 2011).*

- *Lack of confidence in their ethical and legal literacy to challenge the practice of colleagues in their own organisation or the decisions of other agencies, especially without the support of tutors or supervisors (Preston-Shoot and McKimm, 2011b; Preston-Shoot et al., 2011).*

- *Uncertainty as to how to respond to the lack of respect, or to the abuse or neglect they witness (White et al., 2003), especially when victims may not want to challenge the care they have received, because of their own anxiety or lack of decision-making capacity (PCaW, 2011), coupled with loyalty to colleagues and the belief that nothing will change or that their concerns will not be taken seriously (PCaW, 2008; GSCC, 2009).*

- *Managers who are unsupportive and who fail to provide clear and enabling policies, in a context also where unionisation may be discouraged or weak, staff may be on low incomes, and the work and workers relatively unregulated (Pemberton and Tombs, 2008; PCaW, 2011).*

- *Lack of awareness of their rights, absence of support and advice, and a poor understanding of available legal rules and the responsibilities of regulatory bodies (Pinkney et al., 2008; PCaW, 2011).*

BOX **2.4**

Concerns about whistle blowing procedures

Inquiries into breakdowns in patient safety have frequently identified concerns about whistle blowing procedures and the difficulty that staff experience in raising issues about practice standards. However, inquiries do not examine in detail why such a situation might persist and frustrate their well-intentioned recommendations. Arguably, inquiries should include the adequacy of the Public Interest Disclosure Act 1998.

- *Francis (2010) found few instances of whistle blowing and criticised the NHS trust for failing to offer support and respect to those brave enough to speak out. He warned that ineffective responses when staff did raise concerns would discourage others from doing so. He recommended support for staff who raise concerns and indicated that a healthy organisational environment was one where the culture was open.*

- *Kennedy (2001) found that staff were not encouraged to share problems openly and were fearful that doing so would endanger their career prospects.*

BOX **2.4** *continued*

- The CQC (2009a) noted that consultants thought that managers did not welcome critical comment. It advised that staff should be encouraged and enabled to speak up and should be treated fairly when they do so.

- The House of Commons Health Committee (2009a) concluded that the NHS demonstrated a lack of respect towards whistle blowers and recommended government action to improve this situation. Protection for whistle blowers is likely to be incorporated into the NHS Constitution (Santry, 2011).

- Cantrill et al. (2010) found the existence of an informal culture where issues of concern were discussed but not documented. Cantrill coined the term 'a quiet word' to denote a system where problems were addressed within professional groupings rather than through formal structures. The report concluded that a clear and widely understood process for staff to raise concerns about patient care was lacking and that, even after the serious incidents that had triggered the inquiry, people remained unwilling to whistle blow.

BOX **2.5**

Experiences of whistle blowers

The lived experience of whistle blowers demonstrates the truth of the observation that organisations do not welcome staff who point out deficiencies and, consequently, that considerable courage is required when challenging unethical and/or unlawful behaviour (Rodie, 2008; Sercombe, 2010).

- The very first whistle blower to use the provisions of the Public Interest Disclosure Act 1998, Bryan Bladon, worked in a private nursing home. He won his case but lost his job.

- Alison Taylor raised concerns about apparent abuses in children's residential care in North Wales. By the time the government had set up a public inquiry (Waterhouse, 2000), she had been sacked. Although she won damages for unfair dismissal, she suffered stress and ill-health and never worked again as a senior residential social worker.

- Susan Machin was a social worker at Ashworth Special Hospital. She was the only social worker to give evidence to an inquiry into alleged abuses of patients (Machin, 1998). A year later she was suspended and subsequently sacked for helping patients to keep records of alleged ill-treatment. In 1995 an industrial tribunal awarded her compensation for wrongful dismissal. She suffered a nervous breakdown, ill-health and family breakdown. She has not worked in social services since.

- Nevres Kemal claimed that children were being put at risk by being left with alleged abusers, that Haringey council did not act on her concerns, and that she was then treated

BOX **2.5** *continued*

unfavourably. Eventually the council agreed to pay her an undisclosed sum. She has not worked as a social worker since.

• Martin Morton, a social worker who raised concerns about the lawfulness of a council's charging policies, eventually received an apology from Wirral MBC, which accepted the inappropriateness of both its policies and its approach to whistle blowing. This was only after several years during which he had experienced bullying, enforced resignation and organisational denial.

• Margaret Haywood, a registered nurse, found that the NMC appeared more concerned about her alleged failure to protect the confidentiality of those in her care than her experiences of trying to raise concerns about poor professional standards. Whilst raising concerns in a way that is safe for patients is an important goal, an ethical approach may have to be one that prioritises the greater good to be realised by highlighting abuse and neglect.

The evidence currently is that many organisations may be missing opportunities to capture information from which they may learn, to promote procedures for the safe raising of concerns, and to protect whistle blowers. By no means all organisations are willing to address concerns about practice standards when they are first raised, although not all those who raise concerns report negative experiences subsequently (PCaW, 2011).

This significant and troubling mismatch between employers' attitudes and the requirements of professional regulators has led to a recommendation that whistle blowing should be made part of the contract of employment (Preston-Shoot and Kline, 2009). Accountability would be strengthened if such a contractual obligation for employees was reinforced, including where necessary referral to an external professional regulator. Indeed, to tackle the evidence of poor care in some nursing and midwifery settings, it has also been recommended (DH, 2011a) that staff should have the right to speak out and a contractual obligation to raise concerns with a regulatory authority such as the CQC.

Whether or not whistle blowing is an explicit component of an employment contract, open and constructive processes will be required in order to demonstrate to staff that they may question and challenge, without fear of criticism or blame, how organisations are shaping procedures and delivering care and services (Rodie, 2008).

Complaints procedures

Complaints procedures are one responsive form of accountability and one measure of how open an organisational culture is. Some codes of practice or conduct specifically refer to handling complaints, requiring that professionals do not allow critical representations made by service users to affect the care they offer (NMC, 2008a).

The track record on the management of complaints in health and social care is poor, however, leading one report (Parliamentary and Health Service Ombudsman (PHSO), 2010) to conclude that the NHS needs to listen harder and learn more from complaints, and another (House of Commons Health Committee, 2009a) to conclude that the current system for complaints procedures is unlikely to improve the way in which the NHS treats complainants. The latter is scathing about the lengthy and distressing litigation necessary for patients to obtain justice and compensation.

Research across health and social care settings has questioned the effectiveness of complaints procedures and concluded that, as currently implemented, complaints procedures may not be optimally effective in detecting and preventing bad practice and identifying abusive staff (Braye and Preston-Shoot, 1999, 2009). Specifically, researchers have found that people are deterred from complaining because:

- They fear the consequences in respect of the services or care they might subsequently receive, and they feel unsafe (Giordano and Street, 2009; Equality and Human Rights Commission (EHRC), 2011a).

- They believe they will not be taken seriously, they lack confidence and also information about the processes involved, and they are unclear about possible outcomes (Flynn, 2004, Furness, 2006; Marsland et al., 2007; Gulland, 2009; EHRC, 2011a).

- Investigations are delayed and/or poor, procedures are not adequately managed, practice fails to adhere to the legal rules, and ineffective action is taken once the findings are known (Local Government Ombudsman (LGO), 2002; Flynn, 2004, 2006; Gulland, 2009; LGO and PHSO, 2009; Preston-Shoot and Kline, 2009; Francis, 2010; PHSO, 2010).

- Organisational attitudes towards complainants are hostile and/or lacking in compassion, discouraging people from speaking up, and available procedures are not adequately publicised (Flynn, 2004; Furness, 2006; LGO, 2007; Manthorpe et al., 2007; PHSO, 2010).

- Managers are reluctant to acknowledge mistakes and to apologise (Marsland et al., 2007; PHSO, 2010).

It is therefore difficult to dispute the conclusion of Sercombe (2010) that professionals and/or their agencies are inclined to close ranks and protect themselves. A more positive attitude and learning orientation is needed in respect of people who complain.

Governance

Health and social care organisations have been strongly criticised for inadequate internal arrangements for professional and clinical governance. Records of supervision and appraisals, of criminal record bureau checks, and of disciplinary investigations have been inadequate (CQC, 2009a; Hussein et al., 2009a; Cantrill et al., 2010; Estyn and CSSIW, 2011). Concerns have been expressed about recognition, management and learning from serious incidents, safeguarding children and adults, reviewing standards of care in service delivery, and ensuring a workforce fit for practice through training, supervision and opportunities for reflection (Healthcare Commission, 2007b; Marsden and Mechen, 2008; Francis, 2010; Estyn and Care and Social Services Inspectorate Wales (CSSIW), 2011). Engagement with frontline practice and with service users has been sporadic. Patient safety solutions have not been adopted at the front line (House of Commons Health Committee, 2009a).

External governance has also come under the microscope. Commissioning bodies such as primary care trusts have been criticised for exercising too little oversight once services have been purchased and, therefore, for not picking up falling standards (CQC, 2009a; Cantrill et al., 2010; Francis, 2010). Inspections, for example by the CQC, have been criticised for failing to detect abuse, to measure quality of provision, and to challenge internal ratings of performance (LGO and PHSO, 2009; Social Work Task Force, 2009a; British Association of Social Workers, 2011; Munro, 2011).

The relationship between senior managers and council overview and scrutiny committees or NHS governing bodies has sometimes become problematic. Senior managers have been criticised for failing to identify serious issues with the result that concerns have been masked and the opportunity lost for governance mechanisms to exercise independent evaluation. Scrutiny committees and governing bodies, perhaps because of lack of training, have sometimes been too slow to press for information, request reports, challenge senior manager assurances, review action taken in response to concerns, and question organisational compliance with care standards (Marsden and Mechen, 2008; CQC, 2009b; Cantrill et al., 2010; Francis, 2010; ESTYN and CSSIW, 2011). Parliament has forcefully criticised the boards of NHS trusts for failing to drive tangible improvements in services and for allocating insufficient priority to patient safety (House of Commons Health Committee, 2009a).

A duty of care, arguably, requires that everyone in the workforce engages with issues relating to internal and external governance, for which standards of good practice are available. Thus, one way of beginning to consider whether and how an organisation may be providing a safe environment for practice is the degree to which there is openness and clarity about:

- Purpose, goals and outcomes.

- How organisational structures are designed to facilitate delivery of the agency's tasks.

- How, where and by whom decisions are taken, and the openness with which they are recorded.

- Who, where and how scrutiny of these decisions is exercised, for instance in relation to assessment and management of risks.

v Clarity about how the organisation will know about quality standards and the effectiveness of its performance monitoring, and who is involved in providing this information.

- The degree to which all internal and external stakeholders are involved in an organisation's assessment of its effectiveness.

- How open the organisation is to external review and to commentary from frontline staff and service users.

- By whom and how often the state of play is presented to external committees or governing boards, and how they are assisted to exercise independent and effective challenge

(Office for Public Management, and Chartered Institute of Public Finance and Account-ancy (OPM and CIPFA), 2004; Audit Commission, 2005; Braye et al., 2011).

C H A P T E R   S U M M A R Y

The central argument in this chapter is that professional accountability, expressed through active adherence to codes of practise, commitment to a duty of care, promotion of whistle blowing and complaints procedures, and a concern with governance, must become more embedded in everyday practice.

The current accountability framework may be imperfect and incomplete. Not all professions are regulated. The powers available to individual workers and regulatory authorities to hold organisations to account may appear limited or difficult to use. Codes of practice may too readily assume that professionals practise in benign organisational environments, and there-fore seem limited when unethical, unlawful or poor practice is found.

The social and health professions claim to be moral forms of activity with ethics and care for service users at their heart. For these claims to be meaningful, professional integrity requires that practitioners should actively give meaning to accountability and then profess the stand-ards which have been codified.

Chapter 3
Law for professional practice

OBJECTIVES

By the end of this chapter, you should have an understanding of:

- The ways in which law forms a key foundation stone in the architecture for professionalism.
- The legal rules which underpin professional practice.
- Key responsibilities of practitioners and managers.

Introduction

Legal knowledge is highlighted across the benchmarks of different professions. Nurses and midwives must *always* (our emphasis) act lawfully (Nursing and Midwifery Council (NMC), 2008a). This includes disclosing information when someone may be at risk of harm, demonstrating awareness of legislation on mental capacity and safeguarding, and upholding patients' rights to be fully involved in decisions about care and treatment.

Medical practitioners must be knowledgeable about the legal rules concerning confidentiality, consent to treatment, patients' rights and protection of children and adults from abuse (Quality Assurance Agency (QAA), 2002). They must understand and accept the legal responsibilities involved in protecting patients from harm, including when this revolves around the performance of colleagues (General Medical Council (GMC), 2009). Medical practitioners should understand the implications for medical practice of equality and human rights legislation and recognise their legal responsibilities concerning death and dying, drug prescribing, mental health and abortion (UK Foundation Office, 2007).

Social workers must appreciate the significance of legal frameworks for service delivery and for accountability (QAA, 2008). This incorporates understanding the relationship between agency procedures and the legal rules, and an ability to think critically about the legal context when working in partnership with service users and other professionals. Social work practice must also be underpinned by principles of equality, human rights and social justice, with practitioners and managers knowing when to use statutory powers and duties to prevent harm or to protect people from harm (HM Government, 2010). Social workers should regularly update their knowledge, receive from their employers clear guidance about how to balance human rights against risks, and ensure that they and their organisations comply with the legal rules when taking decisions (Changing Lives Practice Governance Group, 2011).

The responsibilities of employers mapped out in Chapter 2, for instance concerning health and safety at work, manageable workloads and professional registration, are required by law. Moreover, service users value professionals who know the law, even when that might mean that statutory authority is used in respect of the problems which they have presented to an agency (Braye and Preston-Shoot, 2006). However, as Chapter 1 uncovered, research consistently identifies deficits about legal knowledge and its use in practice, coupled with anxiety about whether the law supports or undermines professional values.

BOX 3.1

Legal rules

In learning disability services, adult safeguarding procedures have not always been adequately followed, and equality and diversity standards are not consistently achieved (Commission for Social Care Inspection (CSCI), 2007).

Serious case reviews in adult safeguarding identified a lack of awareness across professional groupings of adult safeguarding procedures (Manthorpe and Martineau, 2011), including inter-agency collaboration and information sharing.

A low level of awareness of the law has been found among care-sector professionals (Public Concern at Work (PCaW), 2011), and among medical students and qualified doctors (Preston-Shoot and McKimm, 2011; Preston-Shoot et al., 2011). Newly qualified social workers may also be unclear about the difference between legal rules and agency procedures, may lack knowledge of legislation and may not attribute sufficient importance to it when taking decisions (Drury-Hudson, 1999; Braye and Preston-Shoot, 2009).

Some NHS Trusts and councils with social services responsibilities have failed to observe the provisions in the Human Rights Act 1998 concerning respect and fairness, the duties in the Equality Act 2010 concerning reasonable adjustments and impact assessments, and rules in mental capacity legislation concerning best-interest decision-making (Local Government Ombudsman and Parliamentary and Health Service Ombudsman (LGO and PHSO), 2009).

Some organisations have disregarded their statutory duties towards children in need, looked-after young people, and adults in need of community care provision. This may be because of financial constraints and the impact of performance targets, but possibly too because of lack of knowledge about the requirements (Braye and Preston-Shoot, 2009).

Practitioners find some legal rules difficult to understand and therefore to use, especially those relating to information sharing (Data Protection Act 1998), raising concerns (Public Interest Disclosure Act 1998), and people's rights (Human Rights Act 1998) (Perkins et al., 2007). Managers need greater awareness of the requirements of the legal rules (Skinner and Whyte, 2004), including the rights of whistle blowers (PCaW, 2011).

Reports have identified that both councils with social services responsibilities (Laming, 2009) and NHS organisations (NHS Constitution State of Readiness Group, 2009) may not be fully meeting their legal obligations. Social and healthcare professionals may, therefore, need explanations about the law and its interface with best practice (Manthorpe et al., 2009). This chapter provides information to help social and healthcare professionals negotiate dilemmas that arise in practice, respond to questions from service users, and give an account of their decision-making.

ACTIVITY 3.1

Health and social care practitioners often have an image of the law as intimidating and unlikely to support their values or to assist them to achieve the goals of professional intervention.

- *To what degree do you believe that the legal rules will assist you in practice to:*
  - *Ensure standards of service provision?*
  - *Promote equality and human rights?*
  - *Safeguard and protect children in need and adults at risk in their own homes or in care settings?*
  - *Resolve challenges and dilemmas that arise when working with service users and other professionals?*
  - *Apply professional values and ethics?*

  Note the reasons for the answers you give.

- *Repeat the exercise at the end of the chapter and compare your reflections.*

Structure of the legal rules

Primary legislation lays out specific powers and duties given to the NHS and to councils with social services responsibilities. Because responsibility for health and social services has been devolved to the Northern Ireland Assembly, the Welsh Assembly and the Scottish Government, not all relevant primary legislation is enacted by the Westminster parliament. The provisions within primary legislation often take the form of a skeleton, which is then fleshed out by secondary legislation (regulations and statutory instruments presented by ministers) and government guidance.

Statutory or policy guidance is binding on the organisations to which it is issued, the authority for which in social services in England and Wales resides in Section 7, Local Authority Social Services Act 1970. This requires councils with social services responsibilities to follow ministerial directions. Practice guidance is advisory but should not be lightly ignored (*R v Islington LBC, ex parte Rixon* [1996]).

Sometimes courts have to clarify the meaning, intention or scope of particular provisions (Braye and Preston-Shoot, 2009) and determine whether an organisation has acted in breach of the rules contained with primary legislation, secondary regulations or statutory guidance (for example, *R v Sefton MBC, ex parte Help the Aged and Charlotte Blanchard* [1997]).

Administrative law is also relevant to decisions taken by individual professionals and by NHS trusts and councils with social service responsibilities. The principles within administrative law have evolved as courts have laid down standards by which organisations with statutory powers and duties exercise such authority. These principles become especially relevant when decision-making and the involvement of service users and patients is considered later in this chapter.

Rights

Health and social care in the UK is founded on powers and duties given by legislating bodies to councils with social services responsibilities, and to the NHS. Recent developments with respect to patients' and service users' rights are, therefore, significant in this context.

Rights for patients in England and Wales are enshrined in the NHS Constitution. The constitution has been placed on a statutory footing and must be reviewed every three years for its impact on patients and staff (Health Act 2009):

The NHS Constitution contains several principles:

- Services should be available to everyone, with access based on need not ability to pay.

- Everyone in the NHS should be committed to standards of excellence and professionalism so that services are focused on the patient experience and characterised by quality and effective care.

- Services should reflect the needs and preferences of patients, their families and carers. Consultation and involvement should characterise interactions surrounding care and treatment.

- Partnership working should characterise engagement with other organisations as well as with patients and communities.

- The NHS should provide best value for money and demonstrate accountability.

The NHS Constitution enshrines only three new patients' rights: to choice, vaccinations and rational decision-making about the funding of drugs and treatments. The remaining rights already have some basis in the structure of the legal rules outlined above; however, they are now accompanied by NHS commitments (see Box 3.2).

BOX **3.2**

Rights and commitments in the NHS

- *Right to accessible services which are (mainly) free at the delivery point and available either within maximum waiting times or through alternative providers, if necessary, within the European Economic Area.*

- *Right to expect the NHS to assess the health needs of local communities and to commission services accordingly.*

- *Right to expect services free of discrimination.*

- *NHS commitment to convenient and accessible provision within specified waiting times, with clear and transparent decision-making about how services are planned and delivered.*

- *Right to be treated with professional standards of care by appropriately qualified and experienced staff in organisations which are characterised by safety and quality, and which are effectively monitored.*

BOX **3.2** *continued*

- *NHS commitment to clean and safe services delivered in suitable environments, which aim for continuous improvement and best practice.*

- *Rights to recommended drugs, vaccinations and treatments, with local decisions on funding made rationally.*

- *NHS commitment to provide recommended screening programmes.*

- *Right to dignity, respect and human rights, including privacy and confidentiality, as exemplified by receiving information about possible treatments and their risks and then giving or refusing consent to treatment.*

- *Right to make choices about NHS care, including about which general practitioner to register with.*

- *NHS commitment to offering accessible and reliable information with which to make personal decisions about healthcare, and to show letters between clinicians about your treatment.*

- *Right to be involved in decision-making about personal healthcare, with information given about current and likely future services.*

- *NHS commitment to providing information about future plans and to working in partnership with patients.*

- *Right to use complaints procedures, the Health Services Ombudsman and judicial review, and to receive compensation when harmed by negligent treatment.*

- *NHS commitment to courtesy and support when handing complaints, with no reprisals in terms of future care. Mistakes will be acknowledged and lessons learned.*

The NHS Constitution also outlines patients' responsibilities for their own health and well-being, including to treat staff with respect, provide relevant information and register with a general practitioner.

The NHS Constitution makes commitments to staff, which repeat provisions in employment and discrimination legislation. Commitments cover provision of a safe working environment, professional development, involvement in decision-making, and the right to raise a grievance. Healthcare practitioners and managers must accept professional accountability, maintain high standards of practice, and meet their health and safety obligations. They should engage in training and other forms of professional development, address practice concerns promptly, and only share confidential information when people are at risk of significant harm.

Commissioners and providers of NHS care must have regard to the constitution in all their decisions and actions, reporting to ministers on the quality of services. Statutory recognition is given to the practice principles of dignity, respect and compassion (PHSO, 2011). However, the constitution and the rights it affords are not yet fully embedded in the daily practice of the NHS (NHS Constitution State of Readiness Group, 2009). Proposals have been made to strengthen the duty to involve patients and the duty to promote involvement (NHS Future Forum, 2011). The protection which the constitution gives to whistle blowers may also be strengthened (Santry, 2011).

A similar route is contained within the Patients Rights (Scotland) Act 2011. Scottish Ministers must publish a charter of patients' rights and responsibilities. Healthcare should consider patients' needs and best care or treatment, encouraging their participation in decisions, partly through the provision of information. There are rights to maximum treatment waiting times, to give feedback and to raise concerns with a health provider and/or Scottish Public Services Ombudsman. Staff must maintain a focus on patients and on providing quality care and treatments. Patients have responsibilities too, for treating staff with respect and for attending appointments. Patient advice and support services will be established to help patients know and access their rights, and give feedback.

Rights affecting the provision of services delivered by social and healthcare professionals may also be found in the Human Rights Act 1998. This Act incorporates the European Convention on Human Rights and Fundamental Freedoms into UK law, and applies to organisations that perform public functions. The European Convention rights most applicable to the work of social and healthcare professions are:

BOX **3.3**

Human rights
Article 2 – right to life

Article 3 – right to live free of inhuman and degrading treatment

Article 5 – right to liberty

Article 6 – right to a fair trial or hearing

Article 8 – right to private and family life

Article 13 – right to an effective remedy

Article 14 – right to live free of discrimination

All rights except Article 3 may be limited by the wording of the European Convention or qualified by the state. In the latter instance, any qualification must be according to law and proportionate in terms of the objectives pursued. States are allowed some 'margin of appreciation' in how the articles are reflected in legislation in order to accommodate social and cultural norms. However, states are positively obliged to promote European Convention rights, and legislation may be declared incompatible with them. The rights are meant to be practical and effective rather than theoretical, which may be seen in the sample of judicial decisions about people's health and welfare in Box 3.4.

The Human Rights Act 1998 has rendered public bodies more open to claims for damages arising from how statutory duties have been implemented. The Human Rights Act has strengthened claims to dignity and human empathy. However, this recalibration of power relations, which strengthens service users' procedural rights regarding the use of authority

BOX *3.4*

Protection

- *A flawed assessment that failed to acknowledge the disadvantages for a learning-disabled person living away from home, that disregarded the views of the carer, and that kept the individual in a unit without lawful authority breached Articles 5 and 8 (London Borough of Hillingdon v Neary and Another [2011]).*

- *Children in custody are to be regarded as children in need, to guarantee Article 3 and 8 rights (R (Howard League for Penal Reform) v Secretary of State for the Home Department and the Department of Health (interested party) [2003]).*

- *Failure to protect children from abuse may breach Article 3 (Z v UK [2001]).*

- *Denial of support to destitute asylum seekers which results in intense physical and mental suffering breaches Article 3 (R (Limbuela and Others) v Secretary of State for the Home Department [2006]).*

Quality

- *Unacceptable delays in service provision can breach Article 8 (R (Bernard and Another) v Enfield LBC [2002]).*

- *Failure to review cases of looked-after children and to act on the evidence may breach Articles 6, 8 and 13 (Barrett v Enfield LBC [1999]).*

- *Care should be provided for disabled people at home, when possible, to adhere to Article 8 (R (Gunter) v SW Staffordshire PCT [2006]).*

- *Parents must be involved in decision making and able to answer allegations about the care they provide to their children (Article 8) (TP and KM v UK [2002]).*

- *Ex parte orders, where parents or other potential parties are not present at hearings, should only be used in urgent cases (Article 5, 6 and 8) (Re X (Emergency Protection Orders) [2006]).*

Meeting needs

- *Decisions to close residential homes will be quashed (Article 8) where individuals' needs have not been assessed and where the closure is neither proportionate nor beneficial to them (R (Phillips) v Walsall MBC [2002]).*

- *If a patient who is not suffering from mental disorder is detained for too long pending discharge, this will breach Article 5 (Johnson v UK [1997]). Patients should not be detained longer than necessary (R (KB and Others) v MHRT and Another [2002]).*

Accountability

- *Practitioners and public bodies, when defending claims for negligence, must be able to demonstrate that they did what could reasonably have been expected of them. Article 2 requires that competent staff, trained to high professional standards, adopt safe systems at work, including the proper supervision of patients, and do all they reasonably can to* protect patients from risks that are known or should be appreciated *(Savage v* South Essex Partnership NHS Foundation Trust *[2008])*.

- *A home closure was quashed where residents were not given true reasons and where there had been no consideration of Article 8 rights* (R (Madden) v Bury MBC *[2002])*.

- *Failure to protect children from abuse may breach Article 3* (E v UK *[2002])*.

by public bodies, may not be sufficient to ensure ethical or lawful practice (Braye and Preston-Shoot, 2009).

Equally, there are gaps in the Human Rights Act. The Act focuses on civil and political rather than social and economic rights. It does not cover private placements in residential care[1] or confer human rights obligations on independent care providers and personal assistants, leaving some adults at risk of abuse (Braye and Preston-Shoot, 2009; Galpin, 2010). It is important to recall here that significant numbers of older people, especially, are abused by care workers in their own homes or in nursing care or residential care settings, or in hospitals and sheltered housing (House of Commons Health Committee, 2004; Action on Elder Abuse, 2006).

If not rights, there are principles articulated in other pieces of primary legislation. For instance, in England and Wales the Mental Health Act 2007 requires that practice should respect diversity, the wishes and feelings of patients, and the views of carers. Practice should use effective treatments and promote patient safety and well-being, in part through patients' involvement in their care and treatment. As the section on decision-making below illustrates, mental capacity legislation also enshrines key principles.

Equality

Anti-discriminatory practice is good practice. A failure to meet an individual's needs, to counteract discrimination and to promote equality is, arguably, an act of injustice and a breach of a professional's duty of care (General Social Care Council (GSCC), 2002; NMC, 2008a). Organisations should provide a satisfactory and appropriate service for all communities.

Anti-discriminatory practice is also a legal requirement. The Equality Act 2010 applies in England, Wales and Scotland.[2] It consolidates and extends equality legislation in respect of employment and the provision of goods and services. It covers age, disability, gender reassignment, race, religion or belief, sex, sexuality, marriage and civil partnership, pregnancy and maternity. It adds categories of associative discrimination and discrimination by perception to existing prohibitions concerning direct and indirect discrimination. It extends protection against victimisation, if an employee has made a complaint or expressed a grievance, and harassment. Public bodies have a duty to promote equality by means of policy impact assessments, equality objectives and annual reporting.

Equality duties, including impact assessments, also apply to the provision of goods and services, including the conducting of assessments. Thus, in *R (AM) v Birmingham CC* [2009], a community care assessment was upheld because it had paid proper regard to disability and the need to intervene to protect and promote the service user's interests.

Across the UK, parents of disabled children have the right to request flexible working. Employers do not have to agree to the request but must provide sound business reasons in writing, following a meeting, if they do not (Employment Act 2002). There are also rights to paid and unpaid maternity leave, paid paternity leave, paid and unpaid adoption leave, and unpaid leave to manage unexpected problems involving the care of dependents. These rights apply to same-sex and opposite-sex relationships.

Across the UK, too, changing social norms and moves towards greater equality are also reflected in the Civil Partnership Act 2004 and the Gender Recognition Act 2004. The Civil Partnership Act provides for legal partnerships between adults of the same sex; the Gender Recognition Act enables people who have had gender reassignment surgery to obtain birth certificates in their reassigned sex and to marry.

Judicial reviews, however, have been critical of local and central government concerning their compliance with equality impact assessments when considering changes to policy and procedures.

BOX **3.5**

Judicial reviews

- R (Chavda) *v* Harrow LBC *[2008]* – *a successful challenge by service users to an amendment to a local authority's adult social care eligibility criteria. The local authority had not considered the impact on disabled people of a proposed policy change.*

- R (Kaur) *v* Ealing LBC *[2008]* – *the local authority must perform a race equality impact assessment before changing funding criteria for voluntary organisations.*

- R (JL) *v* Islington LBC *[2009]* – *local authority acted unlawfully when using eligibility criteria to deny a disabled child and family a core assessment. Failed to consider Disability Discrimination Act 2005 duties towards disabled people when creating, implementing or amending policies.*

- R (Boyejo and Others) *v* Barnet LBC *[2010]* – *a decision to withdraw resident warden services was unlawful, because the local authority had failed to complete a rational equality impact assessment, to consult adequately, and to inform decision makers of the content of equality duties.*

- R (Meany & Others) *v* Harlow DC *[2009]* – *cuts to rights advice funding was ruled unlawful because the council had not paid due regard to equality duties and the impact of the proposed change.*

- R (Equality and Human Rights Commission) *v* Secretary of State for Justice *[2010]* – *without documentary evidence, a public authority will have difficulty showing how it complied with equality duties.*

- R (W) *v* Birmingham City Council *[2011]* – *when proposing to raise eligibility levels for community care from substantial and critical needs to critical only, as a result of budget restrictions, there had been a lack of clarity in the consultation material and insufficient regard had been paid to the likely impact on disabled people.*

Inspections of local authority performance in England, relating to progress promoting race, disability and sexuality equality (CSCI, 2008a; CSCI, 2008b; CSCI, 2009), have found the need for positive leadership and the development of staff training in order to challenge discriminatory attitudes. Reviews have been recommended of equality strategies and of policies and procedures concerning assessment, care planning and the provision of information.

Similarly, in England the Healthcare Commission (2009) found variable performance concerning the promotion of race equality. There was some evidence of falling standards with regard to challenging discrimination and respecting human rights. Some black and minority ethnic service users were less likely than others to receive a favourable experience of NHS provision, and black and minority ethnic staff were more likely to be involved in capability reviews and subject to harassment and bullying. The report concluded that there is discrimination within the NHS, that progress with developing race equality schemes and equality impact assessments has been slow, and that adherence to race equality legislation is problematic. The Healthcare Commission report recommended compliance with legal duties, repeated the importance of treating all patients with dignity, and looked to senior managers and governing bodies to exercise leadership relating to workforce monitoring and the involvement of patients and communities in personal treatment discussions and in planning the development of services.

Welfare law also contains principles and duties relating to equality. Thus, in England and Wales, the Mental Health Act 2007 requires that services demonstrate respect for diversity and avoid unlawful discrimination. In England and Wales, those responsible for decision-making concerning the welfare of children must ensure that race, culture, religion and language are considered (the Children Act 1989, and the Adoption and Children Act 2002). The Children (Scotland) Act 1995 and the Children (Northern Ireland) Order 1995 contain similar provisions. Carers have a right to information about assessment (Carers and Direct Payments Act (Northern Ireland) 2002; Community Care and Health Act (Scotland) 2002; Carers (Equal Opportunities) Act 2004).

Some groups, however, remain disproportionately represented in the numbers of looked-after young people or of adults compulsorily detained in psychiatric institutions and prisons. Female and young carers may not receive the support to which they are, in theory, entitled (Braye and Preston-Shoot, 2009). Councils with social services responsibilities have also been criticised for discriminatory and inflexible attitudes towards, for example, financial support for kinship carers (*R (L and Others)* v *Manchester City Council* [2002]), and older people transferring between residential and nursing care settings (*R (Goldsmith)* v *Wandsworth LBC* [2004]).

Extensive patterns of discrimination adversely affect the recruitment, promotion and treatment of staff. Such discrimination is well recorded in respect of gender, disability and ethnic origin in the NHS, although it is less well recorded (but nonetheless present) in local government and for other 'protected characteristics'. Such discrimination adversely impacts on the ability of health and social care services to provide the best possible services (Healthcare Commission 2007b; 2009).

Questions remain, therefore, whether decades of equality legislation have transformed individual attitudes and organisational practices, and whether sufficient attention is paid to anti-discriminatory practice in the provision of care and services.

Standards

All four UK countries have passed legislation designed to improve standards and strengthen the scrutiny of service provision. For social work and social care, legislation has been passed that creates care councils, provides for the registration of social workers and, outside England, some social care workers, enables the publication of codes of practice and frameworks of quality standards, and creates systems and organisations responsible for registration, inspection and deregistration of service providers (Care Standards Act 2000; Health and Personal Social Services Act (Northern Ireland) 2001; Regulation of Care (Scotland) Act 2001).

Increasingly, regulation of quality standards in health is being brought together with that of social care (Health and Social Care Act 2008; Health and Social Care Reform (Northern Ireland) Act 2008), with powers being given to regulators to publish and monitor adherence to quality standards. Thus, in England for instance, the Health and Social Care Act 2008 (Regulated Activities) Regulations 2010 require that health and social care registered settings offering nursing care, maternity care, treatment of disease, injury and disorder, and personal care must have at all times sufficient numbers of suitably qualified, skilled and experienced staff in order to safeguard the health, safety and well-being of service users. The Care Quality Commission (CQC) has a similar requirement in its quality standards (CQC, 2010). This builds on an earlier requirement for social services in England and Wales (Section 6, Local Authority Social Services Act 1970) that there should be sufficient (not defined) staff to enable statutory functions to be performed. It reinforces too the obligations on directors of children's services (Department for Education and Skills (DfES), 2005) and adult services (Department of Health (DH), 2006b) to ensure that there are sufficient resources to maintain standards and discharge statutory functions, and that staff are supported to maintain their code of practice.

The management of professional registers by the care councils is the subject of secondary legislation, for example the Care Council for Wales (Conduct) Rules 2011. Thus the process that may lead to penalties of admonishment, suspension or removal is governed by legal rules. Awareness amongst the general public of the code of practice and registers may be low, however, limiting their effectiveness in raising standards.

The NHS Constitution (PHSO, 2011) requires the provision of high quality care that is safe, effective and focused on the patient's experience. For healthcare professions such as physiotherapy, occupational therapy and paramedics, the Health Professions Order 2001 requires that standards of proficiency are established which govern admission to professional registers. These are standards of conduct, performance and ethics which are regarded as essential and indispensable for safe and effective practice. Nursing and midwifery is currently regulated through the Health Act 1999 and the Nursing and Midwifery Order 2001 (Ackerman, 2011). The NMC was established, and a system created of registration and fitness-to-practise determinations and for midwives' statutory supervision.

Where regulators such as the CQC publish standards as part of their legal powers and duties, these should be followed as statements of good practice. Adherence will certainly be monitored by the regulator and could be used by an ombudsman or judicial review when determining whether practice has met standards of reasonableness. Equally, although the social care employers' code (GSCC, 2002) does not have mandatory status, this too will be used during inspections by the CQC and Ofsted. Thus, quality and safety benchmarks (CQC, 2010) require: people's involvement and consent in their care, treatment and support; standards of safeguarding, which include meeting nutritional needs, cleanliness, infection control, medication management, and protection from abuse; appropriate staffing in terms of numbers and skills; quality management, including accessible complaints procedures; and suitable management in terms of qualifications and attitudes. These benchmarks have their origin in care standards legislation and should be met. Indeed, the CQC publishes media releases on cases where hospitals and care homes have failed to meet these standards, and professional regulators such as the NMC and GMC may initiate fitness-to-practise proceedings when healthcare professionals have failed to provide appropriate standards of care.

The suitability of the workforce has also been the subject of legislation (Safeguarding Vulnerable Groups Act 2006; Protection of Vulnerable Groups (Scotland) Act 2007; Safeguarding Vulnerable Groups (Northern Ireland) Order 2007). Thus, across health and social professions, people must be vetted prior to commencing employment and may be barred as unsuitable to work with children and/or adults at risk. Case law is also now emerging on the degree to which levels of staffing, stress and difficult working conditions may be used as mitigation in conduct hearings (Braye and Preston-Shoot, 2009; Hussein et al., 2009a).

Employers must refer workers who are dismissed, or who resign ahead of the conclusion of capability procedures, for misconduct that has placed people at risk of harm. This misconduct may include neglect, abuse or failure to act. Many referrals emanate from residential and domiciliary care (Stevens and Manthorpe, 2007). However, not all employers have acted upon concerns, and the focus on individual practitioners, whilst necessary, may encourage neglect of fundamental systemic weakness in service cultures and resources (Marsland et al., 2007; Stevens and Manthorpe, 2007; GSCC, 2009).

There are also criminal offences of maltreatment and neglect, which may add to the safeguarding mosaic. Thus, in England and Wales for instance, it is a criminal offence to physically or sexually abuse, harm or cause deliberate cruelty by neglect to a child or an adult (Domestic Violence, Crime and Victims Act 2004); the Mental Health Act 1983 makes it unlawful for staff to neglect or ill-treat a patient; and the Mental Capacity Act 2005 makes it an offence to ill-treat or neglect a person who lacks capacity. However, poor practice rather than criminal behaviour may be the more prevalent challenge (Manthorpe et al., 2009).

In England at least, there is increasing doubt about whether the regulatory framework will be extended to professions which are currently unregulated, such as sports therapy and youth work. Also, the DH (2011a) has not committed itself to legislating for nurses to have protected title, and has stated a preference for voluntary rather than compulsory registration for support workers in the NHS. It argues that employers should take responsibility for service quality which, on the basis of the evidence presented in this book, seems a dubious proposition on its own. In contrast, the NHS Future Forum (2011) has expressed concern that key healthcare workers are not regulated, other than through their contract of employment. The DH (2011b) has also argued that compulsory regulation might constrain the ability of professionals to operate flexibly, and restates the onus on employers and staff to foster professional excellence. It places its faith also in the scrutiny of practice by the CQC, with its inspection and outcome standards relating to practitioners' fitness for practice, and their qualifications and skills. Again, the evidence presented in this book raises question marks over whether there is evidence to justify such an aspiration and whether service users' and patients' interests are adequately safeguarded in such a voluntary system.

In a similar vein, ministers in England have stepped back from previous consideration of the need for regulation a range of social care assistants, notably home care assistants, despite evidence from care settings such as Winterbourne View that service users are abused in care settings and have not been safeguarded by the current system of regulation and inspection (House of Commons Health Committee, 2004; Action on Elder Abuse, 2006; Sheather, 2011). A different approach is possibly emerging in Wales (Welsh Assembly Government, 2011a) which envisages sustainable social services as requiring a move to professionalise managers of care homes.

Decision-making

ACTIVITY 3.2

- *When you consult a professional on whose attitudes, knowledge and skill you rely, what standards do you expect?*

- *What benchmarks would you use when deciding whether you are satisfied? Compare your standards with those that the legal rules recognise.*

Well-established principles in administrative law require that, except where it would place individuals at serious risk, meaningful consultation should occur before decisions are taken with, where relevant, information shared about the decision-makers' powers and duties. Options and their relative merits should be discussed. Information on which decision-takers might subsequently rely must be shared. Those affected should be given time to make representations. Decisions, when taken, must be reasonable, it must be possible to demonstrate how any relevant statutory guidance has been followed, and decisions should preferably be given in writing. Decisions should be based on an assessment of need and supported by adequate reasoning which is in line with best evidence about good practice.

Thus, in a child care case, a local authority had to show that its decisions were not arbitrary, its proposed action was proportionate to the risks identified, and that its recommendations could be justified by reference to an assessment that had weighed all the factors and options in a balance (*Re C and B (Care Order: Future Harm* [2001]). Similarly, a health authority could not evade obligations by waiting until a variation of services was urgently required and then seeking to limit the consultation (*R v North and East Devon Health Authority and North Devon Healthcare NHS Trust, ex parte Metcalfe* [1999]).

Principles of administrative law have been applied to judge the lawfulness or otherwise of decisions about approval of medications (*R (Easai Ltd) v NICE* [2008]), closure of residential care homes (*R v Devon County Council, ex parte Baker and Johns* [1995]), and changes to the funding of voluntary organisations (*R (Capenhurst, Kirby, King, Mistry and Joachim) v Leicester City Council* [2004]).

Where there are competing claims about how an organisation should deploy its resources, often involving competing medical, healthcare or social care opinions, courts are hesitant to interfere unless the decision is unlawful, unreasonable or irrational (*R* v *Cambridge Health Authority, ex parte B* [1995]). Where the legal rules require decision-makers to pay due regard or due consideration to information and assessments, the decision-makers must be able to show what was considered, when and by whom, with the reasons for particular outcomes based on clear and rational reasoning (*R (Chavda)* v *Harrow LBC* [2008]).

Occasionally, primary legislation has articulated principles by which professionals and agencies should approach decision-making. Thus, for England and Wales, the Mental Capacity Act 2005 requires that an adult be presumed to have capacity, and gives adults the right to support in order to exercise that capacity and make their own decisions. Where capacity can be shown to be lacking, professionals must find the least restrictive intervention to preserve the person's basic rights and freedoms – the proportionate response consistent with the risks identified. Equally, across the UK, those involved with assessment under mental health legislation must consider all the circumstances of the case before determining how best to provide care and treatment.

Involvement

One key component of effective decision-making is the degree to which service users feel involved in the care, treatment and services they receive. The NHS Constitution (Health Act 2009) requires that patients are involved in, and consulted about, their care and treatment (PHSO, 2011). However, patients may not be aware of this right (NHS Constitution State of Readiness Group, 2009). Care standards for health and social care service provision (CQC, 2010) include involvement so that people are able to express their views and contribute to decisions about care, treatment and support. At least one jurisdiction is considering how to strengthen involvement, through codifying clear rights to be heard and extending the right to support by advocates (Welsh Assembly Government, 2011a).

Welfare law and statutory guidance promote the idea of people as active partners in assessments and in the design, commissioning, delivery, monitoring and management of services (NHS and Community Care Act 1990; DH, 1990). More recently, this has been framed as expert patients and carers being at the centre of care, with a greater say over where, how and by whom services are provided (DH, 2006a). Research, however, continues to report variable experiences of the quality of advice, support and participation offered (Braye and Preston-Shoot, 2009).

Mental health legislation and guidance – for example, Mental Health Act 1983 (see also DH, 2008); Mental Health (Scotland) Act 1984; Mental Health (Care and Treatment) (Scotland) Act 2003; Mental Health Act 2007 – promote the involvement of patients as far as possible in the formulation and delivery of care and treatment. Patients should be given information about their treatment and their rights. However, research evidence raises questions about the degree of partnership being offered (Braye and Preston-Shoot, 2009).

Decision-making administrative law principles and primary legislation (Children Act 1989; Children (Scotland) Act 1995 and Children (Northern Ireland) Order 1995) require that the wishes and feelings of parents and children are ascertained and considered. However, parents still frequently report being unclear about the procedures in which they have become involved, and may be uncertain about the allegations facing them (Munro, 2011). Children may also not feel involved in processes that are designed to protect them and promote their well-being.

The requirements in professional codes (for example, GSCC, 2002; NMC, 2008a) that patients and service users are given relevant information and support, are endorsed within the legal rules and, indeed, are themselves derived from legislation that has empowered regulators to issue them. Compliance, however, appears variable.

Perhaps in recognition that the balance of power in interactions between service users and professionals may sometimes defeat the intention behind the legal rules, advocacy has been given statutory backing. In England and Wales, learning disabled people and individuals experiencing mental distress have, in certain circumstances, the right to an advocate (Mental Capacity Act 2005; Mental Health Act 2007). In Scotland,[3] similar provision may be found in the Mental Health (Care and Treatment) (Scotland) Act 2003) and the Adult Support and Protection (Scotland) Act 2007. Advocates have helped to improve decision making regarding adult protection, medical treatment, best interest assessments, and accommodation.

The culture shift that independent advocacy entails for NHS and local authority organisations has only just begun, and referrals in some organisations are still low. As yet there is no statutory right to advocacy for all client groups in all situations involving the use of power and authority. Some service users and patients may not have the benefit of an advocate when confronting organisational failures to act lawfully and/or ethically, or when there are disputes between individuals, carers and professionals regarding what might be an appropriate intervention (Braye and Preston-Shoot, 2009; Manthorpe et al., 2009).

Central to a commitment to involvement is consent. Where patients and service users have decision-making capacity, professionals must obtain consent before providing care, treatment or support (NMC, 2008a; CQC, 2010). People's right to accept or decline intervention must be respected. Intervention without consent may constitute assault or battery, depending on whether the individual has been touched (Dimond, 2011). To be valid, consent should be freely given and should be informed, which requires the provision of information detailing all the options and their potential benefits and risks, together with checking what has been understood. This is one aspect of a duty of care. Failure to provide balanced and accessible information might result in a claim for negligence. Such a claim would have to demonstrate a link between the duty of care and the harm experienced.

Thus, social and healthcare professionals must understand legislation regarding capacity (Adults with Incapacity (Scotland) Act 2000; Mental Capacity Act 2005). For those individuals who lack capacity, social and healthcare professionals must be able to show how they have acted in people's best interests, established according to relevant codes of practice (for instance, for England and Wales: Department for Constitutional Affairs, 2007) (NMC, 2008a; Stirrat et al., 2010). Practitioners must adhere to the legal framework that establishes that capacity has to be determined on a situation-by-situation or decision-by-decision basis, using criteria concerning whether an individual understands and can retain relevant information, can use it to reach a decision, and can communicate a decision. For those individuals who might meet these criteria for decision-making capacity but who are acting under constraint, undue influence or coercion, the courts may exercise their inherent jurisdiction to protect them from significant harm (*Re S (Adult Patient) (Inherent Jurisdiction: Family Life)* [2002]; *LA* v *D and E* [2007]).

Involvement also entails respect for the patient or service user's right to confidentiality, as encapsulated in Article 8 of the European Convention (Human Rights Act 1998). Information disclosure, therefore, should normally follow the subject's consent. However, the Data Protection Act 1998, which applies across the UK, allows information to be shared without consent in certain circumstances. These include situations where it is necessary to prevent or to protect individuals from harm, to assist with the prevention or detection of crime, or to facilitate decision-making on what action to take (for guidance, see DH, 2000c; DH, 2008). Case law has also established that a strong public interest can override a professional's ordinary duty of confidentiality (*W* v *Egdell* [1989]; *Re B (Children: Patient Confidentiality)* [2003]), permitting, for example, disclosure to employers and regulatory authorities (*Woolgar* v *Chief Constable of Sussex Police and UKCC* [2000]; *Maddock* v *Devon County Council* [2004]).

Challenges remain, not least regarding practitioners' uncertainty about the lawfulness of sharing information (Laming, 2003; Bichard, 2004; Perkins et al., 2007; Pinkney et al., 2008) and regarding the strength of attachment to the principle of confidentiality, which can impede working together with other professionals and influence whether discretion to disclose is used (Sheppard, 1996; Reder and Duncan, 2003). In response, in the context of children, some regulatory bodies have combined to issue a joint values statement which restates the primary duty to safeguard and promote children's welfare (General Teaching Council (GTC) et al., 2007). In Wales, new legislation may follow to ensure the sharing of information in safeguarding cases (Welsh Assembly Government, 2011a). Thus, for disclosure to be lawful, there should be a legal power in legislation to share information (Data Protection Act 1998), the disclosure should be proportional (Human Rights Act 1998) and the public interest should be capable of justifying it.

Health and safety

Health and social care employers have a general duty to provide a safe working environment for: their employees; others working or training on their premises or otherwise acting in the course of or arising out their employment or training; members of the public, including visitors to the premises; and anyone receiving services, treatment or advice.

An employer's health and safety duties towards staff, service users and the general public include a general duty to have safe systems of work and a safe work environment, a duty to carry out a range of risk assessments of possible hazards, and specific duties laid down in law regarding particular hazards. Employers must involve staff in their health and safety arrangements and, if asked, appoint health and safety representatives with legal rights and protection.

Section 2 of the Health and Safety at Work etc Act 1974 sets out employers' general duties to ensure safe equipment, systems of work, transport, storage, maintenance, training and supervision. The Act requires employers to take steps *so far as is reasonably practicable*. That does not mean, as is sometimes suggested by employers, that they need not do something because it is expensive to do so. It means that the cost of controlling the risk must not be grossly disproportionate to the expected benefits. The onus is on employers to demonstrate that to go any further than they already have would incur costs disproportionate to the amount of benefit provided. Section 3 places a general duty on employers and those who are self-employed to ensure that their activities do not endanger anyone.

Section 7 of the Health and Safety at Work etc Act 1974 requires every employee to take reasonable care for their own health and safety, and for that of other people who may be affected by their acts or omissions at work. This means that, whilst it is the employer's duty that is most important, individual practitioners and managers have some personal responsibility for health and safety and a duty to raise with their employer any health and safety concerns they have, in a similar way that their professional code requires them to raise concerns. At all times, individuals must act within their delegated authority (*R* v *Kirklees MBC, ex parte Daykin* [1996]) and not perform roles and tasks for which they are not competent.

The Management of Health and Safety at Work Regulations 1999 place a duty on employers to conduct assessments of the risks to the health and safety of employees and others. The risk assessments must cover foreseeable hazards, including the consequences of inadequate staffing, lifting and manual handling, and heavy workloads.

The Corporate Manslaughter and Corporate Homicide Act 2007 applies throughout the United Kingdom, although the offence with which organisations can be charged is corporate homicide in Scotland and corporate manslaughter elsewhere. Organisations may be prosecuted for serious failing in their duty of care to employees and/or in the supply of goods and services. Indifference to how risks are managed, care is provided, and health and safety obligations are met are examples of serious failings, for instance in respect of detained patients or offenders, or older people with dementia in residential or nursing care settings. The substantial failing must be at senior level where significant decisions are made for the whole or a substantial part of an agency.

The Health and Safety Offences Act 2008 enables courts to impose greater penalties for breaches of health and safety legislation such as reckless disregard of requirements, death as a result of a breach, and persistent poor compliance. It extends the range of offences for which individuals at any level within organisations can be imprisoned.

Individuals and organisations, therefore, should routinely risk-assess their activities and act to control health and safety risks. Staff competencies should be updated regularly, supported by training and written procedures. Staff should not be exposed to risks to their personal safety, for instance when making home visits or working outside usual office hours.

Raising concerns

There are two aspects to the legal framework here, one relating to employees and the other to service users.

In England, Scotland and Wales, employees who disclose in the public interest information that would normally remain confidential are protected in law (Public Interest Disclosure Act 1998), provided that they act in good faith and not for personal gain, believing their concerns and evidence to be true. The corresponding provision in Northern Ireland is the Public Interest Disclosure Act (Northern Ireland) Order 1998. Permitted disclosures include failures by health and social care organisations to comply with legal obligations, and situations where the health and safety of employees and of service users is endangered by the acts or omissions of employers.

When safe to do so, concerns should normally be raised within the organisation first, but external whistle blowing may be more effective in encouraging employers to act. Case law has established that anonymous statements from staff may be permissible when an organisation is taking action against another employee (*Linford Cash and Carry Ltd* v *Thomson* [1989]; *Ramsey* v *Walkers Snack Foods Ltd* [2004]).

Whether the whistle blower has acted in good faith is ultimately a question for employers and the courts or employment tribunals. The burden of proof lies with the person raising concerns. The legislation does not require organisations to have whistle blowing policies, although they would be advised to do so in order to be seen as having acted responsibly. Employees do not need to have completed a one-year qualifying requirement to pursue unfair dismissal claims arising from a whistle blowing incident.

The law flags the desirability of raising concerns. The law has been used successfully, albeit sometimes at considerable cost to the emotional well-being and job security of those who have blown the whistle (see Chapter 2; Peters et al., 2011), which suggests that the protection provided is inadequate (House of Commons Health Committee, 2009a; Preston-Shoot, 2010a). Research by Public Concern at Work (PCAW, 2011) concluded that clear and accessible pathways are needed, coupled with training and guidance for employers on how to encourage staff to raise concerns, and how then to handle concerns.

All NHS trusts, care providers and councils with social services responsibilities must also have complaints procedures which are accessible to patients and service users. They should actively welcome feedback and complaints. They should have effective systems in place for receiving, handling and responding to complaints, ensuring too that complainants are not subsequently victimised (CQC, 2010).

Patients have the right to complain about unacceptable or inadequate medical and healthcare treatment, long waiting times and discourteous staff behaviour (for example, Health Act 2009, for England and Wales; Patients Rights (Scotland) Act 2011; Health and Social Care Complaints Procedures Directions (Northern Ireland) 2009). Investigations should be efficient and properly undertaken, with the outcomes shared with complainants. The first stage involves an attempt at local resolution, for which assistance is available from agencies such as the Independent Complaints Advocacy Service. Subsequently, referrals may be made for judicial review or to the relevant ombudsman. Referrals are also possible to a regulatory authority such as the NMC, GMC or CQC, in respect of incompetence, breaches of confidentiality or abuse. Indeed, commissioners should report to professional regulators such as the CQC and NMC organisations that do not pay due regard to the NHS Constitution.

Local authority complaints procedures are mandated for children's services in England and Wales by the Children Act 1989,[4] and in adult services by the Health and Social Care (Community Health and Standards) Act 2003.[5] Regulations specify that there should be three stages: informal, formal and review. At different points in the process, panel members who are independent of the local authority are introduced, although there have been criticisms of the degree to which this measure is effective (Braye and Preston-Shoot, 2009). Referrals are also possible to a regulatory authority such as to one of the four social services care councils in respect of abuse, neglect or poor practice.

In all procedures, service users and patients must be given information about how to complain. Procedures must be accessible, efficient and managed with courtesy and respect. Patients and service users should be kept involved in the progress of their complaint. Complaints should normally be made within 12 months of the event (six months in Northern Ireland), and some systems include time frames for the attempted resolution at local level. However, as Chapter 2 discussed, neither NHS organisations nor local authorities are necessarily receptive to complaints. Outcomes for service users may be stressful and disappointing.

Law in action

The first three chapters of this book demonstrate clearly that the law in theory is not necessarily reflected either in the law in action or in what has been termed the law in between (Jenness and Grattet, 2005) – namely how organisations translate legal requirements into agency procedures. For example, there are wide variations in NHS and criminal justice agency engagement with adult safeguarding systems (Manthorpe and Martineau, 2011). Allegations or suspicions of abuse should be reported to the CQC or a similar regulatory body, but staff beliefs, attitudes and anxieties, together with their level of legal knowledge, result in variations in how serious a situation may appear (Furness, 2006).

Accordingly, practitioners and managers should monitor how their organisation translates the legal rules – the law in theory – into procedures, and then how the legal rules are reflected in frontline practice. In particular, where the legal rules permit the exercise of discretion in terms of how statutory powers and duties are implemented, how is this discretion being used? Is the patient or service user benefiting from the exercise of lawful discretion?

ACTIVITY **3.3**

- *Using one or more of the themes discussed in this chapter, compare your setting's policies and procedures against the requirements of the legal rules.*

- *Write a synopsis which details where the agency's approach is, in your judgement, a lawful interpretation of the relevant legal rules, and where, in your analysis, something has been lost in translation.*

ACTIVITY **3.4**

Using the legal rules which have been discussed in this chapter, prepare a resource pack for your team or setting.

C H A P T E R   S U M M A R Y

The purpose of this chapter has not been to imply that the legal rules provide a perfect resource for social and health professionals. Indeed, the law is often a reflection of the political and social processes that contest how particular issues are to be understood, framed and addressed. Far from giving unequivocally clear direction, legal rules often juxtapose competing interests. For example, in adult safeguarding and in community care provision more generally, professionals have to navigate through principles of independence and choice which sit alongside imperatives of protection from harm.

Across health and social care, meeting need sits adjacent to managing within available resources, which creates tensions within decision making which managers ultimately have to defend. Equally, principles enshrined in law, such as autonomy and confidentiality, have to be given meaning; in the processes of meaning-making and decision-taking, practitioners may draw on different ethical paradigms in order to justify the action they decide to take.

The law is one important resource for practice and the management of practice, hence the importance given in this book to legal literacy. Nonetheless, the legal rules must be administered with skill if service users, staff and organisations are to be helped to consider the issues facing them. Equally, professionals must reflect on the values and knowledge that they bring to their practice. That is the focus of the next chapter.

Notes

1 It does, however, cover local authority placements and transfers facilitated in some way by local authorities into private residential care homes.

2 The law on discrimination in Northern Ireland follows the separate legal frameworks that applied elsewhere in the UK prior to the Equality Act 2010. It covers discrimination relating to race, gender, sexuality and disability in employment and the provision of goods and services, and extends this to age, gender reassignment and religion in relation to employment (**www.equalityni.org**).

3 New legislation is being considered for Northern Ireland.

4 The Children (Scotland) Act 1995 and the Children (Northern Ireland) Order 1995 contain similar provisions.

5 NHS and Community Care Act 1990 for Scotland; Health and Social Care (Reform) Act (Northern Ireland) 2009; Health and Social Care Complaints Procedures Directions (Northern Ireland) 2009.

Chapter 4
Practising accountable professionalism

O B J E C T I V E S

By the end of this chapter, you should have an understanding of:

- How practitioners, managers and their organisations might address the types of dilemmas, challenges and problems highlighted in the previous three chapters.

- The knowledge and skills for asserting and for maintaining good practice, which will help you tackle the more specific practice challenges presented in the chapters that follow.

Introduction

ACTIVITY 4.1

- *What does being a professional mean to you? List the attitudes, knowledge and skills which you believe equate with being a professional. Also list those possible components of professionalism that you decide to exclude from your final list.*

- *What has influenced your choice and your decision to give prominence to certain features and to backlight others?*

There is no doubt that practice for healthcare and social care staff is emotionally and ethically demanding. Complexity and uncertainty frequently surround the social and health issues about which they must make fine judgements. Staff must strike a unique balance in each case between person-centred working and the requirements set by job roles and organisational boundaries (Morrison, 2007; Gordon and Cooper, 2010). Staff often act in a context where needs are urgent, possibly life- or development-threatening, and presented with strong feelings. All presenting situations demand attention and both careful and care-full responses. Some people will evoke empathy; others anger or sadness. Some will resonate with the practitioner's own personal experience; others will challenge it in ways that might be painful or stressful. Some service users will be hard to reach, engage and like; others will knock forcefully against a worker's personal boundaries. Staff may feel 'held' by their colleagues and organisation, or abandoned to face alone the tides of emotion and demands which ebb and flow during working hours.

The extent of retention of staff is strongly influenced by individual workers' personal resilience and the working environment provided by the employer, including workload management, support and leadership (Sharpe et al., 2011). Both personal resilience and the working environment are emphasised in this chapter.

This book places at centre stage legal and ethical literacy – the distillation of knowledge, understanding, skills and values that enables practitioners and managers to connect relevant legal rules with professional priorities and the objectives of ethical practice. Of what practice should comprise remains to be teased out. Put another way, what might service users notice if practice is legally and ethically literate?

Earlier chapters have demonstrated that organisations may, consciously or unknowingly, depart from what the law requires. Moreover, it is apparent that attempts to prescribe, control, direct, regulate and standardise practice have not necessarily enabled good practice to flourish (Munro, 2011). Equally, professional codes may not guarantee good practice, partly because the manner in which they are constructed may not help health and social care staff to weigh up situations before deciding how to act (Phair and Heath, 2010), and may not support them to maintain integrity in their professional work (Banks, 2010).

Something more is needed, therefore, if practitioners and managers are to manage the emotional demands arising from their practice, maintain moral and legal integrity in their practice, and demonstrate confidence and willingness to be critical of their agencies when necessary (van Heugten, 2011). The spotlight now turns towards how individuals conduct their practice, focusing on the personal, professional, agency and case-related factors that need to be considered when providing leadership, exercising discretion, undertaking assessments, reaching judgements and intervening in people's lives.

This chapter, then, focuses on supporting the individual worker's authority as well as holding individual workers accountable. It is concerned with enhancing quality, since the quality of professional practice is key when seeking to safeguard and promote people's health and well-being (Dwyer, 2009). It is concerned too with upholding professional integrity (Banks, 2010) and values against a backcloth of complexity, certain uncertainty, intra- and inter-organisational dynamics, and resource constraint. This chapter acknowledges individual responsibility, for example by bolstering reflective sense-making and reliable accountability, but it also recognises that competence is context dependent, and therefore focuses on essential organisational requirements for safe and effective practice.

Although, because groups are often stronger than individuals, collective responses by professionals may be preferable to individuals acting alone, collective responses are not an alternative, but rather an addition, to the personal responsibility that practitioners hold. Staff are personally accountable (National Youth Agency (NYA), 2004; Health Professions Council (HPC), 2008; Department of Health (DH), 2011b), which includes but is not confined to keeping up to date, maintaining accurate records, supervising delegated tasks, and interacting with service users with honesty, respect and integrity. One corollary which follows is that agency managers, trustees and governors have a leadership responsibility which entails creating an organisational culture founded upon support, sincerity, honesty and care.

Professionalism

New emphasis is being placed on professionalism in medicine, healthcare and social work. In medical practice, professionalism embraces the ability to reflect and to reason critically from an informed knowledge and practice base, with the goal of improving a patient's health (Institute of Medical Ethics, 2009). It requires medical practitioners to develop a professional identity that incorporates an in-depth understanding of law, professional ethics and personal values, and how they facilitate patient safety and error reduction (Preston-Shoot and McKimm, 2010, 2011). It includes a duty to speak with authority, a willingness to take responsibility, and a commitment to maintain one's own and the profession's integrity, alongside keeping specialist knowledge and skills updated (Ellis, 2004).

Medical professionalism means putting patients above self-interest or organisational interests (Quality Assurance Agency (QAA), 2002). It is derived from specialist knowledge, clinical and interpersonal skills, and professional competencies, attributes and responsibilities. Appropriate professional attitudes and behaviours include critical evaluation, curiosity and life-long learning, as well as the knowledge and skills to use ethical and legal frameworks (QAA, 2002). In keeping with such responsibilities and attitudes, consultants have raised issues with managers and regulatory authorities concerning patient safety, shortage of nurses and poor standards of patient care (Kennedy, 2001; Francis, 2010).

Similar expressions of professionalism are articulated for healthcare practitioners. They are required to demonstrate effective clinical reasoning and professional judgement, drawing on knowledge and experience (Nursing and Midwifery Council (NMC), 2010b). In addition to knowledge and excellent practical skills, healthcare practitioners should demonstrate kindness, compassion and respect for patients (NHS Future Forum, 2011). In admittedly complex care environments, they should be able to articulate a professional viewpoint effectively and to negotiate with colleagues. They should provide leadership, including challenge, within healthcare and multidisciplinary teams, in order to ensure the delivery of high quality care that is safe, effective and focused on the patient experience (NMC, 2010b; NHS Future Forum, 2011).

Across the range of healthcare professions such as midwifery, nursing, health visiting and physiotherapy, the requirements are intentionally uniform, even if differently expressed (QAA, 2001). Practitioners must adhere to codes of conduct, maintain professional standards and contribute to the safety and well-being of everyone in a work setting. They must take personal responsibility for their professional development and fitness for practice, uphold the principles and practices of clinical governance, and exercise their duty of care to patients. They must maintain the integrity of their profession, monitor standards, and evidence their commitment to high quality patient care. Patients' interests are paramount, with healthcare practitioners expected to recognise the need for changes in practice, to contribute to safe working environments, and to act when care quality might have been compromised. They should think critically, appraise the effectiveness of care, provide leadership, and work collaboratively with other professionals.

Professionalism also features in the capabilities required of social workers (QAA, 2008; Social Work Reform Board, 2010; Welsh Assembly Government, 2011a) and youth workers (QAA, 2009). Social workers are expected to take personal responsibility for their conduct, learning and practice, to contribute to service and organisational development, and to safeguard the profession's reputation. In line with other professional groups, they must use their knowledge, skills, judgement and authority critically and effectively to promote people's safety, independence and well-being, and to scrutinise the relationship between agency policies, legal rules and professional values. Challenge, for example of unacceptable practice, should be constructive wherever possible in order to maintain effective partnerships and to facilitate positive outcomes.

Youth and community workers are also enjoined to commit to their own learning and to safeguard the health and well-being of those with whom they work. Though there is, as yet, no statutory professional regulation, they are expected to engage with legal and ethical frameworks and with critical enquiry and research, partly to manage the boundaries between personal and professional values and spaces.

Noteworthy across these benchmark statements and frameworks is the absence of 'escape clauses' which allow the full impact or force of these requirements to be offset by the complexity of contradictory accountabilities, the demanding nature of the work, and the behaviours and power dynamics in organisations. Across the professional groups there is a requirement to work in partnership with service users, to promote their active involvement in care planning, decisions and delivery. Work must be respectful, boundaries managed, and supervision drawn upon to think through the dilemmas and challenges that work presents. The standards of competence and behaviour are consistent, and as much for senior managers (DH, 2011b) as for frontline staff.

Significant too is the absence of a managerialistic tone. Perhaps that is to be expected when professions codify their standards, as in subject benchmark statements and professional capability frameworks. However, there is perhaps an emerging, if belated, recognition that managerialism has failed to build on the strengths of professionalism, such as ethical orientation (Payne, 2006) and critical challenge to how power is being used. In its emphasis on regulation, procedures, standardisation and numerical targets, managerialism has neglected the importance of the relational and reflective aspects of practice, highlighted what is measurable rather than what it is important to scrutinise, and hindered good practitioners in exercising appropriately informed discretion and innovation in order to meet people's needs (Braye and Preston-Shoot, 2009; Ayre and Preston-Shoot, 2010; Munro, 2011). As the DH (2011b) has recognised, it is not regulatory action (alone) that ensures excellent patient care, but good training, caring attitudes, and well-led organisations which remain rooted in professional values and driven by a commitment to serve. It is on these attributes that the remainder of this chapter focuses.

Reflective resilience

In the organisational contexts which staff may encounter, and given the emotionally charged work which they will have to perform, emotional resilience and moral courage will be required. Gordon and Cooper (2010) refer to practitioners needing to demonstrate persistence in the face of competing priorities if a focus on individual and organisational learning and development is not to be lost. Banks (2010) and Sercombe (2010) refer to needing to display courage in individual situations. Practitioners may have to discuss challenging issues, share difficult information, and take unpopular decisions. They may have to challenge poor practice or comment on how agencies are departing from best evidence.

Benchmark statements recognise this essential attribute of emotional resilience. Medical practitioners and social workers must be able to deal with uncertainty and stress (QAA, 2002, 2008). Youth and community workers must be emotionally literate (QAA, 2009). By emotional resilience, Morrison (2007) means motivation, sensitivity, and rapport with service users and colleagues. It is both intrapersonal and interpersonal, comprising self-awareness, management of self, other awareness and managing relationships. He points to how relationships within and between teams and agencies can become toxic when staff and service users become enmeshed in the dynamics generated by emotional and practical needs, and the personal and organisational response to them. The rules, rituals and procedures which teams and organisations develop, ostensibly to manage the work, may actually be a reaction designed to defend against anxieties triggered by work demands. This may complicate rather than facilitate work with service users and professional colleagues.

Kinman and Grant (2011) found resilience to be a protective factor against distress. Within resilience they distinguished between emotional intelligence, reflection, empathy and social (relationship) competence. Emotional intelligence comprised the ability to self-motivate and to persist when encountering frustrations; to manage anxiety, regulate emotions and to control personal reactions; to analyse and utilise emotional knowledge whilst being able to keep feelings from swamping the ability to think. Reflection, comprising self-reflection, empathetic concern and reflective communication with individuals and within personal and professional networks, is fundamental to professional development. It means being able to reflect on thoughts, feelings and beliefs, to consider the position adopted by others, and to use reflection in communication with others.

ACTIVITY 4.2

Across different occupational groups, Kinman and Grant (2011) identify various components as conducive to building resilience.

- *Reflect on your experience. To what degree is your ability to be resilient affected by the following components? What may help you maintain or build on your resilience?*

  – *Internal locus of control – the degree to which you believe you can control your work surroundings*

  – *Optimism*

  – *Effective peer and social supports*

  – *Setting clear boundaries between work and non-work*

  – *Well-structured work routines*

  – *Effective communication skills which demonstrate empathetic concern*

  – *Self-awareness regarding personal strengths and limitations*

  – *Successful management of emotions and belief systems*

The more practitioners and managers are supported to demonstrate emotional intelligence, to develop reflection and to enhance their skills in social competence and empathy, the more resilient they will be in the face of stress (Kinman and Grant, 2011).

Benchmarks also emphasise the use of reflection in practice. For example, youth and community work practice should be critical and reflective (QAA, 2009). Social workers should reflect on their and others' behaviour, and review their management of boundaries (QAA, 2008). Healthcare practitioners, for example midwives, nurses and health visitors, should demonstrate a critical and reflective approach to practice and to organisational systems (QAA, 2001). Reflective practice for doctors should include auditing and appraising one's own work and the performance of colleagues, as well as being prepared to seek help from more experienced staff and knowing the limits of personal responsibility and capability.

Across professional groups, reflection and resilience equate not (just) to quiet introspection in private moments – they involve engaging with others in supervision, consultation, peer challenge, peer support and sector-led improvement. The focus falls on individual practice and the professional values that motivate it, but also gazes on peers and colleagues for mutual support and challenge in order to assure safe, respectful and effective service provision (DH, 2011b). Reflection and resilience reach into relationships between workers and service users, exploring what is being communicated, how uncertainty and not knowing is managed, and how interpersonal exchanges are understood and experienced. In team and organisational cultures also, reflection and resilience ensure a professional voice in management decisions and highlight the professional standards that should underpin the governance of practice.

The purpose of reflection, including in supervision, is to develop learning (Changing Lives Practice Governance Group, 2011) and to protect patients by promoting best practice, retaining a focus on the humanity of people worked with and maintaining standards embodied in codes of conduct (Bilson, 2007; Ackerman, 2011). It involves people returning to the core purpose of their professional work (Banks, 2010) and questioning whether the roles they are being asked to perform and how they are being asked to work concur with or diverge from the values, knowledge and skills for which they were employed (Payne, 2007; Cousins, 2010).

Resilience and reflection, including space for supervision and consultation, are essential for managers and supervisors too (Cousins, 2010). This acknowledges that supervision and leadership can become entrapped in the emotional impact and communication complexity of the work. The same emotional intelligence, empathetic communication, and awareness of self and others must be embedded throughout the workforce if practice and the management of practice are to be respectful but challenging, and safe rather than dangerous.

Decision-making

Poor decisions can cause harm and have tragic consequences (Duffy and Collins, 2010). Health and social care practitioners exercise power and authority derived from their statutory mandate, position and their expertise on which service users might rely. Unsurprisingly, therefore, decision-making is given some prominence in benchmark statements.

Youth and community workers must be able to reach judgements about complex ethical and professional issues, and to act appropriately in line with professional and ethical codes (QAA, 2009). Harking back to the discussion of reflection, youth and community workers must be willing to question their professional experience and to conduct reasoned argument.

Health visitors and physiotherapists must be able to make confident professional judgements, midwives able to apply evidence to inform their decisions, and nurses able to justify their conclusions (QAA, 2001). Graduate nurses should be analytical and able to plan, deliver and evaluate effective evidence-based care safely and confidently, and challenge unsafe practice when necessary (NMC, 2010b).

Doctors should be able to demonstrate clinical reasoning, including recognising the limitations of their own knowledge (QAA, 2002).

Social workers, who are required to exercise exceptional professional judgement (HM Government, 2010), should be competent in integrating multiple sources of knowledge and evidence, each critically analysed for validity, quality and applicability. This means drawing upon law, values, practice experience, service user knowledge and expertise, research and theory, as well as understanding organisational history and ways of working. These strands must then be applied to each specific situation in order to reach and provide a coherent rationale for decisions (Payne, 2007; Social Work Reform Board, 2010; Changing Lives Practice Governance Group, 2011).

Once again, organisational managers and governors have a leadership responsibility to provide the conditions where staff can develop the confidence to apply their professional judgement (Munro, 2011; WAG, 2011a).

Legal literacy

Social workers, healthcare practitioners and doctors must know when and how to use legal rules in complex situations involving significant harm or the likelihood of significant harm (QAA, 2001, 2002; Institute of Medical Ethics, 2009; Social Work Task Force, 2009b; Social Work Reform Board, 2010). Sometimes the law is implicit in benchmark statements, as when social workers (QAA, 2008) and healthcare practitioners (QAA, 2001) are enjoined to challenge discrimination and to maintain people's rights. Sometimes reference is explicit, to practise according to current legislation and to maintain awareness of legal rights and responsibilities (QAA, 2001) such as whistle blowing when concerned that agencies may be failing to protect children from significant harm (Care Quality Commission (CQC), 2009b).

Levels of knowledge of the legal rules, and confidence in drawing on them, appear disappointingly low (Braye et al., 2007; Perkins et al., 2007; Pinkney et al., 2008; Preston-Shoot et al., 2011). Instead, organisational procedures are often drawn upon even though these may not accurately translate the legal rules into practice guides. Lack of continuing professional development, informal organisational cultures (Preston-Shoot, 2012), the impact of agency priorities, politics and resources, and lack of knowledge may all affect how practitioners regard the law for practice.

ACTIVITY 4.3

- *Draw up a list of legal rules relevant to your role (examples are available for doctors (Preston-Shoot et al., 2011) and for social workers (Braye and Preston-Shoot, 2006).*

- *Reflect on how confident you feel about your knowledge of these legal rules and your skills in using them. What learning needs can you identify and how might you access the detailed expertise you feel you need?*

- *Finally, compile a list of resources that would enable you to build on your legal literacy in your present role.*

Ethical literacy

Benchmark statements also emphasise professional values and ethics. Youth and community work is an ethical activity in which practitioners must act appropriately in line with ethical codes (QAA, 2009). Healthcare is a moral and ethical practice in which practitioners must understand their ethical responsibilities, recognise moral dilemmas and create a safe working environment for patients and colleagues (QAA, 2001). Doctors should recognise the impact of their own value judgements and beliefs, which should not be allowed to prejudice patient care (QAA, 2002). Harking back to reflection, doctors should adopt an inquisitorial attitude towards their practice and that of their colleagues. Social work is a moral activity (QAA, 2008) in which practitioners and managers should be knowledgeable about the profession's values and ethical standards, and able to apply them in practice (Social Work Reform Board, 2010).

Professional codes also promote the importance of ethical literacy. Youth workers must demonstrate ethical awareness and reflection as part of acting with integrity and justifying difficult decisions (NYA, 2004). Doctors and social workers must be capable of managing ethical issues and upholding ethical standards in practice (General Medical Council (GMC), 2009; Social Work Reform Board, 2010).

Using nursing as the focus, although his arguments may be capable of generalisation across professions, Woods (2011) captures how, to survive the challenges thrown up by practice, practitioners must find ways to maintain an ethic of care. He argues that, alone, an ethic of care is insufficient as an impetus to act; it requires courage to maintain safe, efficient and ethical care. Practitioners need moral commitment and a determination to establish purposeful relationships, maintain people's trust, advocate for others and deliver expert care. Such qualities are required by professional codes (for example, NYA, 2004; HPC, 2008). Practitioners are enjoined to place service users' interests above professional and organisational loyalty, and to challenge colleagues and employers in order to uphold ethical and lawful practice.

Concerns have been expressed about whether sufficient time is allocated within professional education and training to ethics (Holt, 2006; Preston-Shoot and McKimm, 2010). Concerns have been expressed too about whether sufficient reflective space is created within organisations so that the value base of the workplace can be made explicit and analysed for its impact on people's moral functioning (Branch, 2000; Payne, 2006; Dunworth and Kirwan, 2009). Without an opportunity when training to apply taught ethical models to practice, and without reflection in practice, practitioners and managers may not develop the skills to participate effectively in ethical decision-making. Equally, commitments expressed in social policy – such as to personalisation, autonomy, independence and choice – might, if applied uncritically, support discriminatory or unreflective approaches when the complexities surrounding safeguarding, rights and risks, and people's decision-making capacity require a more nuanced and care-full response which draws on rather than obscures the contribution of different ethical theories (Braye and Preston-Shoot, 2009; Galpin, 2010; Jones, 2011).

For such reasons, commentators advocate the importance of workplace spaces in which to reflect on and debate attitudes – for example to risk, if risk aversion is not to outweigh ethical principles (Spratt, 2001) – and emotions such as unease or anger which might indicate the existence of a dilemma that needs a thoughtful and considered response (Bilson, 2007). Such spaces are essential if, as Branch (2000) suggests, practice is to integrate moral sensitivity (the recognition of ethical issues), moral commitment (the determination to do what is right) based on moral reasoning (weighing up rights and principles), and moral behaviour (skills at implementation).

ACTIVITY 4.4

Take a case that is presenting a dilemma, as evidenced in the emotions it arouses and the tensions it evokes between right and risks, needs and resources, or welfare and justice. Draw on different ethical theories – for example utilitarian or deontological – to shed light on how the dilemma might be understood and resolved.

Orientations

Narrow or fixed professional views are often implicated in reviews of serious incidents (Healthcare Commission, 2007c). Favoured ways of thinking about and responding to situations can easily become traps that blinker vision, restricting consideration of alternative options and confining practitioners and agencies to particular practices. Spratt (2001) identifies orientations which agencies may demonstrate. These include the degree to which organisations: encourage narrow or broader involvement of staff and service users in decision-making; anticipate need or respond to referred cases; and embrace knowledge-informed risk-taking in order to promote learning. Organisations may also be noted for the degree to which they openly discuss dilemmas and practice knowledge as opposed to relying on formalised procedures delivered through hierarchies.

Braye and Preston-Shoot (2007, 2009) have shone the spotlight on orientations which individual practitioners bring to their work. These may include a preference for: doing things right, which emphasises, for example, the technical content of the legal rules; doing right things, which prioritises values and ethics; or right thinking, which gives prominence to human rights, equality and social justice. Put another way, practitioners may emphasise the technical (legal rules), people's needs (assessment), rights (equality) or procedures (agency rules).

No one orientation is necessarily correct. All have something to offer practice, especially in challenging situations. The danger arises when one orientation is followed to the exclusion of what other approaches might offer. Thus Payne (2006) recommends examining opposites, for example the continuum between confidentiality and open sharing of information. Sercombe (2010) stresses the importance of thinking spaces and networks of support in which the demands of professional practice, and the cultures in which that practice operates, can be explored critically with a view to protecting and enhancing standards.

Relationships

Whether focusing on healthcare or social work, the voices and experiences of patients and service users need to be hard wired into professional and organisational systems at policy-making, management and operational levels (Munro, 2011; NHS Future Forum, 2011). Relationships are, indeed, central to practice (Morrison, 2007) and decision-making. Failures to listen and to explore different viewpoints are often implicated in serious case failures (Healthcare Commission, 2007c). Dialogue is an essential tool which comprises openness and honesty, respectful listening and learning, promotion of involvement, and allocation of time to provide information and deal with responses. Dialogue also comprises recognition of the expertise and strengths as well as needs and emotions that service users bring to any encounter (Manthorpe et al., 2009; Sercombe, 2010). It must incorporate respectful uncertainty (Laming, 2003) or a curiosity which balances appropriately in each unique situation challenge and support. Dialogue focuses on the individual outcomes and goals which people express, but considers them in a social and community context.

Once again, benchmark statements capture the essence of core standards. Healthcare practitioners must maintain respectful relationships, communicate effectively and involve patients in decisions (QAA, 2001). Youth workers must be able to form trusting relationships (QAA, 2009), and social workers must be committed to the involvement of service users (QAA, 2008; WAG, 2011a). Like doctors (QAA, 2002), all health and social care practitioners are expected to respect different cultures and to demonstrate compassion, respect and consideration in their relationships.

Such principles – including fairness, dignity and the involvement of service users in planning and in decision-making – are also upheld in the legal rules (Human Rights Act 1998; Health Act 2009; Equality Act 2010; Health and Social Care Act 2008 (Regulated Activities) Regulations 2010). Accordingly, inspectors working on behalf of regulatory bodies will be investigating the degree to which service users are enabled to take decisions, to access advocates and support when appropriate, to express views without recrimination about the care they have received, and to receive personalised care (Care Quality Commission and Equality and Human Rights Commission (CQC and EHRC), 2011).

Moreover, if these are at least some of the essential elements that should characterise relationships between practitioners and service users, they should also be embedded in the relationships between practitioners and their managers. Managers too should encourage conversations without hierarchy.

Organisational effectiveness

Alongside the focus on individual practitioners and the knowledge, skills and attitudes they bring to their professionalism, a gaze must also be cast on the characteristics of an effective organisation or employer. The work environment can foster or undermine performance, motivation, quality, reflection, reporting, and learning from errors, and also the professional values of care and empathy (Branch, 2000; Kroll et al., 2008; Preston-Shoot, 2010a; DH, 2011a, 2011b; Munro, 2011). Reliance on individual commitment alone will be insufficient to guarantee and underwrite quality practice standards (Audit Commission, 2008).

There is clear evidence that effective performance is influenced by the supportiveness of colleagues and managers. This supportiveness is indicated in staffing levels that enable people's needs to be met, training which covers equality and human rights, induction, and supervision that extends beyond case oversight to professional development and the lived experience of work (CQC and EHRC, 2011; Sharpe et al., 2011). However, researchers continue to express concern about the variability of arrangements for induction, training and supervision (Bates et al., 2010; Preston-Shoot, 2010a; Worsley et al., 2010; Sharpe et al., 2011); employers are still ready to assume and demand that practitioners are fit for all the demands and complexities of practice at the point of qualification, rather than recognising their responsibility to facilitate newly qualified staff to manage the transition between qualifying education and practice.

A clear expression of what good looks like in terms of organisational context and the leadership provided by managers can be generated from close reading of reform initiatives and inquiries (for example, Social Work Reform Board, 2010; NHS Future Forum, 2011). Employers need to understand the context in which accountability and professionalism can thrive, and to have the skills and commitment to provide that context. As a minimum, this context comprises a number of components, outlined below.

Effective governance

This comprises clarity about standards and outcomes, about the indicators by which progress will be measured, and about how monitoring of effectiveness will be undertaken. This component includes effective audits of professional practice and the management of practice, via case files, supervision records, analysis of action plans following complaints or serious incidents, and minutes of meetings. It includes: use of feedback from staff and service users; the leadership that managers provide; the role-modelling and the personal and organisational values that managers demonstrate; and the support they too receive (White et al., 2003; Marsland et al., 2007; Audit Commission, 2008; Office of Public Sector Information (OPSI), 2010; Social Work Reform Board, 2010; Changing Lives Practice Governance Group, 2011; NHS Future Forum, 2011).

Workforce planning

This comprises analysis of where there are key gaps in organisational capacity (Commission for Social Care Inspection (CSCI), 2007) and the management of staff working conditions, and analysis of the lived experience of work (White et al., 2003). It includes workload and resource management, monitoring compliance with legal rules and professional codes of practice, and maintaining transparent systems to safeguard staff and promote their well-being (OPSI, 2010; Social Work Reform Board, 2010; Changing Lives Practice Governance Group, 2011). It means taking action to minimise the risks that arise from staff shortage, for example on hospital wards, and to promote a quality workplace focused on the safety, dignity, respect and involvement of service users.

Nonetheless, especially for newly qualified staff, the experience of workload and caseload management has been variable (Worsley et al., 2010; Sharpe et al., 2011). Regulators should consider whether staffing levels are sufficient to enable people's needs to be met and rights to be respected (CQC and EHRC, 2011).

Staff development

There are several elements which together assist an organisation to develop the capability and capacity of its staff (OPSI, 2010). They include a focus on developing and maintaining open and trusting relationships, with staff feeling they can influence organisational deci-sion-making and contribute to improved outcomes (Audit Commission, 2008). There will be a focus on formal and informal supervision, oriented towards learning as much as agency accountability and targets, and focused on improving and supporting the quality of practice and decision-making as much as on workload management. This focus on supervision, pro-fessional development and appraisal will be aimed at developing people's knowledge base, supporting reflection on tasks and roles, and thinking through the impact of their emotional response to work demands (Marsland et al., 2007; Cantrill et al., 2010; Social Work Reform Board, 2010; Munro, 2011).

Staff development also includes access to research, guidance and to continuing professional development. Again this is aimed at developing practitioners' knowledge base and skills, but also their ability and confidence to recognise and report where quality standards are being undermined (Marsland et al., 2007; Stevens and Manthorpe, 2007; Public Concern at Work (PCaW), 2011), and their ability to develop and maintain emotional resilience, learning and creativity (Changing Lives Practice Governance Group, 2011). Where training and other initiatives are taken, they will be evaluated for their impact on practice and how the organi-sation has facilitated the introduction of new knowledge and practice into its procedures (Richardson et al., 2002; White et al., 2003; Preston-Shoot, 2010a).

Recent attention, for example in social work (Social Work Reform Board, 2010), to the stand-ards that employers should meet regarding supervision, induction, appraisal and post-regis-tration training is welcome. However, the standards are voluntary rather than enforceable. Over the decades there have been continual reminders of the stresses involved in frontline child protection and mental health practice, and the essential importance, therefore, of the provision of regular high-quality supervision alongside caseload management, training and safety-at-work risk assessments (Stevenson, 1974; Blom-Cooper, 1985; Butler-Sloss, 1988; Sheppard, 1996; Leslie, 1997; Social Work Task Force, 2009a, b). Voluntary standards for employers appear insufficient to guarantee the well-being of staff and, therefore, service users.

Staff development also includes the openness of the organisation to scrutiny and challenge (Audit Commission, 2008; Francis, 2010; Social Work Reform Board, 2010). Individual prac-titioners and managers must feel able to raise concerns without fear of recrimination, retali-ation and bullying. The culture must be capable of supporting questioning, reflection and challenge, and ethical and legal deliberation (DH, 2011c; Parliamentary and Health Service Ombudsman (PHSO), 2011; PCaW, 2011), otherwise the organisation will witness ethical erosion (Kroll et al., 2008; Preston-Shoot, 2012).

Culture

Here the focus is on the degree to which the organisation is open or closed – engaged with its professional community, multi-agency networks and service users or isolated (CSCI, 2007; Social Work Reform Board, 2010; Changing Lives Practice Governance Group, 2011; Manthorpe and Martineau, 2011). A healthy culture is one that recognises practitioner advocacy for patients and service users, and welcomes complaints and other kinds of feedback from which it can learn. It is one which admits mistakes and serious incidents, and apologises for and seeks to learn from these (DH, 2011c). Key mechanisms to assist organisations to remain open and to assess risks to compliance with safeguarding and other standards include peer challenge and peer review, and deep conversations with staff and with service users (Furness, 2006; Marsland et al., 2007; NHS Constitution State of Readiness Group, 2009; Local Government Group et al., 2011).

Professionalism includes understanding organisational structures and when these are (or are not) supporting quality standards and practice (QAA, 2001). It includes not being entrapped by or colluding with an organisation, because otherwise professional practice risks being distorted by the organisation and losing its ability to deliver the transformational caring objectives on which it is based (Payne, 2006).

Leadership

This emphasis on organisational culture and on support for frontline staff highlights the skills and conduct required of managers at all levels. There is clear evidence that good leadership and management benefits both staff and service users, for example contributing to patient satisfaction and reduced mortality rates (Borrill et al., 2001; Boorman, 2009; Sharpe et al., 2011).

One code for NHS managers stresses the importance of being patient centred as well as performance oriented, partnership focused and responsive to needs, inclusive of patients and practitioners as well as open to accountability (National Leadership Council, 2010). Research and inquiries have also linked service quality outcomes with collegial work environments where practitioners believe that managers appreciate the importance of their health and well-being (Stevenson, 1974; Leslie, 1997; Boorman, 2009). There is also a link between staff retention and a work environment that enables workers to implement their practice values (Sharpe et al., 2011). Additional important leadership qualities for managers include the ability to build and maintain teams and organisations where staff feel involved in organisational decision-making, where there is clarity about and commitment to shared objectives, where supervision and appraisals are well structured and promote a sense of being valued by the organisation, and where accountability is observed through open questioning, feedback and routine reviews of performance (Borrill et al., 2001).

There is now powerful and authoritative evidence, therefore, for an approach to management and leadership that promotes the values identified in the first four chapters of this book as epitomising professionalism. This approach is transformational rather than having a 'command and control' style, creating a context where workers can engage and perform well. It is marked by an emphasis on: personal qualities of openness, availability and self-awareness; effective communication and partnership building, and working which promotes trust and encourages contributions; planning, resource, performance and people management, improvement and innovation, in order to ensure patient safety and service users' well-being; and evaluation in order to set and review direction (National Leadership Council, 2010).

By contrast, the evidence from major public inquiries in the NHS (Kennedy, 2001; Francis, 2010) has identified the antithesis of transformational and support management as one root cause of resultant deaths. Many serious case reviews found that the inability of organisations to 'learn', to be open about mistakes, and to listen to staff and service users similarly prevented them avoiding potentially avoidable mistakes (Braye and Preston-Shoot, 2009).

Good leadership and good management will not prevent mistakes and accidents, although they may well reduce their numbers. What they will do is create a culture in which organisations learn from mistakes and from the knowledge and experience of their staff and those who use services. Such organisations inevitability treasure professional accountability and the willingness of staff and service users to speak out and raise concerns, as means of improving services.

C H A P T E R   S U M M A R Y

This chapter represents one response to the causes for concern that were expressed in the opening chapter of this book, alongside the values and legal rules that support accountable practice, which have also been explored in detail already. This chapter specifically encourages an exploration of the experience of work with service users and colleagues. Practitioners and managers have an obligation to make their evidence count. That requires an obligation to articulate the issues as they see them, to appraise and learn from service performance, to comment critically and reflectively on the complexities and ambiguities that arise in practice, and to question how social issues are defined, sources of knowledge prioritised and orientations to problems valued.

Thus far the book has begun to articulate the commitments that social care and healthcare professionals (should) bring to practice. It has rehearsed the standards that patients and service users have a right to expect, and that professional groups have captured in ethical and practice codes. It has identified the legal rules that support accountable professionalism and pointed to how quality outcomes may be shaped and secured by practitioners, managers and service users working together.

Implicit at the very least throughout has been the idea that accountable professionalism requires leadership at every level of health and social welfare organisations. At the heart of leadership must be a vision of what good looks like. However, the development of leadership expertise is gradual. Readiness for such practice is not achieved at the point of initial qualification (Bates et al., 2010) but is gradually accumulated. As practitioners accumulate experience, they deserve and need the support of their managers, policy makers and academic researchers and teachers.

Leadership should occur at all levels within professions and organisations, irrespective of the formal positions which people hold. Effective leadership demonstrates clarity about purposes, values and goals, and engages in quality improvement through planning, service design and delivery, and evaluation. It offers mentoring, facilitation, co-ordination, innovation, direction and monitoring as situations arise and demand. It accepts responsibility for tackling issues, questioning resources and practices, and promoting interaction between practitioners, managers and board members, and between staff and service users.

ACTIVITY 4.5

Return to the work you did for Activity 1.1.

- *How would you respond if you encountered similar practices to those which have been discussed throughout the opening four chapters?*

- *How has your training and your work experience equipped you for the transition between qualifying education and practice, and between graduating from being newly qualified in practice to seniority in terms of expertise?*

- *What further training needs can you identify and how much you access them?*

The book now turns towards exploring particular practice challenges in more depth.

Chapter 5
Workloads and skill mix

OBJECTIVES

By the end of this chapter, you should have an understanding of:

- The contractual, common law and professional accountability framework within which workloads and the delegation of work should be considered.

- The responsibilities of health and social care professionals (and students) when facing a shortfall of resources or inadequate staffing.

- The responsibilities of health and social care professionals when faced with an inappropriate skill mix or delegation either to themselves or by themselves or colleagues.

Introduction

The medical and surgical wards at the trust had a history over at least three years of low staffing levels and a relatively low proportion of qualified nurses [. . .] Staff across several professions commented that shortages of nurses contributed to the spread of infection because they were too rushed to communicate with their colleagues, wash their hands, wear aprons and gloves consistently, empty and clean commodes and clean mattresses and equipment properly.

(Healthcare Commission, 2007a, p.108)

Excessive workloads and inappropriate delegation of work are major obstacles to safe and effective practice in health and social care. Excessive workloads can also undermine the duty of care to patients or service users, or the employer's duty of care to its staff. Health and social care staff have a duty to report concerns arising from the impact of excessive workloads and hours on their duty of care to others or the employer's duty of care to themselves.

Health and social professionals must meet their duty of care to service users and carers. They must do this by providing a service of no less quality than that to be expected from someone with the skills and responsibilities of an ordinarily competent qualified social worker or healthcare worker of their particular profession.

Workloads and the duty of care:What must professionals be able to do?

Chapter 2 discussed what the duty of care of all health and social care professionals requires them to be able to do, including to:

- Keep their knowledge and skills up to date and follow accepted approved practice based on best evidence and current knowledge.

- Take reasonable care at all times.

- Keep accurate and contemporaneous records of their work, to the standard expected in their particular area of work.

- Not delegate work unless they are confident that the person(s) to whom they delegate the work is competent to carry out the work in an appropriately safe and competent manner. Health and social care professionals should also not accept delegated work unless they are confident they can undertake it in a safe and skilled manner.

- Protect confidential information, other than when the wider public interest or their duty of care could justify disclosure.

- Inform their manager when they are unable to do work to the above standards.

If excessive workloads or inappropriate delegation mean health and social care professionals are unable to meet this standard, then they risk breaching their duty of care.

Lord Laming said of the working conditions of social workers:

> *However, there are significant levels of concern that current practice, and in particular the pressure of high case-loads for children's social workers and health visitors, has meant that staff often do not have the time needed to maintain effective contact with children, young people and their families in order to achieve positive outcomes.*

(Laming, 2009, p. 22)

Faced with limited resources, staff and their managers are expected to use the various duties, powers, thresholds, policies and procedures to set priorities and allocate resources. The Care Standards Tribunal in considering issues around Victoria Climbié's death made clear that:

> *Workload issues demand action, whether by prioritisation, seeking to delegate or asking for help/reallocation of files.*

(*LA* v *General Social Care Council* [2007], para 125)

> *The issue of workload is a recurring theme in social work practice. Tasks have to be prioritised, and help sought if there are problems.*

(*LA* v *General Social Care Council* [2007], para 14)

It would not be acceptable practice, for example, for staff time to be spread so thinly that it is reasonably foreseeable that the duty of care to service users or staff may be breached.

The courts will not substitute their own judgement for assessments and priorities set by skilled professionals, unless the allocation of resources or assessment is entirely unreasonable or is a breach of public duties. In setting priorities, it is essential that what it is agreed will be done, can be done safely.

It is important to note that priorities which are applied incorrectly can themselves lead to a charge of negligence. So, for example, setting priorities which accord with the requirements of external performance targets ahead of priorities which are necessary to ensure the safety of service users would be questionable. Employers must ensure that professional staff are able to meet the healthcare professional or social worker's duty of care to service users, and to comply with their professional code. If the resources available are insufficient to ensure that this is the case, then senior management and staff should act proactively and urgently to remedy the situation.

There is a connection between workloads and the duty of care owed by employers under the Health and Safety at Work etc Act 1974. Employers must ensure the safety, health, and welfare at work of their employees and others on their premises. They must also seek to ensure their employees' acts and omissions do not endanger others, and that employees are able to comply with their duty of care towards colleagues, themselves and service users. The health and safety impact of excessive workloads is discussed further in Chapter 9.

ACTIVITY 5.1

Why might you be entitled (indeed required) to question and challenge an instruction or expectation to carry an excessive workload?

Contracts of employment and workloads

Employees cannot be required to give up statutory rights such as a limit on maximum working hours. Nor should they agree to undertake unlawful instructions such as working when it is clear that the proposed work is unsafe to themselves or others.

Both employers and employees need to ensure that employees can work in accordance with reasonable and lawful instruction and exercise skill and care in the performance of their work.

Instructions or expectations must be challenged if they are such that professionals cannot work safely because such instructions or expectations conflict with implied contractual duties including the duty of care to themselves, colleagues and service users, and compliance with their professional code.

CASE STUDY

John qualified as a social worker a year ago. Since then his caseload in a child protection team, including some very complex child protection cases, has increased substantially. Workload pressures are compounded by the fact that two of the team of ten are newly qualified social workers, and two are on long-term sick leave.

John's manager is supportive but she has become increasingly stressed. One consequence of her increased workload is irregular supervision. John's manager has asked for additional support for the team, the members of which have average caseloads of 29, but has been told that the budget is already overspent.

ACTIVITY **5.2**

What should John and other team members (described in the case study above) do?

In the circumstances described in the case study above, team members should start by referring to their professional code. For social workers (all professions have similar obligations) this states they must:

(Bring) to the attention of your employer or the appropriate authority resource or operational difficulties that might get in the way of the delivery of safe care.

(General Social Care Council (GSCC), 2002, para 3.4)

Sometimes statutory guidance sets standards. Thus, *Working Together to Safeguard Children* (Department for Education, 2010) states that staff in England and Wales undertaking both initial assessments (Children Act 1989, Section 17) and core assessments within a Section 47 investigation should be 'qualified and experienced' social workers. The two newly qualified workers in John's case study are, therefore, restricted in their child protection role, and the supervision difficulties will not help them gain further experience.

In the case study, the manager's stress is likely to spread to other staff, thereby compromising the employer's duty of care to them. Caseloads of 29 in children's social work are much greater than official inquiries have recommended (and at the upper end of social work caseloads recorded by the Social Work Task Force) (Baginsky et al., 2010). Team members should set out their concerns in writing in preparation for a group supervision meeting with the manager. The manager herself would be well advised to draw their concerns and her own to the attention of her manager.

What should you do if workloads are unsafe or may become unsafe?

The first priority here is to make sure that effective workload and caseload management systems are in place. Many employers have a workload management policy to help ensure that safe and effective staffing levels exist. This can also help to identify any work which cannot be safely allocated. Employers have probably had (or should have had) input from staff and their professional bodies and trade unions.

The systems are specific to each service, profession or setting and may vary between the four countries of the UK. In the NHS, some professions have national guidance on staffing ratios and workloads (Critical Care Programme Modernisation Agency, 2003).

Some settings, such as nursing homes or residential homes for older people, have minimum staffing ratios linked to particular categories of staff, depending on their qualifications, or to certain minimum standards. Some minimum standards have a statutory basis, for instance the National Minimum Standards for Children's Homes (Department of Health (DH), 2002a). For many professions, settings and services there will be good practice models of calculating safe staffing levels, but their status will not be mandatory. In the NHS, you can check these out by asking the relevant professional body or checking within your own organisation. For social workers in England, the employers' standards (Social Work Reform Board, 2010) offer a number of ways to calculate safe staffing on the grounds that the appropriate staffing ratios will be different in, say, children's services and adult services. In Northern Ireland, there is a recommended model for social workers and healthcare professionals working in the community (Department of Health, Social Services and Public Safety, 2008).

For any profession, setting or service it may be possible to work out a method of estimating safe workloads. You should know whether this has been done where you work. When you start in a new workplace, it is essential to check whether there are recommended staffing ratios as well as finding out about local clinical or service protocols. A workload management policy may have guidelines on how much time staff should spend on specific duties or roles, and include a workload weighting tool to help calculate the level of demand on staff according to the risk, time or complexity of the cases or roles they are undertaking. The policy may set out guidance on what qualifications are needed for certain tasks or roles, especially if there is statutory guidance. Guidance may also be given on the use of students, trainees and less skilled staff, and on team-working, management, allocating and prioritising tasks, and access to training and supervision.

If there is no workload management system where you work and you have concerns about the duty of care, then a short staff survey to establish workload pressures, unmet needs, and risks to patients, service users and staff can be a good way to ensure the issue is taken seriously. You can find advice on conducting a staff survey on the website (see Introduction for navigation instructions).

ACTIVITY 5.3

You are just starting a new job with a new employer where you know workloads are high. Taking your own profession and current role, what policies and guidance might you want to read as part of your induction to ensure you know how to work safely when workloads are high? What guidance can you find nationally on staffing ratios and protocols that might be helpful?

Statutory duties and workloads

Employers must risk-assess the main foreseeable hazards facing staff and service users. Hazards would certainly include the health consequences of excessive workloads, excessive hours and inadequate staffing (The Management of Health and Safety at Work Regulations 1999). Chapter 9 explains risk assessments further.

The Working Time Regulations (1998, as amended by the Working Time (Amendment) Regulations 2007) set out legal protection for employees to not have to work more than 48 hours a week on average, unless they choose to, as well as legal rules around night working, rest breaks and holidays. Many healthcare and social work professionals work long hours to keep on top of their work. As part of a staff survey (see above), it is helpful to ask staff how many hours they actually work each week.

Employers must have 'due regard' to the equality impact of their decisions (Equality Act 2010). Excessive workloads are often linked to intensification of work patterns, often combined with a less supportive working environment. If most administrative posts have disappeared or there is a use of 'hot desks', then your workload and stress may have increased. Substantial changes to working arrangements, for example shift patterns, will affect staff and/or service users (Maben, 2010). It is important, therefore, to consider the equality implications, for example on service users and staff with disabilities or with carer responsibilities.

Before making substantial changes to working patterns, staffing levels, skill mix, and location of services or service provision, employers are obliged to consult with staff, trade unions and/or service users. Consultation with staff and service users is discussed in Chapters 3 and 6. There are specific legal procedures if redundancies are planned.

CASE STUDY

Speech and language therapists

Speech and language therapists in a primary care trust were concerned that their heavy workloads meant it was impossible for them to meet their duty of care. The only way a service kept going was through the use of ten fixed-term-contract staff – a quarter of the workforce.

The trust then decided that, as part of a deficit reduction programme, all ten fixed-term contracts would end after three months. Staff met and decided to collect evidence showing how workloads were already at breaking point with serious implications for the service, their duty of care and compliance with their professional code.

The staff produced a briefing note with evidence explaining their concerns. When that failed to stop the redundancies, they took the almost unique step of going on strike for one day to show how strongly they felt. Soon after, the trust changed its mind and agreed to keep six of the ten fixed-term-contract staff. Whilst this fell short of what staff wanted, they felt vindicated and believed they had helped to protect the local service.

Students and trainees

Students and trainees cannot be professionally accountable in the way that fully trained registered practitioners are. They are not expected to reach the standards of the 'ordinarily competent' practitioner, and should always be supervised effectively by an appropriately qualified member of staff. Although not qualified, students and trainees do have a duty of care, although the standard of care they are expected to reach is less than that of a qualified practitioner (Nursing and Midwifery Council (NMC), 2010c). As their experience and knowledge increases, students and trainees will not always be directly accompanied or supervised.

The student or trainee should always make it clear that they are not yet qualified. Service users have the right to refuse to be treated or cared for by a student or trainee.

Students and trainees should raise concerns if their workload or delegated roles undermine their own safe practice. They should do so initially with their supervisor, and if necessary with their course tutor. The healthcare professionals they work with should also raise concerns if students and trainees, or their service users, are placed at risk.

What if excessive workloads lead to complaints from service users?

Your professional code requires you to always place the interests of service users first. Sensible organisations listen to the concerns of service users to improve services. For social workers, the GSCC Code of Practice (GSCC, 2002) includes helping service users and carers to make complaints, taking complaints seriously and responding to them or passing them on to the appropriate person. Similarly nurses and midwives, like other professionals, must act as advocates for those in their care, helping them to access relevant health and social care, information and support (NMC, 2008a; Health Act 2009). Chapter 6 discusses complaints in some detail.

Managers and excessive workloads

Resources are finite in health and social services. Local authorities are not required to provide care for all who may need social services, but they are required to draw up eligibility criteria which set out for each year, within those duties and powers, what they plan to do. However, where local authorities set eligibility criteria and adopt procedures to manage within their available resources, they must consider in each case whether to exercise discretion and to provide a service in response to need. Put another way, blanket policies, identified when a local authority *always* does something or *never* does something else in a particular situation, will be challengeable in law. Equally, care must be taken as to when resources may lawfully be taken into account when deciding what assessment or service provision approach to take in particular cases (Braye and Preston-Shoot, 2009).

Similarly, the NHS is not required to provide care to all who may need it. However, it must:

- Provide a comprehensive and integrated health service.

- Demonstrate that within available resources, appropriate priorities are chosen.

- Ensure that those providing care are able to practise safely and carry out their duty of care (and that of the employer) to each patient.

If, within the available resources, it is difficult to deliver to a safe standard the priorities set out, then managers need to analyse the risks raised, listen to staff, take advice and respond to ensure that appropriate priorities are set and staff can practise safely. There may also be concerns about whether the priorities themselves raise questions about equality and human rights for service users, to which managers must respond. This is discussed further in Chapters 3 and 7. Guidance for inspectors has been issued (Care Quality Commission and Equality and Human Rights Commission (CQC and EHRC), 2011) linking expected care standards in health and social care settings with equality and human rights measures. Senior managers, councillors and NHS boards all have a duty to create an environment in which staff can practise safely. As discussed in Chapter 3, local government duties in relation to staffing are contained in statutory guidance (Department for Education and Skills (DfES), 2005; DH, 2006b).

Employers operate within a framework of vicarious liability whereby they would almost certainly be held responsible for negligence by their employees for harm resulting from breach of the duty of care owed. The obligations of both employees and employer are to:

- Ensure that what is done is done safely and appropriately.

- Make clear what cannot be done, or at least cannot be done safely.

- Ensure that service users are treated with appropriate urgency.

- Prioritise statutory duties over other responsibilities.

Within this framework, should resources fall short of what is needed, managers must:

- Clarify why staff (or service users) believe that the situation is potentially unsafe. This means sitting down with staff in an environment where staff are able to voice concerns. Supervision sessions are the most appropriate environment in which individual staff can raise concerns initially. If the concerns affect more than one member of staff, then a team discussion may be more appropriate, with the concerns set out in writing to assist discussion and effective action.

- Determine (in the light of priorities set by the employer, the available resources, and relevant protocols) whether or not to respond positively to the concerns raised and determine priorities and working methods so that what is done can be done safely. This may involve considering whether things could be done differently, or deciding that certain tasks or roles will not be performed until it is safe to do so. It will almost certainly involve setting priorities for staff, a written plan of action and a review date.

- Ensure staff will be able to undertake their work in a safe manner.

Managers must ensure that no statutory duties to service users are at risk of being compromised, and that compliance with professional codes is not undermined. When concerns are raised, the response must be set down so everyone is clear who is doing what, by when, and how, and whether a review period or monitoring arrangements have been agreed. If managers have their own concerns, they should raise them in a similar manner.

ACTIVITY 5.4

Imagine that workloads for each member of your team rise by 20 per cent. Draft a letter to your line manager setting out your concerns, then compare it with the model letter on the website.

A manager is expected to take active steps to identify potential or actual problems rather than wait for them to occur. Failure to do so could place managers and staff at risk if workers subsequently were to fail to observe their duty of care. Managers may be held responsible if harm is caused by inadequate resources and they failed to take appropriate measures to prevent foreseeable risks arising.

CASE STUDY

A patient on a maternity ward complained that the level of care during her first pregnancy fell below the standard she was entitled to expect, when a suture was not removed promptly once labour commenced. The staff and hospital response was that the care provided was appropriate because the ward was extremely busy that evening.

The court asked to see the notes (in confidence) of all patients on the ward that evening. The notes confirmed that the ward was very busy, but did not show that the doctors could not have conducted a vaginal examination and removed the suture.

The court decided it was not sufficient to show that professionals were very busy, and awarded damages to the patient. It decided it was also necessary to show how priorities were determined by professionals in a rational way using their professional skill and knowledge.

(Deacon v McVicar and Another [1984])

Support for managers

Besides concerns about staff workloads, managers may have concerns about their own workloads. Employers have the same duty of care to managers as they do to other staff. Managers need supervision, continuing professional development, training, support and effective management. They need manageable workloads so they can give the support needed to the staff they manage. If staff or managers are unable to resolve concerns through supervision or other informal means, they may need to consider taking out a grievance or using other means, which are discussed in Chapter 10.

Skill mix

The proper and well-thought-out allocation of cases is a central component of the effective management of a social work team. [. . .] It would appear that Victoria's case was allocated to Ms Arthurworrey by Ms Baptiste without any consideration of the sort of factors I have previously described. In the first place, there would seem to have been no assessment of whether Ms Arthurworrey had the requisite capabilities to handle the case. Ms Arthurworrey told me that at the time she found Victoria's case file lying on her desk, she had never completed a section 47 Inquiry, never dealt with a child in hospital and never taken a case through to case conference. For present purposes, what concerns me is not whether Ms Arthurworrey was capable of handling Victoria's case in a competent manner, but that no assessment of her capabilities would seem to have been made by her manager before allocating the case to her

(Laming, 2003, p. 201)

ACTIVITY **5.5**

As a group, discuss whether you have had work inappropriately delegated to you.

- *How did you respond emotionally to being expected to manage work for which you did not have the appropriate training or competence?*

- *What did you do?*

- *If it happened again tomorrow, what would you do?*

When work is delegated, its allocation requires the exercise of professional skill and judgement. No professional works alone. Social workers, for example, work in teams with other social workers and social care staff, and alongside doctors, health visitors, occupational therapists, psychologists, nurses, the police and teachers. Every professional works with, and relies on, colleagues.

All professionals also have work delegated to them by other colleagues, most notably their team leaders or other managers. They in turn delegate work to other staff such as technicians, social work or healthcare assistants, and administrative staff. Increasingly, some of these staff work for other employers such as private contractors or voluntary organisations, in which case the arrangements for delegating work should be set out in a document commissioning services. Delegation to contractors does not remove from commissioners all responsibility for what is then undertaken.

CASE STUDY

A United Kingdom Homecare Association survey also identified safety concerns for staff. Two-fifths of councils and trusts have reduced funding for the doubling-up of care workers on visits, despite some providers' risk assessments stating that two care workers were required, for instance in getting a client into a bath.

One senior home worker said the times for visits are getting worse. . . . the use of 15 minute slots for visits took away all dignity and humanity. She had seen a social worker in tears explaining that a package of care for an older woman would no longer include any time for the care worker to buy her any groceries.

(Dunning, 2011, p. 6)

ACTIVITY **5.6**

If you were the social worker, and your employer delegated work to a contractor with inadequate resources, what should you do?

When a council or NHS trust delegates work to a contractor, it retains responsibility for how the standards of the contract are to be met, when and by whom. The council or NHS trust must monitor the contract to ensure that its duty of care to those receiving services is met.

If social workers or health service staff become aware of unsafe, discriminatory or otherwise poor practice, possibly affecting service users' human rights, then they must establish quickly what is happening and challenge the contractor directly or through the contractor's manager. They must do so in a way that protects the staff or service users who have raised concerns. As always, a written audit trail is essential. A sample of service users should be interviewed by the employer to see how widespread the concerns may be. The contractor should be held to account by imposing penalties or even ending the contract.

Four categories of people are affected by the delegation of work, in addition to those receiving services. They are:

- Staff, including students and trainees who are not qualified professionals, undertaking work delegated to them by professionals.

- Staff who are newly qualified or who otherwise may not possess the specific skills required for the delegated responsibility.

- Qualified professionals and their managers who are asked to accept or delegate work themselves.

- Staff who work in settings where they are a minority amongst other professionals, or in multi-agency or multi-professional teams where role boundaries may change.

There has been much talk in recent years about 'remodelling' or 'modernising' public services, but the proposals put forward often appear to be driven more by the need to make savings or in response to staffing shortages. This can result in 'viruses' impacting on lawful and ethical decision-making (*R (CD and VD)* v *Isle of Anglesey CC* [2004]; Preston-Shoot, 2010b).

In many organisations – sometimes as a result of carefully planned new ways of working, but increasingly as a result of financial pressures – role boundaries are changing. Changes in roles may involve expanding the breadth of a job by working across professional divides or creating new jobs by introducing new types of workers, for instance combined occupational therapist/social worker posts in adult social care teams. Many roles in the NHS are themselves 'new' roles which have evolved, such as operating department practitioners, whose role now substantially overlaps with that of theatre nurses. Role changes may also occur when delegating work, by moving a task up or down a role hierarchy often involving an extension of responsibilities for those to whom work is delegated. For example, a family support worker or social work assistant undertaking roles previously done by social workers, or a call centre where non social workers handle the initial referral. Similarly, in health care, assistant practitioners now undertake many tasks previously undertaken by registered nurses, whilst nurses undertake roles previously designated as medical.

Principles underpinning the delegation of work

General principles which apply across all professions are set out in guidance on delegation from the NMC, which states that:

The delegation of nursing or midwifery care must be appropriate, safe and in the best interests of the person in the care of a nurse or midwife.

Prior to agreeing to delegation, the nurse or midwife has the responsibility to under-stand this advice . . . . the decision to delegate would be judged against what could be reasonably expected from someone with their knowledge, skills and abilities when placed in those particular circumstances.

(NMC, 2008b)

Those who consider delegating work to other staff must have first undertaken an assess-ment of the needs to be met and how they should be addressed. Only then can they deter-mine the knowledge, skills and understanding required to perform the delegated task.

Helpful guidance has been published which examines how this applies to nursing and pro-fessions allied to medicine (Royal College of Nursing (RCN) et al., 2006).

CASE STUDY

Unsafe delegation

Angela is a district nurse with a heavy caseload. She was asked to take on additional cases to cover long-term sickness. Her manager was under pressure to cover these cases, and eventually suggested they be given to a district nurse assistant and only nominally allocated to Anne's caseload. Angela wasn't happy but could see no alternative. Two months later, a serious misjudgement by the district nurse assistant led to Angela facing disciplinary action. She had not put her concerns in writing nor explicitly objected to the nominal allocation of the case to herself. She was suspended pending possible disciplinary action.

ACTIVITY 5.7

As a group, discuss what difference, if any, it would have made if Angela (described in the case study above) had put her concerns in writing – and what should those concerns have been.

Who decides what should and should not be delegated, and how and when?

Many professions have very specific protocols or guidance setting out who may or may not undertake certain roles, tasks or procedures. In Scotland, there are particular functions or 'reserved roles' that can only be undertaken by social workers:

Social workers should assess, plan, manage the delivery of care and safeguard the well-being of the most vulnerable adults and children, in particular, those who:

- *are in need of protection; and/or*

- *are in danger of exploitation or significant harm; and/or*

- *are at risk of causing significant harm to themselves or others; and/or*

- *are unable to provide informed consent.*

To do this social workers must:

- *carry out enquiries and make recommendations when necessary as to whether or not a person requires to be the subject of protection procedures; and*

- *be responsible for the development, monitoring and implementation of a plan to protect the person, in particular, identify and respond appropriately to any risks to the achievement of the plan and/or any need for the plan to be revised because of changing circumstances.*

(Scottish Executive, 2006, p. 30)

In England and Wales, only approved mental health professionals can exercise powers under the Mental Health Act 1983 and Mental Health Act 2007 to admit a person into a psychiatric setting compulsorily. You must be familiar with guidance and policy documents setting out the functions or roles that must only be performed by your profession, or which must not be undertaken by your profession.

ACTIVITY **5.8**

Where do you think you would find information about functions, roles or tasks that must only be carried out by a qualified professional in your own profession? Begin to compile a catalogue of legal rules – including statutory guidance, case law and policy documents – which set the standards for lawful and safe working.

Many professions have protocols about what may or may not be delegated. For example, the principles of good practice for biomedical scientist involvement in histopathological dissection state:

During specimen dissection the duty pathologist must be available should the biomedical scientist require assistance. Departmental protocols should reflect a low threshold for seeking advice. Examples of this would be if:

- *the specimen complexity is beyond the biomedical scientist's experience and competence*

- *the specimen is of usual complexity but shows unusual features*

- *the specimen has not been previously encountered*

- *there are important or unusual features in the request form, clinical information or past history*

(Institute of Biomedical Science and the Royal College of Pathologists, p. 5)

In nursing, significant work has been undertaken on what might be safe and appropriate ratios of qualified nurses to unqualified staff, as part of a wider examination of workload models (RCN, 2010). The benchmark average on general hospital wards is two qualified nurses for each unqualified staff member. However, one common feature of major scandals such as those in the Mid Staffordshire (Francis, 2010) and Maidstone Hospitals (Healthcare Commission, 2007a) has been a much lower ratio of qualified nurses to unqualified staff.

The example of administration of medicines

The administration of medicines is a role that relies on appropriately trained staff following strict procedures to ensure safe practice. The National Patient Safety Agency seeks to ensure accurate reporting and analysis of healthcare-related incidents. Its first report (National Patient Safety Agency, 2005) suggested that 10 per cent of all untoward incidents reported across the NHS were medication-related, and it highlighted concerns that the teaching of how to administer medicines is not well done.

Many NHS trusts have local arrangements to test nurses' competence in the safe administration of medicines prior to allowing them to undertake clinical practice. In a hospital ward or nursing home, detailed and comprehensive procedures and standards must exist in order to encourage safe, legal and effective practice. These should take account of relevant legal and professional frameworks such as the Medicines Act 1968 and guidance from the NMC (2007), General Medical Council (GMC) (2008) and other professional bodies as appropriate. In secondary care, medicines administration is usually the responsibility of a registered nurse; in the community, however, healthcare support workers may be responsible for the administration of medicines such as eye drops. The NMC recommends that medicines administration by nursing students is countersigned by the supervising registered nurse.

Who should decide what should be delegated?

The day-to-day supervision of the work delegated by a professional to someone who is not a qualified professional is likely to be the responsibility of the professional. However, the decision as to whether it is appropriate to delegate work to another member of staff is a management decision to be taken by a manager or more senior professional, albeit in close consultation. The distinction is important. That manager is accountable for the safe delegation of the task or role, and the professional is responsible for such supervision as is delegated to them. In some cases the person to whom the work is delegated may not even be managed by the professional and may not even be employed by the same organisation.

The worker to whom the work is being delegated is also accountable for the delegated task or role, and is responsible for their actions in carrying it out as long as they have the skills and knowledge to undertake the delegated work competently. Service users are entitled to know who is providing services and to expect that those who provide their treatment, care or support are competent. It is essential that there is no confusion as to who is a registered professional and who is not.

No one is more dangerous than someone who does not know what they don't know. Supervision of the person to whom work is delegated is crucial and must be appropriate to the work delegated. For example, if the delegation of some visits to, or work with, a child in need or subject to a child protection plan is considered, then closer supervision and clearer feedback will be required than in some other roles. Clear, accurate and contemporaneous record keeping is essential when work is delegated so that it is clear who is responsible for what, and when, whilst the professional or manager remains accountable overall. Record keeping is discussed further in Chapter 8.

Within any team, an individual member of staff must refuse to accept a role until competent to perform it. Staff who are newly recruited or newly qualified, or who have had an extended absence through maternity leave, sickness or a career break, should be sure they have sufficient training, support and supervision. However, if the work can reasonably be regarded as resting within their contract of employment, then the employer can insist on more training to ensure they are competent to undertake it. If someone within a team acts beyond their level of competence and is negligent and causes harm, they could be liable – but so could the person who delegated work to them in the first instance.

What if the concern is that the role delegated is questionable because the request or instruction is itself unsafe?

CASE STUDY

Rosemary is a midwife. She notes that forceps are likely to be necessary to complete a delivery. She prepares a trolley for the doctor she has alerted and makes sure all the equipment is available, including the Neville Barnes forceps that the hospital protocol requires as the normal forceps to be used. Only consultants are allowed to use Kielland forceps, following a baby death when they were inappropriately used.

The registrar on duty is called and asks for Kielland forceps. Rosemary explains he should be using the ones she has prepared. The registrar says he is instructing the midwife to get him the forceps he prefers to use. Rosemary explains that the hospital protocol means he must call the consultant, and that she is not willing to get them. He insists he is instructing her and will call her manager if she does not follow his instruction. Delivery is imminent.

ACTIVITY 5.9

In the case study above, what should the midwife do next?

Individuals remain accountable for their own professional conduct. In some circumstances, if an inexperienced worker consults a more experienced worker within the team, it may be held that the more experienced member of the team is negligent if something subsequently goes wrong. As in other situations, contemporaneous recording of both instructions and any concerns is essential.

All members of a team must work within their level of competence and make it clear if they are not competent to undertake a task or role. Similarly, senior staff should not delegate without being able to confirm that the person to whom the task or role is delegated is competent to perform it. This applies to circumstances where professional boundaries may be blurred – between social workers, occupational therapists, doctors and physiotherapists for example – as much as to the delegation of work to support staff.

In the case above, Rosemary should urgently contact her manager to explain the situation and her concern that she believes unsafe practice is imminent. Good practice would lead the senior midwife to challenge the registrar over Rosemary's concerns. If Rosemary is convinced the practice is unsafe, then she should consider refusing to get the wrong forceps. If instructed to get them by her own manager, she may need to take further advice or follow the instruction having made her concerns clear. Rosemary must place her concerns on the record as soon as the immediate care needs are resolved.

Where agencies work together, delegation and good communication are essential. The independent Longcare inquiry on the care of vulnerable adults noted that the goal (of multi-agency working) should be that:

> There have to be agreements on lead responsibilities, specific tasks, co-operation, communication and the best use of skill. Those interagency arrangements must be in place so that they can be activated quickly when needed.

> However, no individual agency's statutory responsibility can be delegated to another. Each agency must act in accordance with its duty when it is satisfied that the action is appropriate. Joint investigation there may be but the shared information flowing from that must be constantly evaluated and reviewed by each agency.

> (DH, 2000a, p. 29)

Students and the delegation of work

The principles set out below for student nurses are broadly applicable to all healthcare and social work students.

> At all times, you should work only within your level of understanding and competence, and always under the appropriate supervision of a registered nurse or midwife, or a health professional with a registered nurse or midwife providing mentorship.

> As a pre-registration student, you are not professionally accountable in the way that you will be after you come to register with the NMC. This means that you cannot be called to account for your actions and omissions by the NMC. So far as the NMC is concerned, it is the registered practitioners with whom you are working who are professionally responsible for the consequences of your actions and omissions. This is why you must always work under direct supervision. This does not mean, however, that you can never be called to account by your university or by the law for the consequences of your actions or omissions as a pre-registration student.

> There may be times when you are in a position where you may not be directly accompanied by your mentor, supervisor or another registered colleague, such as emergency situations. As your skills, experience and confidence develop, you will become increasingly able to deal with these situations. However, as a student, do not participate in any procedure for which you have not been fully prepared or in which you are not adequately supervised. If such a situation arises, discuss the matter as quickly as possible with your mentor or personal tutor.

> (NMC, 2006, p. 3)

ACTIVITY **5.10**

As a student, were you ever asked to undertake roles for which you were not sufficiently trained or supervised?

What did you do if you were?

Newly qualified professionals may also be restricted in certain roles. For example, newly qualified social workers in England should note this extract from the relevant statutory guidance.

Safeguarding children roles that cannot be delegated

5.34 Local authority children's social care should ensure that the social work practitioners who are responding to referrals are supported by experienced first line managers competent in making sound evidence based decisions about what to do next.

5.41 The initial assessment should be led by a qualified and experienced social worker who is supervised by a highly experienced and qualified social work manager.

5.62 The core assessment is the means by which a section 47 enquiry is carried out. It should be led by a qualified and experienced social worker.

(Department for Education, 2010, pp. 144–155)

What should you do when delegation is proposed?

Proposals for delegation may affect just one individual or, more usually, be part of wider role changes. If you are not sure, you must ask for advice from a more senior professional, your colleagues, your professional body or your trade union. Do not agree just because you are worried that you might seem to be causing trouble.

However, what if the person seeking to delegate an unsafe task which you refuse to undertake decides to carry out that task themselves? Consider another incident that happened in one hospital two decades ago.

CASE STUDY

A nurse works on a special care baby unit. The paediatrician asks her to administer a dose of potassium. The nurse says the dose is far too high given the baby's weight, and is unsafe. The paediatrician insists he is instructing the nurse to administer the dose. The nurse refuses and says the doctor must administer that dose himself. The baby subsequently died.

ACTIVITY **5.11**

In the case study above, what would the nurse's position have been if she had complied with the instruction?

There are nine areas to consider before making a decision to delegate work.

First find out precisely what is proposed. Any proposal to delegate work should set out in writing:

1. What is proposed and which staff are affected directly or indirectly by it.

2. Who proposed it.

3. Why it is proposed, including any evidence that the proposal will improve or at least not worsen outcomes and standards of care – incorporating any examples of similar proposals elsewhere that have been looked at.

4. How the proposal relates to any relevant clinical or service protocols or guidance issued at national or local level.

See the pro-forma letter on the website asking for such information.

Ask questions and find out more. The staff to whom work is to be delegated may be highly committed, knowledgeable and skilled, but when considering whether it is safe or appropriate to delegate work, you should ask:

5. Has there been an assessment of needs and risk and a determination of appropriate action by a competent person?

6. Is the worker to whom work is being delegated judged by the person responsible for the delegation to be trained, qualified and competent to carry out the work?

7. Is the worker to whom the work is being delegated confident that they are appropriately qualified, trained and competent to perform the work?

8. Does the delegation of this work come within the policies and protocols of the workplace?

9. Is the level of supervision and follow-up feedback appropriate?

Make sure there is time for consultation and ensure that the process is thorough. This is to ensure there is appropriate time for all staff affected to consider the proposals, take advice, ask questions and possibly make alternative proposals or amendments to the proposals. At every stage, the questions summarised above should form a template against which any proposal should be considered. Also consider the following:

• Find out from your union, professional body or via the web whether similar proposals have been introduced elsewhere, how they worked, and what changes workers have made to them since its introduction.

• Has 'due regard' been given to the equality impact of the proposals on service users or staff?

• Can the proposals be piloted? If the proposals appear to be safe and well thought through, then it is still worth seeking to pilot them or have them introduced for a trial period at the end of which there will be a proper review of what worked and any changes needed or whether the change should be withdrawn.

- Have all affected staff been kept informed and had a say in whether the proposals are introduced? There is nothing worse than a set of cosy discussions between a few people at the end of which, magically, the proposals are agreed, probably with minor changes.

- How do the proposals affect pay terms and conditions, especially if they involve an intensification of work as well? Proposals that involve more shift work, redundancies or pay cuts need clarity and need to be challenged, as they may impact on services as well as staff.

- Is the necessary training, support and equipment in place? If the proposals are introduced, make sure that before they are, there is a budget for sufficient training and that proper professional supervision arrangements are in place alongside clear protocols setting out who does what.

- Are the proposals subject to monitoring and a review period? Any sensible management will want to monitor how the proposals work and review them to tackle any concerns that arise. Make sure your union or professional body is part of that review, alongside the staff affected.

If those putting the proposals forward cannot satisfactorily answer these questions, then the proposals should be withdrawn.

C H A P T E R   S U M M A R Y

After reading this chapter, you should understand the contractual, common law and professional accountability framework within which workloads and the delegation of work should be approached. You should have formed some appreciation of your responsibilities as a health and social care professional when faced with a shortfall of resources, inadequate staffing or an inappropriate skill mix.

Chapter 6
Advocacy

OBJECTIVES

By the end of this chapter, you should have an understanding of what health and social care professionals must do:

- To help service users raise concerns, including formal complaints about their care or the lack of it.

- To ensure service users are aware of, and able to obtain, their rights to involvement in their assessment and care.

- To ensure carers understand their right to raise concerns and be involved in the assessment and care of those for whom they care.

- To assist service users and their representative organisations understand their entitlement to be consulted on changes to the range, nature or means of service delivery.

Introduction

The NHS Constitution offers clear commitments to patients. These include:

You have the right to have any complaint you make about NHS services dealt with efficiently and to have it properly investigated.

The NHS commits, when mistakes happen, to acknowledge them, apologise, explain what went wrong and put things right quickly and effectively.

The NHS commits to ensure that the organisation learns lessons from complaints and claims and uses these to improve NHS services.

(Health Act 2009 – NHS Constitution, p. 3)

For social workers, their code obligations include:

3.1. Promoting the independence of service users and assisting them to understand and exercise their rights;

3.2. Using established processes and procedures to challenge and report dangerous, abusive, discriminatory or exploitative behaviour and practice;

3.5. Informing your employer or an appropriate authority where the practice of colleagues may be unsafe or adversely affecting standards of care;

3.7. Helping service users and carers to make complaints, taking complaints seriously and responding to them or passing them to the appropriate person.

(General Social Care Council (GSCC), 2002)

This chapter's focus on advocacy aims to empower staff to stand up for patients and service users. It also aims to assist staff in helping patients and service users to speak their truth to professional and organisational power. Health and social care providers must ensure that service users and carers who wish to complain or raise concerns are encouraged to do so.

Professional accountability and advocacy – what professionals are required to do

Advocacy is not an optional extra; it is at the heart of professional accountability. In language similar to that of other professional codes, the Nursing and Midwifery Council (NMC) Code (NMC, 2008a) requires nurses and midwives to act as advocates for those in their care, helping them to access relevant health and social care, information and support. This chapter looks at how service users must be assisted to protect their interests and exercise their rights by those who work with them.

CASE STUDY

Margaret Haywood, 58, a nurse for more than 20 years, who became a whistle blower by secretly filming the neglect of elderly patients for a television documentary, was struck off the nursing register despite Sussex University Hospitals NHS Trust issuing a public apology admitting 'serious lapses in the quality of care'.

ACTIVITY 6.1

On what possible grounds, having looked at the NMC Code, do you think that the NMC might have found Margaret Haywood guilty of misconduct?

This case sparked outrage, resulting in a compromise which, in effect, exonerated Margaret Haywood and prompted new guidance on raising concerns. This new guidance emphasises that nurses and midwives have a duty to prioritise the interests of those in their care and to act to protect those in their care if they consider them to be at risk (NMC, 2010a; Health Professions Council (HPC), 2011).

Figure 6.1 How a learning organisation enables service users to raise concerns and exercise their rights

What must be done when service users and patients raise concerns and make complaints?

Raising concerns and making complaints are an essential part of improving services and holding service providers and their practitioners to account. When care falls below the standards that service users are entitled to expect, organisations and staff should learn from that experience. The guide to the Local Authority Social Services and NHS Complaints Regulations 2009 explains that:

> *When someone is unhappy with your service, it is important to let them know their rights when it comes to making a complaint. In the NHS, these rights are articulated by the NHS Constitution.*

> (Department of Health (DH), 2009a, p. 15)

Thus, directors of adult social services *should ensure that nationally recognised professional codes of conduct and practice are observed by staff delivering care services in the community . . . (and are) responsible for ensuring that staff providing care services exercise a duty of care and that the personal dignity of service users is upheld* (DH, 2006, pp. 10–11). Directors of children's services have similar responsibilities (Department for Education and Skills (DfES), 2005). Systematic reporting of concerns by practitioners and managers is a precondition of directors effectively discharging this function.

Similarly, the NHS Constitution (Health Act 2009) requires that NHS trusts:

> *should aim to be open with patients, their families, carers or representatives, including if anything goes wrong; welcoming and listening to feedback and addressing concerns*

promptly and in a spirit of co-operation. You should contribute to a climate where the truth can be heard and the reporting of, and learning from, errors is encouraged.

(DH, 2010, p. 108)

Unfortunately, this guidance makes no further mention of the duty that healthcare professionals and social workers have to assist with complaints, and it remains the experience of many patients and service users (and staff) that complaints are seen as a problem rather than an opportunity to learn.

ACTIVITY **6.2**

Obtain and read a copy of your employer's complaints procedure. Consider what your employer expects you to do if someone complains about their care or that of another person.

The Local Authority Social Services and NHS Complaints Regulations 2009 set out a two-stage complaint process. Local resolution requires that local NHS trust or local authority complaints procedures are used to raise a concern, in writing or in person, with the nurse, doctor, therapist or social worker concerned, or with their immediate manager. Most cases are resolved at this stage. If the complainant is still unhappy, they can refer healthcare matters to the independent Parliamentary and Health Service Ombudsman (PHSO). In some, limited cases there may be the further option of a judicial review. Appeals concerning social services are made to the Local Government Ombudsman.

These regulations are helpfully detailed and prescriptive. Health and social care professionals should draw service users' and carers' attention to them. Service users and carers should know that the regulations state that:

- Verbal complaints not resolved within one working day will be required to be put in writing <u>by the responding body</u> and forwarded to the complainant.

(Section 13)

- Complaints made verbally but not successfully resolved within one working day, and those made in writing or electronically, such as by email, will need to be acknowledged within three working days, which can be done either verbally or in writing.

(Section 13)

- In the acknowledgement, the responding organisation must offer the complainant the opportunity for a discussion at a mutually convenient time.

(Section 13)

- The purpose of the discussion is to determine how the complaint is to be handled and the timeframe in which to seek resolution.

(Section 13)

- The responding body is required to investigate the complaint in a manner appropriate to *resolve it speedily and efficiently and, during the investigation, keep the complainant informed, as far as reasonably practicable, as to the progress of the investigation*.

(Section 14)

- The complainant must be sent a written response signed by the *responsible person* which describes how the complaint has been considered, what conclusions have been reached and what actions, if any, have or will be taken as a result. (The 'responsible person' in the NHS is the chief executive or someone deputed by him.)

(Section 14)

- The normal time limit whereby people can raise their complaint is extended to 12 months, and can be longer depending on the circumstances.

(Section 12)

(Local Authority Social Services and NHS Complaints Regulations 2009)

NHS and social services organisations must keep records of complaints and publish an annual report summarising complaints and outcomes (The Local Authority Social Services and NHS Complaints Regulations 2009, Sections 17 and 18).

CASE STUDY

Mr L was 72 and suffered from Parkinson's disease. He had been a fit architect, and had stopped taking medication to manage his symptoms because this disturbed his mental health. Mr L experienced further episodes of hallucinations, paranoia and aggressive behaviours, which led his daughters to administer diazepam and take him to Epsom General Hospital A&E department. He was then transferred to the trust's West Park Hospital, which specialised in assessing elderly patients with mental health difficulties.

On arrival, he was said to be in a'calm and pleasant mood', but nevertheless he was given 10mg olanzapine, an antipsychotic drug. Mrs L visited her husband later the same day and was 'devastated' by what she saw. He had been 'turned into a zombie – a ragdoll'. Over the next few days, despite his family's concerns, Mr L was given more antipsychotic and tranquillising medication, which his family say robbed him of his dignity.

(PHSO, 2011, story number 9)

ACTIVITY 6.3

If you had responsibilities (as a nurse, pharmacist or hospital social worker) for the case above:

- *What should you do to advise the family how to raise their concerns?*

- *What would you say to your manager?*

Mr L's treatment appears to be a possible breach of the hospital's duty of care and of his human rights. Moreover there appears to have been no consultation with his family regarding his treatment, so there may also be issues around consent. In such circumstances, it is essential that you record the family's concerns and immediately draw them to the attention of the staff concerned and/or their managers, as well to your own manager. If inappropriate care is being given, then it should be stopped as a matter of urgency. You should refer the family to your manager but explain to them where they can find the hospital's complaints procedure if the discussion with your manager does not satisfy them.

Specific rights to complain

In addition to the general right to complain, some service users have specific rights to complain or to access advocacy support and advice.

Children

Section 26(3) of the Children Act 1989 requires local authorities to establish a procedure to respond to complaints about the exercise of their functions made by children or made on their behalf. The procedure must be explained to any potential complainant. Local authorities must give complainants information about advocacy services and monitor the outcomes of these complaints so that they can then improve services. The Children Act 2004 goes further and requires local authorities to consider the views of children prior to deciding on intervention (*Pierce* v *Doncaster MBC* [2007]). The 2004 Act strengthened advocacy support for children in care, partly as a consequence of the inquiry findings into widespread abuse in children's homes in North Wales stretching back 25 years (Waterhouse, 2000; Children's Commissioner for Wales, 2003).

The Children's Commissioner in England and the equivalent office in Wales are responsible for reviewing the complaints procedure, whistle blowing, and the provision of advice, information and advocacy.

Adults

The Community Care Assessment Directions 2004 regard the participation of users and carers as central to the assessment process. Personalisation has accelerated this process. Statutory access to an independent mental health advocate who exists to help and support patients to understand and exercise their legal rights is available to patients subject to certain aspects of the Mental Health Act 1983 (see Mental Health Act 1983 (Independent Mental Health Advocates) (England) Regulations 2008). Independent mental capacity advocates are intended to safeguard the most vulnerable people who lack capacity and have no family or friends to support them when serious decisions are taken in their lives (DH, 2009b). Research continues to identify the need for, and beneficial outcomes of, advocacy in challenging the balance of power between service providers and users. Assessment and service provision practices are not infrequently criticised in ombudsmen and judicial review decisions. Attitudes towards complainants remain variable, with local authorities and NHS trusts having been censured for mishandling complaints (Braye and Preston-Shoot, 2009).

Practical support from professionals

If service users or carers wish to raise concerns or complain then, as a registered professional, you should bear in mind your professional code and the relevant statutory and employer policies, and then:

- Listen carefully to the service user or carer and then explain how to raise a concern or make a complaint.

- Find out if the complaint is one that should be resolved immediately. If it directly affects the care of the person on whose behalf the complaint is being made (for example, it relates to important safeguarding visits missed, unchanged soiled hospital or care home linen, or unsafe waiting times), then the matter should be addressed immediately. This need not be instead of pursuing a complaint, but is in addition to doing so. If immediate action is needed, be sure to draw your manager's attention to the concern.

- Reassure the complainant that there will be no adverse consequences as a result of making a complaint.

- If the matter can be resolved informally, then do so, but ensure it is recorded. If not, give complainants the contact details of the person to whom the service user or carer should complain (the complaints manager), a copy of the complaints procedure, and the relevant contact details and, if it seems appropriate, explain how they can access an independent advocate.

- Explain any time limits – 12 months is usually the upper limit, but if the matter is urgent the complaint should be made as soon as possible.

- Make a note of the advice provided and alert your manager.

- If, in the course of listening to the complaint, you realise that your duty as a registered professional requires you to take the matter further, then you should do so (see Chapter 10).

In Mr L's case (above), his condition deteriorated and he died. The family took his case to the Health Ombudsman (PHSO, 2011).

It may be possible to challenge the final decision on a complaint by taking court action called a judicial review. Judicial review is not a form of appeal focused on the merits of the decision itself. Rather, it is concerned with whether decisions have been made lawfully, rationally and following reasonable procedures. Judicial reviews can be expensive and should not be considered without careful legal advice. There are strict time limits for submitting a claim (see **www.publiclawproject.org.uk**).

In England a new organisation, Health Watch, will have a role in NHS complaints advocacy as part of new arrangements which will eventually replace the Independent Complaints Advocacy Service (see **www.pohwer.net**). The role of the supervisory body regarding hospitals under the Mental Capacity Act Deprivation of Liberty Safeguards (DOLS) will pass from primary care trusts to local authorities.

The Care Quality Commission (CQC) does not handle individual complaints, but does have powers (though not necessarily the resources) to ensure that all registered NHS providers and adult social services providers are handling complaints properly. However, the CQC and Ofsted (for children's services) both have whistle blowing procedures for staff, users, patients and carers who have tried to raise concerns within their local organisations. The CQC guidance summarises the statutory arrangements for a number of settings including care homes, domiciliary care, nursing agencies, children's homes, adoption, foster care and residential family centres (see CQC, 2011).

ACTIVITY **6.4**

*Visit the website of the Local Government Ombudsman (**www.lgo.org.uk**) or Parliamentary and Health Service Ombudsman (**www.ombudsman.org.uk**). Find a complaint that has been upheld and ask yourself what the organisation involved should have done to instead learn from the complaint and thus avoid the matter ever being referred to the ombudsman.*

The importance of raising concerns

Safe systems depend on staff, patients and service users being encouraged to raise concerns. All organisations benefit by learning from complaints and analysing adverse incidents and mistakes, especially if there is a pattern to them. NHS complaints procedures should complement NHS clinical governance and the National Patient Safety Organisation's adverse incident reporting procedures (see **www.npsa.nhs.uk**).

In social work a similar mix of robust complaints procedures, audit and professional supervision should be in place. Across health and social care there should be effective professional supervision so that staff can talk through concerns, complaints and near misses.

Clinical governance and good supervision help employers to become 'learning' organisations. Managers responsible for health and social care services have been encouraged to create learning organisations following a series of scandals in the NHS, and by the Laming inquiry (Laming, 2003) following Victoria Climbié's death. The culture of openness, transparency, clear accountability, genuine co-operation and sharing of skills and knowledge within teams and organisations that this requires, complements professional codes, all of which require that staff work openly and co-operatively with colleagues and treat them with respect (GSCC, 2002).

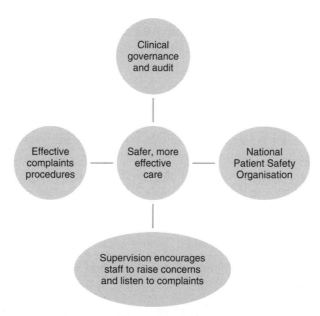

Figure 6.2 Good practice in advocacy assists good quality care

CASE STUDY

The NHS commissioned research, which also has implications for social care, exploring the impact of good appraisal schemes, collaborative team working, and strong training practices on patient care. As well as benefits to staff morale and role clarity, the research showed a direct link between good management and reduced hospital deaths in the two areas of care examined – deaths after admissions for hip fracture and deaths within 30 days of emergency surgery.

The results showed that a hospital appraising 20% more staff is likely to have 1090 fewer deaths per 100,000 admissions – or 12% of the expected total. The link between better training and effective collaborative teams was also clear, though less so. Where all hospital staff had access to a formal training policy, mortality was 3.5% lower than would otherwise have been expected, whilst where 60% worked in formal teams, mortality was 5% lower than would be expected.

(Borrill et al., 2001, pp. 215–230)

When staff raise concerns as advocates for service users, managers have contractual responsibilities in addition to those they may have as registered professionals. They must:

- Listen carefully and be clear why staff (or others, including service users and carers) believe the situation is potentially unsafe.

- Respond positively to the concerns raised in the light of the employer's priorities, the available resources and relevant protocols and standards. The manager should decide, probably after taking advice from other managers or specialists, whether the concerns need to be addressed and how.

- Make sure that whatever steps are taken, staff can undertake the work they are expected to do in a safe manner, for both service users and themselves, so that no one's professional accountability, common law duty of care or any statutory duty owed by the employer is compromised.

Clinical governance

Clinical governance is a systematic approach to maintaining and improving the quality of patient care within a health system. Learning from complaints and mistakes is a crucial part of clinical governance. It has become the norm within the NHS after the 1995 Bristol Royal Infirmary scandal where doctors covered up a high mortality rate for paediatric cardiac surgery (Kennedy, 2001). NHS trust boards subsequently assumed a legal responsibility for the quality of care alongside their other statutory duties. Clinical governance is how that responsibility is discharged, and includes:

- Clinical audit, which seeks to continuously refine clinical practice and measure performance against agreed standards.

- Clinical effectiveness, which measures whether a particular intervention works and whether it is appropriate and cost-effective.

- Education and training, especially continuing professional development.

- Research and development, undertaken routinely.

- Public scrutiny, linked to open processes.

- Risk management, which seeks to protect service users and staff by critical event audit and by learning from complaints within a framework of professional accountability, part of which will be captured within a risk register.

Adverse incident reporting and risk assessment

Systems failures are often the root cause of safety incidents within the NHS. However, the most common response to serious patient safety incidents is instead to suspend and then discipline the staff involved. This can be unfair to staff and diverts management attention away from identifying contributory systems failures. The NHS has been encouraged to move away from a blame culture towards one where underlying causes of incidents are analysed to help managers and senior clinicians:

- Decide whether it is necessary to suspend staff from duty following a patient safety incident.

- Explore alternatives to suspension, such as temporary relocation or modification of duties.

- Consider other possible measures to be taken as the investigation progresses.

Tools such as the Incident Decision Tree (see **https://report.npsa.nhs.uk/idt2**) and the Root Cause Analysis toolkit have been developed to focus on system failure, not just individual failure. In social care, internal investigations should have a similar 'systems' focus, but often do not, whilst the lessons of Serious Case Reviews are certainly not always learned beyond the organisation concerned. Accordingly, trends similar to those in the NHS are being advocated for social care (for example, in Munro, 2011).

ACTIVITY **6.5**

If you worked in any environment where professionals effectively ignored abuse and poor practice, what do you think your starting points for challenging such poor practice would be?

Professional supervision

One crucial aspect of ensuring that services learn is professional supervision. The Victoria Climbié inquiry report (Laming, 2003) described supervision as the *cornerstone of all good social work practice*. The 2009 Laming report reiterated the importance of supervision:

> *there is concern that the tradition of deliberate, reflective social work practice is being put in danger because of an overemphasis on process and targets, resulting in a loss of confidence amongst social workers. It is vitally important that social work is carried out*

*in a supportive learning environment that actively encourages the continuous develop-
ment of professional judgement and skills.*

(Laming, 2009, p. 32)

In every organisation providing health and social care, good professional supervision should:

- Ensure that the employer's policies, national guidance and the relevant professional code are understood, applied and safely implemented, and are a lawful translation of the statutory duties and powers.

- Enable staff to understand work pressures, provide support to staff, and be an opportunity for staff to draw attention not only to difficult or complex cases and overall workloads, but to any concerns about training, support, inappropriate delegation or management.

- Help staff to think about their work and about current research, policy and evidence, and include consideration of individual cases and help ensure professional development.

- Promote shared decision-making involving a review of decisions made and encouraging mutual knowledge and development, helping both staff members and managers to take responsibility for their actions whilst accepting scrutiny from their peers, their employer and service users. Shared decision-making has implications for the manager's duty of care, since the manager will also be accountable for decisions jointly made and implemented.

ACTIVITY 6.6

In a group, discuss how many of you have regular supervision in which the agenda is jointly prepared, the decisions are jointly agreed, which is not interrupted, and in which you feel you can safely raise concerns about your own practice or the environment of care.

How should someone who does not have this go about getting it?

Ensuring service users and carers are involved in assessment, treatment and care

In recent years, public services policy has sought to make service users' experiences and wishes central. This has prompted changes to the statutory arrangements for consultation, involvement and complaints (see Braye and Preston-Shoot, 2009). The reasons for this are well documented:

- If inequality and discrimination are to be challenged, then the institutional and social causes need to be addressed, not just the individual consequences.

- Groups representing disadvantaged people have insisted that their experiences and knowledge must influence what services are provided, how, by whom, when and where.

- The views of 'experts by experience' are important and must be considered alongside the skills and knowledge of practitioners, and the policies and procedures of organisations providing care, support and treatment (Commission for Social Care Inspection (CSCI), 2008c).

Carers play a vital role in asserting the rights of those they care for and ensuring that authorities carry out their duty of care. They have significant advocacy and employment rights.

CASE STUDY

Helping carers know and obtain their rights

Tariq has become increasingly concerned that the local authority has made it very difficult for carers of older people to have their needs addressed. When he and other team members raise this as a concern with their manager, they are told that although the manager is sympathetic, senior managers have made it clear that there is no funding for carers except in the most exceptional cases.

Tariq has a new referral today, and it is clear that the carer is central to the continued independence of the adult concerned, who has learning disabilities, but the manager says that the budget for learning disabilities is already heading towards an overspend.

ACTIVITY 6.7

In the above case study, what should Tariq and other team members (and the manager) do?

Tariq should remind himself of carers' legal entitlement to have their own needs addressed. The carer is entitled to be consulted about the user's assessment under the Community Care Directions 2004, and to be involved in mental health decision-making (Department of Health (DH), 2008). Carers may have their needs assessed under the Carers (Recognition and Services) Act 1995 if providing regular and substantial amounts of care. The Carers and Disabled Children Act 2000 strengthened the right of carers to request an assessment of their needs, by removing the requirement that the cared-for person had accepted an assessment or services for their own needs. The Carers (Equal Opportunities) Act (2004) requires that carers are informed of their rights, including their entitlement to a carer's assessment. Moreover any risk to carers should be addressed when making eligibility decisions under the Fair Access to Care Services guidance (DH, 2002b).

In the light of these entitlements being denied, the professional code for Tariq and other team members requires them to draw to their manager's attention the failure of the council's policy to meet its statutory duties. Tariq should also advise the carer, in accordance with his professional code and the council's duty to provide information to those in need, of the shortcomings in the council's policy. Since this is not an isolated case but is the result of a mistaken policy, Tariq should contact his union, which should approach the employer to ensure the policy is brought into line with the employer's statutory duties.

Moreover, since the learning disabilities budget is heading towards an overspend (part of a national pattern of under-resourcing learning disability services), the union should ensure that local campaigning groups for both carers and those with learning disabilities are aware of the general problem, if they are not already. Tariq and his colleagues could also remind managers of the legal rules surrounding resources (see Braye and Preston-Shoot, 2009), both in terms of the artificiality of internal budget divisions of what is, in fact, one corporate budget, and in respect of when resources may and may not be taken into account when deciding whether to apply eligibility criteria to a case, how to assess need, and what services to provide.

Assisting service users and representative organisations to know their entitlement to be consulted on changes to local services

Ombudsman reports and the courts have been critical of local authorities that fail to involve and consult those entitled to receive services. The courts have made it clear that individual users and representative organisations must be consulted when proposals (or assessments) are at an early stage (*R v Devon County Council, ex parte Baker and Johns* [1995]; *R (Haringey Consortium of Disabled People and Carers Association) v Haringey LBC* [2002]).

The courts have said that consultation on public service changes must:

• be undertaken when the proposals are still in a formative stage;

• provide adequate information to enable those being consulted to respond properly;

• allow adequate time in which to respond; and

• demonstrate that the decision-maker has given conscientious consideration to the response to the consultation (*R (Haringey Consortium of Disabled People and Carers Association) v Haringey LBC* [2002]).

Consultations may be open to challenge if these principles are not followed, especially if the consultation also fails to take account of equality duties (see Chapters 3 and 7).

CASE STUDY

Flawed consultation

• *Oldham Metropolitan Borough Council's consultation on changes to care service charges failed to tell service users exactly what the proposals were. The council claimed that to give consultees the full information might prejudice the cabinet's eventual decision. The ombudsman said this was 'as absurd as informing neighbours that a planning application has been received but that they cannot know what the application is for as it might prejudice the decision of the planning committee'. In addition, the consultation letter was 'extremely difficult to understand, complex and unfocussed'. It was hard for respondents to know what they were being consulted on – and as this letter was going to some very vulnerable people, it was exceptionally ill-considered.*

• *The ombudsman upheld a complaint from a man whose wife used a day centre one day a week, and whose service charge rose from £1 (plus £6.50 transport and meal charges) to £46 a day for the same service. The council has agreed to undertake a new, proper consultation exercise, apologise and pay compensation to the complainant.*

• *'Mr Howard' (not his real name for legal reasons) is the sole carer for his wife, who suffers from dementia. They do not receive home care, but Mrs Howard uses a day centre one day a week, for which Mr Howard was paying the full charge. He complained about the way the council increased charges for its care services, and particularly about its consultation process. The ombudsman recommended to the council that it should undertake a new consultation.*
(Local Government Ombudsman decision 05/CO/8648, 2007)

Individual and collective advocacy

The role of health and social care professionals as advocates is not, and should not be, confined to support and advice for individual complaints. Service users and their representative organisations within the NHS and social services are entitled to be consulted on many aspects of changes to services. The legislation governing the health service imposes a duty on NHS bodies to make arrangements in order to secure public involvement in relation to the planning, development, delivery and range of services for which they are responsible. Consultation must be with anyone to whom those services are being or may be provided (NHS Act 2006, Section 242).

> You (patients) have the right to be involved, directly or through representatives, in the planning of healthcare services, the development and consideration of proposals for changes in the way those services are provided, and in decisions to be made affecting the operation of those services

(DH, 2010, p. 54)

For example, users must be involved in the development of a range of options for the way community services could be provided within an area, not just asked for their opinion on a model developed behind closed doors by health professionals and managers. Users must be involved where a decision will change the way a service operates if the change affects the manner in which those services are delivered or the range of services offered. Examples might include the time a family planning clinic is open or when an NHS trust plans to provide a service from a different hospital or site.

The arrangements for advising complainants and scrutinising the performance of local health providers have been in turmoil, and seriously under-funded, in recent years. Local involvement networks (LINKs) are being replaced by local HealthWatch bodies. Where people need help in making their complaints, independent advocacy support in the NHS is provided by the statutory Independent Complaints Advocacy Service (ICAS). This is a free, confidential service which helps people to understand their rights and make informed choices. It assists with making complaints.

There is also a very widespread concern that the process of making GP commissioning central to NHS planning and delivery will make many of these arrangements even less effective than they currently are. Another element in the consultation jigsaw is the statutory requirement imposed on NHS bodies (DH, 2007; Local Government and Public Involvement in Health Act 2007) which requires NHS organisations to consult with local authority overview and scrutiny committees when they are considering substantial health service changes locally.

Organising communities and professional accountability

Some groups of staff, primarily those involved in public health and social care, may have a professional role in supporting local communities and not just individuals. Social workers, health visitors, youth workers and public health doctors have a responsibility to help individuals, families, groups and communities through the provision and operation of appropriate services, and by contributing to social planning and obtaining or keeping essential resources and services such as youth clubs, day care centres and children's centres, or tackling environmental concerns such as poor housing. Such work requires the involvement of those who use those services.

In the current environment, health and social work professionals will increasingly need to consider not just how to respond to individual circumstances where safe practice is compromised, but also to wider proposals to curtail or close whole services, especially if consultation on the proposals is flawed or if the proposals undermine equality and human rights.

A health provider or local authority cannot simply change the services it provides overnight. It is required to follow a consultation process to ensure that, if resources are scarce, they are actually distributed according to need. The withdrawal of care services by a council without it first reassessing the individual care needs of service users is unlawful (*R* v *Gloucestershire County Council, ex parte Mahfood and Others* [1995]).

A line that cannot be crossed

Whilst the courts recognise the financial difficulties that local authorities and the NHS now face, there are some services that must be provided, either driven by specific pieces of legislation, notably on disability, or where proposals clash with equality and human rights law. In adult services in England, for example, local authorities determine eligibility to receive services using the fair access to care services criteria (DH, 2002b), which set four levels of need: low, moderate, substantial and critical. When Birmingham City Council sought to set a fifth 'supercritical' criterion, it ran into conflict with disability and human rights requirements (*R (W)* v *Birmingham City Council* [2011]).

Whatever the severity of funding pressures, councils cannot justify a failure to comply with a statutory duty because of budgetary pressures. A Northern Ireland court decision made clear that budgetary pressures on the Western Health and Social Care Trust were no defence to a failure to carry out carers' assessments (*JR30's (HN, a minor) Application* [2010]). A similar view was taken in a case involving home tuition for a sick child when the education authority reduced the hours provided for financial reasons (*R* v *East Sussex County Council, ex parte Tandy* [1998]).

So what must you, as health and social care professionals, do when those to whom you provide – or ought to provide – services or support are not receiving the quality or range of care they (or their carers) require?

CASE STUDY

A celebrated trumpet player who featured on the soundtracks to Star Wars and the Harry Potter films died after a hospital feeding tube was mistakenly inserted into his lung, causing fatal pneumonia, an inquest heard.

Poplar coroner's court heard that a junior doctor, Jonas Woo, overruled a nurse who questioned the procedure, despite a radiologist's report saying the tube was in the wrong place. Juliet

Boateng said she became concerned when she could not remove fluid through the tube. An X-ray was performed and Dr Woo, a registrar in general medicine, told her to start feeding.

Radiologist Dr Naheed Mir saw the X-ray and filed a report flagging up the error, the inquest heard. Over the next few days, Dr Woo still thought Mr Murphy was being fed successfully. Ms Boateng said: 'I spoke to the doctor again and asked him to confirm if the tube was in the correct position. He said to me, "You don't have a brain to remember that I told you to start the feed as the tube is in the right position."' Mr Murphy became increasingly unwell and died within 24 hours.

(This is London, *27 January 2011, p. 1*)

ACTIVITY **6.8**

When an incident occurs, what responsibility do staff have to let the patient or the patient's carers know?

In every ward and hospital theatre, an incident book should be kept to record accidents and incidents. The nurse should ensure any incident is recorded, even if doctors or the nurse's manager are unhappy about this. The National Patient Safety Agency (see above) operates a national reporting system for adverse incidents. It should normally be the responsibility of the nurse's manager or the consultant to inform the patient or the patient's carers of any untoward incident. The nurse's job is to ensure that is done.

If the nurse manager or consultant fails (or refuses) to inform the patient or carers, then besides recording the incident, the member of staff needs to raise their concerns at a higher level, including if necessary drawing attention via the employer's whistle blowing procedure. Both the nurse and radiologist have a duty – arising from their professional code and from the hospital's own procedures – to ensure their managers and the consultant are frank with the patient or the patient's carer.

When mistakes happen (and they will), it is impossible to learn from them if they are denied or covered up. There are many pressures which lead professionals to stay silent or collude in poor practice. The power of the employer is immediate, and the risk of disapproval from colleagues or even losing one's job is real. Nonetheless, health and social care is rooted in an ethical approach to practice as well as in contractual duties. As discussed in earlier chapters, when a duty of care conflicts with instructions or expectations, then those instructions or expectations must be questioned, challenged and in some cases refused, and concerns recorded and drawn to the attention of an appropriate person within the organisation. So you must:

- Advise service users and carers how to raise individual concerns and complaints.

- Alert your manager to what you have done and, if you share the concerns of service users or carers, make clear you do so, and why, in writing.

- If proposals to change services are considered and you have concerns about their safety or impact on service users or staff, then you should, either individually or collectively with colleagues, make your views known with your employer.

- If asked by service users and carers or their representative organisations for your professional views on the changes, first take advice from your union or professional organisation, but nevertheless be prepared to offer your views, making it clear they are your personal views.

CASE STUDY

Abuse goes unchallenged in name of partnership working

The poor quality of one care home in particular was known and discussed by social workers. . . . Yet none of this was challenged at the time, through agency reporting lines or safeguarding forums. Instead, social workers (and nurses) continued to place older people there.

Social workers infrequently challenged the views of other professionals in safeguarding cases. The disrespectful treatment of older people in hospital was something to be managed, not confronted. This was the way of things: social workers knew that every agency was in the same boat. Rather than being dysfunctional, this lack of challenge had an internal logic. It may have done little for older people enduring their final months being sworn at by care home staff, but it reflected an uncritical accommodation with underfunding.

(Community Care, *28 March 2011, p. 11*)

C H A P T E R   S U M M A R Y

Having read this chapter, you should be clearer about when and why you ought to assist service users and carers in making their voices heard, including making complaints. You should be clearer about the advice to give if you believe the quality and/or range of care and support is poor, or if plans and proposals are likely, in your judgement, to have an adverse effect, undermining or compromising the quality and/or extent of provision.

Chapter 7

Equality, human rights and the duty of care

OBJECTIVES

By the end of this chapter, you should have an understanding of:

- Why challenging discrimination and promoting equality and human rights is necessary for both good service provision and the fair treatment of staff.

- What employers are required to do to promote equality and challenge discrimination and promote human rights.

- What staff are required to do to promote equality and challenge discrimination.

- The implications of the Equality Act 2010 and Human Rights Act 1998 for professional practice and employer actions.

Introduction

Tackling discrimination and promoting equality is a contractual obligation for health and social care professionals and is integral to the:

- Duty of care of the employer to service users, carers and staff.

- Duty of care of staff to service users and carers.

- Duty of care of staff to each other.

Discrimination is widespread in health and social care and affects:

- The need for, access to, and provision of health and social care services.

- The care, treatment and support provided to service users.

- Entry into the health and social care professions and other staff groups.

- The employment and treatment of staff.

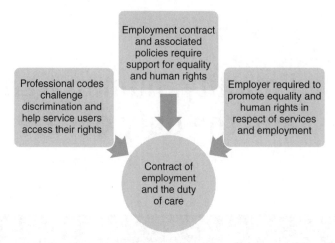

Figure 7.1 Equality and human rights and the staff duty of care

The law and equality

Chapter 3 summarised the equality statutory framework primarily set out by the Equality Act 2010. Discrimination is unlawful:

- In access to health and social care services.

- In all aspects of how patients and service users are treated by staff or the organisation.

- Against carers who must not be treated less favourably because of who they are or because the person they are caring for has a protected characteristic.

- Against staff and by staff.

Public authorities – as defined by Section 6 (3) (b) of the Human Rights Act 1998 – including NHS organisations and local authorities, have an additional legal responsibility to positively promote equality. Private sector and voluntary organisations have the same obligations as public sector employers to tackle discrimination where they are performing 'functions of a public nature', including within contracted-out services. If a company runs an independent treatment centre for NHS patients but also runs a private hospital for paying patients, the NHS patient function is covered by the general duty, but any private work undertaken is not.

Public sector equality duty

The new public sector equality duty (Equality Act 2010, Section 149) states that a public authority must, in carrying out its functions, have 'due regard' to the need to:

- Eliminate discrimination, harassment and victimisation as prohibited by the Equality Act.

- Advance equality of opportunity.

- Foster good relations.

Advancing equality of opportunity is further defined as the need to:

- Remove or minimise disadvantages connected with a relevant protected characteristic. (For instance, addressing under-representation of black staff in management positions.)

- Take steps to meet the different needs of people who have a protected characteristic. (For example, addressing the particular needs of older people who may be vulnerable to abuse.)

- Encourage people who share a relevant protected characteristic to participate in public life or any other activity in which they are under-represented. (For example, encouraging disabled people to apply for training courses.)

Fostering good relations is further defined as:

- Tackling prejudice, for example against lesbian, gay, bisexual or transgender patients.

- Promoting understanding, for example of the needs of service users from the gypsy and traveller community.

Specific equality duties

The public sector equality duty is underpinned by further, specific duties that apply to certain identified public authorities (see the Equality Act 2010 (Specific Duties) Regulations 2011). There are two specific duties that most public authorities have to comply with. Public authorities must show they are complying with Section 149 duties (as listed above), by publishing equality information about their employees (if employing 150 or more staff). The Equality and Human Rights Commission (EHRC) has produced non-statutory guidance on information gathering under this duty (available at: **www.equalityhumanrights.com/ advice-and-guidance/information-for-advisers/codes-of-practice**). The EHRC recommends that this information should include:

- The race, disability, age and gender composition of the workforce.

- The likely composition by sexual orientation and religion or belief, provided no individuals can be identified.

- Issues that transsexual staff are likely to face in the workplace.

- Gender pay gap information.

- An analysis of grievances and dismissals by race, disability, age and gender.

The EHRC also states that it would be useful to publish maternity return rates, flexible working data, recruitment and promotion rates for different groups, pay gaps by other characteristics, length of service including by grade, and information on other terminations of employment. Such information can be very useful.

Public authorities must publish one or more specific and measurable objectives they believe they should achieve to have due regard to the need to eliminate discrimination and harassment, to advance equality of opportunity, or to foster good relations. Different (and arguably better) provisions apply in Wales (Welsh Assembly Government, 2011b) and Scotland (EHRC Scotland, 2011).

Ask for a copy of the most recent annual equality report produced by your employer.

• *Check how much of the information recommended by the EHRC is provided.*

• *What do you think is the single most striking piece of information in the report?*

Understanding what 'due regard' means is important for professionals. Public bodies:

• Must consider how to advance equality and not just how to avoid discrimination.

• Must give consideration to any likely impact on equality *before* any decisions that may have equality implications are made, and to the implementation and review of policies.

• Must 'carry the can' even if the policy is implemented by someone else (such as a contractor).

• Must ensure that those making a policy decision take a fully informed view of the likely impact on equality, either through an equality impact assessment or by other means so long as there is sufficient information to assess the equality impact on those affected.

• Should properly record the process of having 'due regard' and be transparent.

How relevant a decision or policy is to equality concerns will determine how comprehensive the assessment of equality impact needs to be. If a negative impact or a risk of one is identified, then the public authority must consider whether it needs to discontinue or change the policy or proposal. The equality duty requires public authorities to listen to the most vulnerable people at a formative stage of the decision-making process and to ensure that policies and practices do not cause disadvantage. Professionals and their organisations, such as trade unions and professional bodies, should help service users to influence policy. When a public authority is considering a new decision or an existing policy, any member of staff, their trade union or professional body, or service users can ask for a range of information using the Freedom of Information Act 2000 if they believe the decision raises equality concerns. A model letter is available on the website.

Equality and discrimination in service provision

The equality duty developed from the concept of 'institutional discrimination', strongly profiled by the Macpherson report on the murder of the black teenager Stephen Lawrence. The report revealed 'institutional racism' in the Metropolitan Police, which was defined as:

> *The collective failure of an organisation to provide an appropriate and professional service to people because of their colour, culture or ethnic origin which can be seen or detected in processes; attitudes and behaviour which amount to discrimination through unwitting prejudice, ignorance, thoughtlessness and racist stereotyping which disadvantages minority ethnic people.*

(Macpherson, 1999, para 6.34)

Prior to the introduction of the race equality duty, which resulted from the Macpherson report, the emphasis of equality legislation was on remedying cases of discrimination and harassment *after* they occurred, not preventing them from happening in the first place. The race equality duty was designed to shift the onus from individuals to organisations, placing for the first time an obligation on public authorities to positively promote equality, not merely to avoid discrimination.

Equality and anti-discrimination legislation has been criticised for not being robust enough, for failing to substantially alter the pattern of inequality and discrimination (for a review, see Braye and Preston-Shoot, 2009). However, it can be helpful in questioning and challenging cuts and changes in provision. There have been a number of successful legal challenges (see Chapter 3) because public authorities have failed to adequately consider equality when making decisions. In such cases, the public authority will normally be required to start the decision-making process again, with proper consultation and evidence gathering to identify the impact on particular groups (EHRC, 2011b).

Equality and service impact

Even when the context of decision-making is financial resources in a tight budget, that does not excuse compliance with the (Public Sector Equality Duties), and there is much to be said for the proposition that even in straitened times the need for clear, well informed decision-making when assessing the impacts on less advantaged members of society is as great, if not greater.

(*R (Rahman)* v *Birmingham City Council* [2011])

Many aspects of health, well-being and care are affected by protected characteristics. Gender makes a difference to health and life expectancy. In social care, women take most responsibility for the upbringing and care of children and older people. That is one reason so many women work part-time. Single parents are overwhelmingly women, and it is women who are the main victims of domestic violence. Women are much more likely to suffer from anxiety and depression. On the other hand, men live for five years less than women on average and develop heart disease ten years earlier on average (House of Commons Health Committee, 2009b).

People with learning disabilities or mental health problems are much more likely than other citizens to have significant health risks and are less likely than the general population to receive certain standard checks when they are ill (Disability Rights Commission, 2006). Many disabled people also encounter multiple discrimination because of the combination of gender, sexuality, race and age. For example, people with mental health conditions who are also from black and minority ethnic communities are significantly more likely to be compulsorily admitted to hospital as a result of their condition, and are likely to stay longer. They are also more likely than white people to be prescribed drugs or electroconvulsive therapy rather than psychotherapy or counselling (for a review, see Braye and Preston-Shoot, 2009).

The EHRC provides specific guidance for the health and social care sectors in England and Wales. Ending discrimination is about more than making buildings accessible by constructing ramps or producing health information in alternative formats. It is about systematically identifying barriers and reducing inequalities. Social care services have a fundamental role to play in helping to secure the participation of disabled people by providing support that promotes independence and social inclusion, and enables choice and control for all disabled people. The care of people with learning disabilities has been repeatedly found to be 'impoverished and completely unsatisfactory', with care that was 'simply not acceptable' and characterised by widespread 'institutional abuse' (Healthcare Commission, 2007d, pp. 48–54). A national report on race equality in healthcare similarly called for 'urgent action throughout the NHS in England to identify and eradicate racial discrimination against ethnic minority patients' (Healthcare Commission, 2009, p. 39).

ACTIVITY **7.2**

Do you know what your own employer is doing to actively reduce discrimination and promote equality in the service you work in?

Where would you find out?

Age discrimination has received more attention as the treatment of older people in health and social care has been repeatedly investigated, with the same depressing outcomes (Age UK, 2011). The treatment of young people in care has similarly been heavily criticised (Broad, 2005; Scott and Hill, 2006). Discrimination on the basis of the sexual orientation of patients, service users and staff has been better reported in recent years,although many patients and staff still do not want to self-identify because of the discrimination they fear they may suffer (Commission for Social Care Inspection (CSCI), 2008a).

Equality and discrimination in employment

Discrimination against staff, or by staff, can directly impact on how services are provided, not least since failure to treat workers fairly can mean service users being deprived of the best possible practitioners, and result in good staff being made ill or leaving through discrimination, harassment or bullying (Borrill et al.,2001).

If staff themselves face discrimination or victimisation for assisting service users, patients and carers in asserting their equality and human rights, that is unlawful. There is no qualifying period of employment before their legal protection begins. Harassment and bullying are, unfortunately, common in health and social care – as discussed in Chapter 9 on health and safety – and often disproportionately affect ethnic minority staff (Balloch et al., 1999). Discrimination is widespread, and the pattern of institutional discrimination affects:

- Who enters training courses and degree programmes, and what qualifications students get.
- What employment people obtain and the pay they receive.
- People's chance of promotion.
- The likelihood of being disciplined.
- The chances of being selected for redundancy.

Although most employers have policies promoting equality and challenging discrimination, proving that discrimination has happened is very difficult, because much of it is not deliberate discrimination but unthinking patterns of behaviour that cannot be identified unless sufficient equality data are collected and analysed. Discrimination in the recruitment and selection of staff, in their terms and conditions, their treatment, in dismissal or any other kind of detriment is unlawful and adversely affects the care provided to patients and service users. Similarly, it is unlawful to harass staff or victimise someone for challenging discrimination (their own or someone else's). In all types of discrimination, the motive of the person or organisation discriminating is irrelevant; it is the impact of the discrimination that counts.

Employers must ensure they prevent discrimination in all aspects of employment, including appointments, promotion, dismissal, treatment, sick leave and training opportunities. They must be aware of not discriminating against part-time and fixed-term staff, who may be disproportionately female or from ethnic minorities.

CASE STUDY

Catherine is a senior nurse manager, with two degrees, well regarded by staff and her own managers, with outstanding appraisals and a track record of innovative work. She applied for a post as assistant director. She didn't get the post. She was told by one panel member (all three were white) that she didn't get the post because 'she spoke too quickly at interview in giving her presentation' and then told her she didn't get it because she 'lacked key business skills'. No one could believe either explanation, as she regularly deputised for the assistant director on budgetary issues and was well known as an excellent presenter.

Her daughter persuaded her to question the decision. When her trade union representative looked at the pattern of management appointments in the trust it was clear that the chance of a Trinidadian applicant (or indeed any Caribbean applicant) being successful at interview was three times less than that of a white applicant with similar qualifications and experience.

What should Catherine do?

Those who discriminate are often surprised or defensive when questioned about it. Catherine does not need to show that her discrimination was the result of the panel having racist views. It is the outcome of the decision that matters, not its motive. Courts accept that proving discrimination is difficult (*Anya* v *University of Oxford* [2001]). The law places importance on what equality data show about an employer's practices. If Catherine can show that on the face of it there has been discrimination, then the burden of proof switches to the employer to show that it did not discriminate (*Brunel University* v *Webster* [2007]). If Catherine's union can show from the panel's scoring of interviewees, from the application forms, and from the pattern of treatment of past Caribbean applicants that she may well have been discriminated against, then she has a better chance of winning her claim. If the employer sees sense, it will recognise it has unconsciously discriminated, take action to compensate Catherine, and ensure she gets fair treatment in future. If it doesn't see sense, then it will eventually lose an outstanding member of staff and demoralise other black and minority ethnic managers.

If discrimination is suspected, the employer's equality data can be invaluable in showing that discrimination is likely to have happened. The employer's various policies on equality will accord with legal requirements, so holding the employer to its own policies should be the starting point of challenging discrimination. Finally, if any employer discriminates against its own staff, for whatever reason, it is quite likely it also 'unconsciously' discriminates in service provision. Moreover, if the best people are not being recruited and promoted, irrespective of their gender, disability, race or other protected characteristics, then that prevents service users accessing the best possible staff. Fair treatment of staff leads to better support for patients and service users.

Carers at work

Working parents of children under 17 or disabled children under 18 have a statutory right to request flexible working arrangements from their employer. Similarly, an employee who is caring for an adult who is a relative or a person who lives at the same address has a statutory right to ask their employer for flexible working. Working parents and carers also have the right to take (unpaid) time off work to deal with domestic emergencies relating to dependants.

Returning to work after being a carer may have an impact on any entitlements and benefits a person receives as a carer.

Most carers are women. Women repeatedly suffer discrimination when pregnant, and as the prime carer for children or for elderly parents (House of Commons Health Committee, 2009b).

CASE STUDY

Maternity double think?

Carmen has been shortlisted for a midwifery post in a small private hospital. The hospital has a serious staffing shortage, and Carmen's CV is outstanding. At interview, she is asked whether she is thinking of having a baby. She says she hopes to have a baby within five years. The body language of the panel chair changes. Carmen is not appointed.

Should Carmen complain?

In the case study above, Carmen is entitled to complain because less favourable treatment on the grounds of maternity is unlawful. She should make a careful note of what happened and the discussion about her possible maternity, and then write asking for the reasons for her not being appointed. She can say it is so she can learn for any future interviews. Carmen must do so reasonably quickly, as any claim must be made promptly. If there is any delay in the hospital responding, she should take legal advice from her trade union or elsewhere. Using a statutory discrimination question form she can (with her lawyer) ask detailed questions about her treatment, the training of the panel, the treatment of other candidates and other background information. Carmen should be able to remedy her own poor treatment, and hopefully her challenge will also help prevent similar occurrences.

People from ethnic minorities and those with disabilities

Ethnic minority students and staff face systematic discrimination throughout their careers. People from ethnic minorities find it harder to gain entry to university courses, and their progress through them is marked by inequality (Hussein et al., 2009b). They face discrimination when seeking employment and in their treatment once employed. Senior positions in social services and the NHS are overwhelmingly held by white staff (Local Government Association, 2010). There is evidence that disciplinary processes and referrals to the General Social Care Council (GSCC) are influenced by ethnic origin (Kline, 2011). Discrimination against staff means that valuable knowledge and experience that could inform and assist better health and social care for black and minority ethnic service users is lost.

Disability discrimination is another barrier to fairness at work. Even where their qualifications are the same as those of other applicants, disabled people find it harder to enter work and harder to progress to more senior roles (EHRC, 2011c).

Ensuring compliance with the duty

To meet the general equality duty, public authorities should 'engage' with people who are likely to be affected by their decisions (EHRC, 2011c). It is not entirely clear what 'engage' means, but it appears to mean 'consult'. The principles of administrative law clearly specify that organisations must consult when proposals are at a formative stage and well before any decisions have been taken. Organisations must share information on which they may later rely when taking decisions, they must give people sufficient time to prepare and present representations and, when decisions are taken, written explanations must be given and time allowed for any appeals (*R* v *Devon County Council, ex parte Baker and Johns* [1995]; *R (Chavda)* v *Harrow LBC* [2008]; Braye and Preston-Shoot, 2009). This engagement should be with former, current and potential service users, staff, staff equality groups, trade unions, equality organisations and the wider community.

There have been a number of successful legal challenges arising out of a failure to consult and have due regard to equality when making cuts in social care, such as closures of services, increases to user charges and restrictions on eligibility criteria. An important case in which four disabled people won a landmark legal challenge against Birmingham City Council's plans to cuts its adult social care budget illustrates how a public authority's duties to consult and have due regard to its equality duty can together be helpful to service users. The case (*R (W)* v *Birmingham City Council* [2011]) was brought by the families of four disabled adults concerned that they were being told that any needs which were not considered 'critical' would no longer be paid for, which would result in essential care and support needs being unmet.

The court decided that Birmingham Council had:

- Breached Section 49a of the 1995 Disability Discrimination Act (the case was brought prior to the Equality Act coming into force) by failing to sufficiently question the proposals.

- Failed to have 'due regard' to the elimination of discrimination, the promotion of equality, the need to promote positive attitudes, the need to encourage participation by disabled people in public life, and the need to take account of a disabled person's disabilities.

- Failed to comply with its duty to consult properly.

Although the council produced an equality impact assessment, it was inadequate and not shared with all decision-makers. The council had to pay legal costs of £100,000 and consult again with due regard to its equality duty.

As discussed in Chapter 3, there are a range of statutory duties in health and social care, for example requiring councils to ensure that the best interests of children are the primary consideration in decisions affecting them, and the need to have regard to children's safe-guarding and welfare. In another judicial review of eligibility criteria, brought by the family of a disabled child whose care package was drastically cut, the borough's application of a new set of criteria in 2007 was found to be unlawful after it resulted in the family's home care and short breaks services being halved from 24 hours a week to 12 (*R (JL)* v *Islington LBC* [2009]). Mrs Justice Black ordered Islington Council to reassess the 14-year-old's needs and urged a review of the authority's 'fundamentally flawed' criteria. The judge concluded the criteria were not compatible with either the Chronically Sick and Disabled Persons Act 1970 or the Disability Discrimination Act 1995. She found that social workers had failed to make a genuine assessment of his needs by sticking to the eligibility criteria so rigidly.

ACTIVITY 7.3

If you had been one of the social workers described above and you thought the assessment was flawed but found that the other social workers disagreed with you:

- *What do you think you would (or should) have done?*

- *Would you have known what advice to give to the family?*

- *Would you have told your employer you were giving the family advice?*

Equality and human rights legislation can delay unlawful changes and force a rethink to proposals to cut local health and social care services. This is particularly the case when the decision-making process is flawed. Courts are generally reluctant to intervene and instruct councils or health service providers how to spend their money and prioritise spending, but they will intervene when proposed cuts infringe human rights or are clearly discriminatory such that they deny disabled people the most basic services. In the above case, moreover, social workers should have advised the council that eligibility criteria must not function as blanket policies but, rather, whether or not to apply them should be considered in each referred case (Braye and Preston-Shoot, 2009).

In another case the Court of Appeal stressed:

> It is the clear purpose of Section 71 [Race Relations Act 1976] to require public bodies . . . to give advance consideration to issues of race discrimination before making any policy decision that may be affected by them . . . Compliance should therefore never be

treated as a 'rearguard action following a concluded decision' but exists as an 'essential preliminary', inattention to which 'is both unlawful and bad government'.

(R (Bapio Action Ltd v *Secretary of State for the Home Department* [2007])

If as a result of an 'impact analysis' a public authority concludes that unlawful discrimination will be the result of a proposal, it cannot lawfully proceed with it and must evaluate the extent of such effects on affected persons and consider whether they can be mitigated. The process of 'due regard' must be documented and transparent, as was shown in another case:

The process of assessments should be recorded . . . Records contribute to transparency. They serve to demonstrate that a genuine assessment has been carried out at a formative stage. They further tend to have the beneficial effect of disciplining the policy maker to undertake the conscientious assessment of the future impact of his proposed policy, which section 71 requires. But a record will not aid those authorities guilty of treating advance assessment as a mere exercise in the formulaic machinery. The process of assessment is not satisfied by ticking boxes. The impact assessment must be undertaken as a matter of substance and with rigour.

(R (Kaur and Shah) v *Ealing LBC* [2008])

Human rights and health and social care

The NHS Constitution and the Human Rights Act 1998 enshrine human rights into NHS practice and UK law for both health and social care. The values embodied in human rights legislation mean that service users, carers and staff must be treated with fairness, respect, equality, dignity and autonomy (the FREDA principles). The promotion of human rights lies at the heart of good service provision and employment practice in healthcare and social work (British Institute of Human Rights and Department of Health, 2007).

The Human Rights Act 1998 applies to all 'public authorities', including the NHS and social services departments, as well as central and local government agencies, courts, tribunals and prisons. The Act also applies to any person or organisation 'whose functions are of a public nature', including private organisations such as companies or charities when they perform a public function. For example, a private hospital might detain someone under the Mental Health Act 1983, whilst Section 145 of the Health and Social Care Act 2008 also provides that human rights protection travels with a user who is placed in an independent care home by a local authority.

Chapter 3 summarises ways in which the Human Rights Act 1998 requires employers and staff to ensure, for example, that:

- Procedures which determine how users are treated must be fair and robust.

- Those detained or in residential care are not detained without good reason.

- There is no discrimination in how services and advice are provided (for example on the basis of age or ethnic origin or disability).

- There is no degrading or inhuman treatment, for example in residential or children's homes.

- Users must be involved in decisions about their lives.

Health and social care staff are required to ensure these principles are embedded in their work, whilst staff need clear guidance and training on the implications of the Act for the provision of services. Neglecting people's human rights can adversely affect their health and well-being (Ministry of Justice, 2006). Public authorities have a positive duty to take proactive steps to protect people from treatment that breaches the Act, no matter who is causing the harm, and even if it is not directly caused by their staff members. For example, if a public authority is aware that a relative or friend who is caring for an older person at home may be abusing them, it has a duty under the Human Rights Act to investigate or intervene. Article 3 has been interpreted as imposing a positive obligation upon state bodies to *take steps that could reasonably be expected of them to avoid a real and immediate risk of ill-treatment . . . of which they knew or ought to have had knowledge* (*Z* v *UK* [2001]). Reasonable steps must be taken by a care provider to avoid the development of an environment in which abuse can flourish. The treatment does not need to be deliberate. It is the impact it has that matters. For example, if staff in a care home unintentionally leave residents in soiled bed sheets for long periods because they are understaffed, this may still amount to inhuman or degrading treatment.

The European Convention contains a right not to be discriminated against in the enjoyment of any other convention right. This might require changes to policy or practice, for example through a commitment to improving mental health services for people from black and minority ethnic groups, or by ensuring that people are not denied treatment solely on the basis of their age. Public authorities cannot use budgetary pressures as a means of avoiding statutory duties. The Western Health and Social Care Trust of Northern Ireland was told (*JR30's (HN, a minor) Application* [2010]) that the trust must comply with the statutory duty to carry out carers' assessments.

To know when to act, professionals must know what to look for. The relevant articles of the European Convention include:

- Article 3 prohibiting inhuman or degrading treatment such as neglect leading to pressure ulcers, failing to offer assistance with eating or drinking, excessive force used for the purpose of restraint, calls for help being routinely ignored, leaving people unwashed or unclothed without regard to their dignity, or treatment without consent.

- Article 5 providing a right to liberty and security, especially relevant to those detained or facing detention under the Mental Health Act 1983.

- Article 6, the right to a fair trial, which is relevant to how case conferences are conducted, professional conduct allegations are handled, and statutory powers are exercised, including how complaints are dealt with.

- Article 8, the right to respect for family and private life, which should mean, for example, that those detained or in residential care are not denied access to their family without good reason. Public authorities must take proactive steps to ensure that respect for private and family life is fulfilled. This may mean providing extra resources such as adequate support to enable an older person to remain living at home rather than moving into residential care. The use of seclusion – keeping and supervising a patient alone in a room that may be locked – usually involves an interference with the right to respect for private life, unless it can be justified as being lawful, necessary and proportionate.

- Article 9, the right to freedom of thought, conscience and religion, which may raise issues around dress codes or exemption from participation in specific workplace procedures such as terminations.

- Article 14, which prohibits discrimination in the enjoyment of these human rights. For example, locked-up children must not be discriminated against in respect of their human rights, and people should not be denied services or treatment solely because of their age.

When making decisions where human rights are concerned, staff must ask whether there are alternative solutions to the issue being addressed. For example, if a child is removed from her mother because of concerns of neglect, and as a result all contact is forbidden, this has to be a proportionate step. Therefore, depending on the circumstances, it might be appropriate for the local authority to consider other options such as allowing supervised visits and family support. The option that is most appropriate is the proportionate one.

CASE STUDY

Abuse at leading care home leads to police inspections of private hospitals

Inspectors have been called in to private hospitals that care for people with learning disabilities after exposure (by BBC Panorama) of a regime of shocking abuse by staff at a unit run by one of Britain's leading care companies. The chief executive of the company, Castlebeck, said he was ashamed of what had gone on at the unit. Thirteen employees have been suspended and police have arrested three men and one woman as part of an ongoing investigation.

Workers routinely slapped and kicked patients, pinning them to the floor and drenching them with cold water. Staff, sometimes with qualified nurses watching, used forms of restraint that an expert described as closer to martial arts rather than any approved technique.

Panorama focused on Winterbourne View after being approached by Terry Bryan, a former senior nurse at the unit who had tried and failed (repeatedly) to raise his concerns within Castlebeck and with the CQC. The regulator said it recognised that 'there were indications of problems at this hospital which should have led us to taking action sooner'.

(The Guardian, *1 June 2011, p. 8*)

ACTIVITY 7.4

What human rights issues does the case study above raise?

Why do you think that only one nurse blew the whistle about these terrible conditions?

If you were a clinical psychologist, nurse, occupational therapist or social worker and were faced with this situation, what should you report and to whom?

Abuse like that described above is a breach of the home's duty of care and of the residents' human rights, a criminal offence and an act of discrimination. You should challenge such behaviour there and then, and immediately report it to the manager on site, keeping a copy of your report. You should make a careful note of what has happened, if possible getting your account corroborated by others present, and send it to your own manager. You should also discuss with your manager the urgent reporting of what you witnessed to the Care Quality Commission (CQC); if your manager is not willing to do so, you should do so yourself. Failure to do all of these things would be a breach of your professional code and might lead to your being accused of colluding in such abuse by not robustly reporting it.

Professional practice and equality and human rights

Equality and human rights are not an optional extra for employers or professionals in health and social care. Working for equality and against discrimination is an essential element of effective health and social care. It is a statutory requirement, and has a prominent place in professional codes, both in respect of how staff are treated and how services are provided. The GSCC Code (2002), for example, requires registrants to promote equal opportunities for service users and carers, and use established processes and procedures to challenge and report dangerous, abusive, discriminatory or exploitative behaviour and practice.

When confronted by actual or possible discrimination or breaches of human rights, health and social care professionals have contractual responsibilities to:

- Ensure public authorities' equality and human rights duties are complied with.
- Respect the rights of service users with regard to equality and human rights.
- Respect the equality and human rights of colleagues.
- Assist service users to understand their rights and access complaints and consultation processes when equality and human rights are at risk.

Health and social care professionals cannot do this unless they understand how and why they may and must raise concerns about equality and human rights on behalf of service users or assist service users to raise them themselves. The rights of service users to be consulted (or in the new jargon,'engaged with'), to use complaints procedures and be assisted by health and social care professionals are explored in some detail in Chapters 6 and 10. If you believe that patients, service users or carers are being discriminated against or that service provision is discriminating, or is likely to discriminate, then you have a duty to draw that to the attention of your employer and to assist patients, service users and carers in raising their concerns.

Last but not least, those charged with training staff, and the respective professional registration bodies, trade unions and other professional bodies, must also embrace equality and human rights requirements.

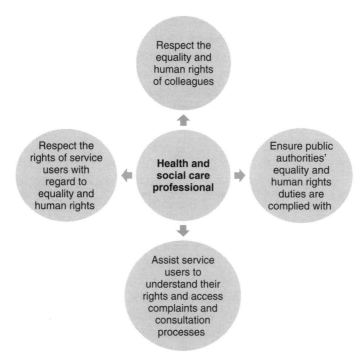

Figure 7.2 Health and social care professionals and equality and human rights

---

Responding to discrimination

Judith's team has received a number of complaints from ethnic minority carers who believe that those they care for have not got aids and assistance that they should have, unlike other white local residents. Judith is an experienced social services manager. She does not believe this can be due to racism, but when she asks to see the monitoring statistics on the proportion of those assessed for aids and assistance who were successful, she is surprised that there is a significant difference between services provided following assessments of white and (especially) Asian people.

During supervision sessions and then at a team meeting, it becomes clear that, faced with hopelessly high thresholds, staff are trying to bend the rules to help people, and are inadvertently helping those whose cases are presented most insistently, and that these are disproportionately white.

What should Judith do?

Staff may be creating the disparity described above out of good intentions, but Judith decides that, if staff members feel they need to regularly bend the rules, then the current thresholds prevent real and important needs being met, and this must be placed on the record with her own manager. The council is in breach of the Equality Act 2010 by allowing such a disparity to arise. In effect, Judith has conducted an equality impact assessment on assessment outcomes within her team. The local authority has a duty to monitor its service provision. Judith now feels confident to approach her own manager and argue that a review of the thresholds and the budget that underpins it is essential, and suggests that monitoring data across the authority should be scrutinised for similar patterns. In any case, the local authority should be monitoring the impact of its policies. Judith will need to bear in mind that not only does the employer have equality duties, but her own professional code states that she must promote the interests of service users and carers, including promoting equal opportunities for service users and carers.

C H A P T E R   S U M M A R Y

This chapter has set out the equality and human rights framework within which public authorities must act. Whilst the prime concern is the welfare of service users, it is impossible to separate the treatment of staff from that of service users. Staff who are bullied and harassed, who are denied appropriate employment and promotion, who are not given fair access to training and professional development, or who are treated unfairly within the disciplinary process or for raising concerns about the treatment of service users, cannot give of their best to service users. Accordingly, fair and equitable treatment of staff is a precondition for the fair and equitable treatment of service users.

Professional responsibility, like human rights and equality duties, is not reactive. It must be proactive. This means that professional staff must not only respond to circumstances where equality and human rights have been breached, but must seek to anticipate where they might be breached. In a climate where cuts in services are increasing, there is a greater likelihood of risks of breaches. Practitioners and managers must remain vigilant on their own and service users' behalf, ensuring that all future proposals, as well as current practice, meet the standards required.

The EHRC website for England has a wealth of useful information: **www.equalityhuman-rights.com/advice-and-guidance/public-sector-equality-duty**

For guidance on how the duty applies to devolved Welsh public authorities see: **www.equalityhumanrights.com/wales/publications/guidance-on-the-equality-duty-for-the-welsh-public-sector**

For guidance on how equality and human rights duties apply to devolved Scottish authorities see: **www.equalityhumanrights.com/scotland/public-sector-equality-duty-in-scotland**

The Scottish Human Rights Commission is also a useful source of information. See: **www.scottishhumanrights.com**

For guidance on how the duty applies in Northern Ireland, see: **www.equalityni.org**

Also useful is the Trade Union Congress (TUC) Equality Duty Toolkit, available at: **www.TUC.org.uk**

Chapter 8
Confidentiality and record keeping

OBJECTIVES

By the end of this chapter, you should have an understanding of:

- What type of information about service users is collected and why.
- What constitutes good record keeping practice and why it is so important.
- Using and disclosing service user information.
- The duty of health and social care professionals, students and others to assist service users to exercise their rights to confidentiality.
- The rights of staff and students to access service user information necessary to provide safe, competent and effective health and social care, including the right of access to occupational health information held about themselves by their employer.
- What to do if the duties or rights of staff, and rights of service users are not met.
- The importance of consent and its link to good record keeping.

Introduction

Good record keeping and maintaining confidentiality are essential for good health and social care. They are also a prerequisite when staff, service users and relatives wish to understand, question or challenge treatment, care and support.

Good record keeping is essential to enable competent care to be provided and to demonstrate that you have discharged your duty of care. The standard of care is that set out in Chapter 2 (*Bolam v Friern Hospital Management Committee* [1957]) and is the standard of the ordinarily competent professional.

In England, each health and social care organisation will have its own policies and procedures which you should check to follow the guidance set out by the Department of Health (DH) (2000c, 2003, 2006d). Good record keeping is underpinned by an understanding of confidentiality and is essential to service user consent.

Figure 8.1 Record keeping, confidentiality and the duty of care

Record keeping and the duty of care
Why keep records?

Write down what happened on a visit you made or in a case you dealt with last week. Then compare what you have written with what your notes of your visit or case say, taking note of any gaps in memory.

Record keeping is not an optional extra. If it isn't recorded, it hasn't happened. There may be no other evidence of your involvement with a service user, so records must be sufficiently detailed and relevant to demonstrate your involvement. The main purpose of records is to keep an account of the care given to a service user, to assist in monitoring progress, to help with developing care, treatment and support, to allow continuity of care and to enable the service user's relevant history to be understood. Professionals must record decisions made and the reasons for them.

> *A four-year-old child suffered cardiac arrest and brain damage during an arthroplasty operation. The theatre team claimed that the patient's pulse had simply stopped abruptly, but this was rejected by the court since there was nothing in the patient's records showing what happened in the period immediately before the pulse stopped. The health authority was deemed to have been negligent.*
> (*Saunders v Leeds Western Health Authority* [1984])

Much of the contact that professionals have is on a one-to-one basis without other professionals being present.

A patient claimed after an operation that she had not been told about the relatively high risk associated the procedure. The surgeon undertaking the operation was able to show from the records written at the time that the risks had been both explained to the patient and understood by her. The case failed. The records were crucial evidence in convincing the court that the patient had probably been told about the risks she faced.

(*McLennan v Newcastle HA* [1992])

Record keeping presents many challenges. The universal use of computerised record-keeping systems (to some degree alongside manual records) has created its own problems. One review of safeguarding practice (Munro, 2011) has recommended ending numerous centrally imposed targets and giving practitioners more autonomy to exercise professional skills and judgement, partly because of concerns that computerised recording systems have become one obstacle to good practice.

Recording is regarded by many practitioners as a necessary evil. It is resented as a distraction from the real work. In one inquiry after another, recording has been identified as an area of concern. Practitioners complain about the amount of paperwork that increasingly dominates the job, about cumbersome and unreliable electronic recording systems, and that recording is seen essentially as an administrative task and back-covering exercise. Yet, despite this, many practitioners can become reflective when asked to consider the many complex and problematic aspects of the recording task. As one interviewee explains, '[Recording] is on the one hand pointless, on the other absolutely essential.'

(O'Rourke, 2009, p. 11)

Delegation of record keeping

Many roles or tasks are delegated, but professional responsibilities (including record keeping) continue. When roles and tasks are delegated to other staff such as unregistered care assistants or students, those delegating must ensure records are completed to a reasonable standard, by countersigning record entries. Health professionals who delegate roles and functions to other non-registered staff have a responsibility to ensure all such staff understand the principles of confidentiality and local policies to implement it.

Health and social care support worker employment contracts will include a confidentiality clause. A registered professional must ensure their own record keeping is competent and complies with the standards set out by their professional body and by their employer. They must also countersign the records of staff to whom they have delegated tasks or roles. A student or non-registered member of staff must take reasonable care to record accurately and comprehensively. A manager of professional staff should, through audit, supervision, training and support, ensure that professional staff records are competently undertaken to the required standard.

If for any reason, notably because of workloads, any member of staff feels unable to complete records in a timely manner to the required standard, then they must inform their manager.

Good record keeping

Some general principles of good record keeping may be identified. All staff, contractors and volunteers must be aware of their responsibilities and ensure that service user information is:

- Recorded accurately and consistently.

- Kept physically secure.

- Used and disclosed with appropriate care.

- Processed as lawfully and as transparently as possible.

Those who use services, and their relatives and carers, must be able to:

- Understand how and why personal information is used and processed.

- Give their consent for the disclosure and use of their personal information.

- Trust those holding and handling information.

- Understand their rights to access information held about them.

What practitioners and managers are required to do has also been codified. Standards for record keeping are set out in statute, case law, contracts of employment, and professional codes. Throughout the UK, codes of practice for health and social care records have been published (Department of Health, Social Services and Public Safety, 2004; Scottish Government, 2008; Welsh Assembly Government, 2005), which local protocols should follow. Additional guidance is available for certain mental health conditions, child protection and occupational health (Royal College of Nursing (RCN), 2003/2007, 2005; Department for Education, 2010). In each NHS organisation, a 'Caldicott guardian' or lead information governance manager oversees access to patient-identifiable information, and has responsibility for ensuring compliance with these standards (DH, 1999).

Staff must understand confidentiality and seek training or support where necessary. They must respect the rights of patients and facilitate patients to exercise their right to have access to their records. They should report possible breaches or risk of breaches. Contractors, agency staff, volunteers who are not employees, and students are also under an obligation of confidentiality.

ACTIVITY *8.2*

You are a student nurse on placement in an older persons' ward. You realise there are significant gaps in the liquid and food intake records of several patients. What should you do?

If you are a student nurse on placement in the situation described in Activity 8.2 above, first establish the facts. Make a note of the gaps and draw them to the attention of the member(s) of staff responsible for the patients – usually the named nurse, if present. It is possible the gaps represent poor record keeping, or they may be symptomatic of a more fundamental problem. Report the matter informally, but ask what steps are to be taken to ensure there is no repetition, and how this will be done. You should make a note of what has happened, and discuss it with your university tutor and/or placement supervisor. If nothing is done and the problem continues, you should formally place your concerns on record, in writing, keeping a copy.

Standard of record keeping

All health and social care employers should have policies and procedures, underpinned by training, supervision and audit processes, which make clear the standards expected of staff and the access provided to records for patients, service users and others. However, the Audit Commission (1999) study of record keeping in the NHS highlighted shortcomings, reflected in subsequent reports in both health (Kennedy, 2001) and social care (repeatedly in serious case reviews), including in the inquiry following the death of 'baby Peter' (Laming, 2009).

Professional accountability

Every professional code (Nursing and Midwifery Council (NMC), 2010d) and its linked guidance set out similar requirements on record keeping standards. However, poor record keeping remains a major source of disciplinary action and professional misconduct cases.

CASE STUDY

Physiotherapist suspended for one year for incomplete or non-existent clinical notes

The Health Professions Council's Conduct and Competence Committee [2009] heard that the physiotherapist's notes lacked case histories, clinical reasoning, patient consents, treatment plans and advice, as well as clinical outcomes and records of referrals and discharges. Between 2005 and 2006, 74 sets of notes were found to be deficient including five patients for whom 'no notes whatsoever' had been written.

The panel heard that Mr Taylor was experienced and his knowledge and skills were of a 'high standard'. The problems emerged during a search for case notes after solicitors requested a report on a patient's physiotherapy treatment in connection with a compensation claim.

(www.hpc-uk.org/complaints/hearings/index.asp?id=1541&showAll=1)

Health and social care records should:

- Be written as soon as possible after an event has occurred.

- Be written clearly, legibly and so that they cannot be erased.

- Be accurately dated, timed and signed, with the name of the author printed alongside the first entry.

- Be written such that any alterations or additions are dated, timed and signed in such a way that the original entry can still be read clearly.

- Be readable when photocopied.

- Be written, wherever applicable, with the involvement of the patient or carer.

- Be clear, unambiguous, without unnecessary jargon, and written in terms that the patient or service user can understand.

- Be in date order with no line gaps.

- Use standard coding techniques and protocols for electronic records.

- Be written to comply with the Equality Act, especially in respect of race discrimination and disability discrimination.

- Not include meaningless phrases, irrelevant speculation, offensive subjective statements or irrelevant personal opinions.

- Not normally be taken home, except where this cannot be avoided, and where it is in accordance with local procedures for safeguarding the information.

Illegible records

In a case involving a pharmacist, a badly written prescription led to a patient being given the wrong drug, which in turn resulted in harm. The pharmacist was held to be 75 per cent liable for the harm, whilst the GP was found to be 25 per cent liable, for his poor handwriting. The Court of Appeal held that there is a duty to write clearly so that busy or even careless staff can read your records (Prendergast v Sam and Dee Ltd [1989]).

Good records should include:

- The name and address of closest relatives or carers (and in mental health, the details of the nearest relative).

- Medical and other healthcare observations, including records of examinations, tests, diagnoses, prognoses, prescriptions, other treatments, feeding, liquid intake, progress or otherwise.

- Social care observations and records of engagement with the service user and relevant carers, relatives and dependents by the social worker and others.

- Relevant disclosures by the patient or service user which might assist understanding causes or effecting cure/treatment.

- Information provided by other professionals or the service user.

- Views expressed by the service user or others parties.

- Information and advice provided to the service user.

- Details of any telephone calls made to or received from the service user or their carer.

- Details of any unsuccessful attempts to speak with or visit a patient or service user or their carer.

- Details of any disagreement with another health professional or other staff (including managers) about the provision of care, treatment, support or advice, including the reasons for any such disagreement, and what follow-up action was taken.

- Concerns raised by a patient, service user or carer.

- Details of any other legal requirement or form completed in your presence, such as a consent form.

- Decisions to disclose information and the justification for so doing.

ACTIVITY 8.3

Take a case record that you are currently working with. Using the checklist above, write down details of any aspect of the record where the standard is not met.

Record-keeping difficulties

A common explanation for poor record keeping is the pressure of other work.

CASE STUDY

A social work team has been hit by a 'perfect storm' of vacancies, staff sickness and increased referrals and case loads. The manager is under pressure and is proving unsympathetic, and the entire team have been warned they may be disciplined if they don't get the records up to date within four weeks.

What should staff say at their team meeting next week in response to these pressures in order to comply with their duty of care to service users and themselves?

Keeping accurate, comprehensive and contemporaneous records is an essential part of good practice. If the record keeping difficulties arise from an increase in referrals, for example, and risk compromising safe practice, you must draw your manager's attention to your concerns. The General Social Care Council (GSCC) Code of Practice, for example, requires registrants to 'bring to the attention of your employer or the appropriate authority resource or operational difficulties that might get in the way of the delivery of safe care' (GSCC, 2002, para 3.4).

Concerns are best raised during professional supervision, but if this is not regular and frequent, or does not include genuine discussion of concerns, you should put your concerns in writing so that they are discussed at your next supervision meeting. Placing concerns on the record lays an audit trail and should be done sooner rather than later.

If concerns relate to an increase in referrals, you should suggest a team meeting with the manager. The underlying problems need to be tackled, notably rising workloads. If workloads compromise safe practice, your manager must reduce them by delegating some work, reducing certain functions or duties, or finding different ways for the additional work to be done (such as bringing in extra staff). It is not good enough to simply issue instructions without acknowledging the underlying reasons. You should document the work pressures and insist they be addressed, involving your trade union if necessary. A sample letter you can adapt is available on the website. In one case (*Deacon* v *McVicar and Another* [1984]) the judge ordered disclosure of the notes of other patients in a maternity home to see how busy doctors were on a particular evening. That decision to order disclosure is a reminder that in litigation your records may well be subjected to scrutiny, and that you have no right to withhold records from the court.

To be reliable, records must to be completed at the time of the matter they are recording or as soon as possible afterwards. Retrospective alteration of records is unacceptable.

> *An ambulance took some 30 minutes to arrive at an emergency, but the crew recorded the journey as taking just nine minutes. The court held that the record had been falsified and found in favour of the patient.*
>
> *(Kent v Griffiths and others* [2000])

Poor records have consequences for the professional too

Poor record keeping undermines your duty of care to service users, placing you and your employer at risk in any claim for negligence. Your defence in any professional misconduct or employer's disciplinary proceedings is seriously weakened, especially if you wish to claim that you drew attention to excessive workloads, inappropriate instructions, unsafe skill mix or a dangerous work environment, but there is no record of this. Allegations concerning shortcomings in record keeping are amongst the most common category of alleged misconduct heard by registration bodies. At least one in three health professionals will be involved in some kind of legal proceedings at some point in their career.

Crucially, poor record keeping undermines the rights of service users providing information (and those they give permission to access their records) to know and understand the treatment, care and support they are receiving. If you have cared for hundreds of service users, you cannot possibly remember the details of each case weeks, months or even years later, but those details may well still be fresh in the memory of the person raising a complaint in a court, misconduct or disciplinary case. Good documentation is therefore a vital means of recollection for nurses and social workers faced with litigation. The detailed evidence (or lack of it) contained in contemporaneous records may be decisive in reaching conclusions about what happened and where responsibility lies. Courts and disciplinary hearings take the view that if it is not recorded, it did not happen.

Supposing you are not there?

Records enable others to understand the circumstances of each individual service user and then know what to do when you are not there. Your colleagues must be able to rely on your record keeping. Shift patterns and staff turnover may further complicate the sharing of information, as may the use of a call centre to filter calls. A good test is: if a nurse, doctor or social worker were coming to care for or support this person for the first time, are my records good enough for them to know what to do next?

The rights to confidentiality of those who use services

The Data Protection Act 1998 protects the right of service users to confidentiality and gives them a right to access information held about them. Article 8 of the European Convention makes clear that there needs to be a specific reason to prevent individuals having access to information which forms part of their private and family life (*Gaskin v UK* [1989]).

A confidential service that is trusted is good for patient care. Health and social services must do everything possible both to safeguard confidentiality and ensure service users' involvement and access to information so that they can fully understand the choices they face. If patients do wish to impose access restrictions, then any potential risks to well-being must be explained and their choice recorded once the options and the consequences have been explored.

Every health and social care professional must understand their own employer's policies on data collecting, processing and access if they are to respect confidentiality and be able to ensure that service users' rights are respected. Breaches or possible breaches of record confidentiality should be reported by staff.

CASE STUDY

The wayward son

Susan is an elderly patient whose relationship with her adult son broke down after she discovered he was stealing money from her bank account. When she was taken to hospital following a serious accident, the ward nurse had an extended conversation with the son, explaining his mother's condition, the prognosis, and how long she would be in hospital. Susan was furious because confidential information had been disclosed to her son, and in addition he now knew the house would be empty for two weeks, and there was a risk he would enter the house and remove valuables.

What should the nurse have done?

In the case above, if Susan had told the hospital that the relationship with her son had broken down or that only other named people should have information shared with them, then there has been a breach of patient confidentiality. The hospital should have checked who was Susan's nearest relative or carer, and should have been much more cautious in disclosing any information before being clear what information staff had permission to disclose.

Consent

The recommendations of the inquiry into baby deaths at Bristol Royal Infirmary (Kennedy, 2001) insisted that:

- Informing the patient and obtaining consent is a process and not a one-off event consisting of obtaining a patient's signature on a form.

- The process should apply not only to surgical procedures but to all clinical procedures and examinations which involve any form of touching.

- Patients should, except when they have indicated otherwise, be given sufficient information about what is to take place, the risks, uncertainties, and possible negative consequences of the proposed treatment, about any alternatives and about the likely outcome, to enable them to make a choice about how to proceed.

- Patients should be given the opportunity to ask questions to which they should receive answers.

Professionals seeking consent must know sufficient about the patient to give competent advice. The need to know about patients may have implications for the use of rotating shift patterns, extended use of agency staff, and excessive workloads, which might systematically limit such knowledge. Consent applies not only to surgery but to all activities that involve touching, such as assisting with washing and dressing, applying dressings, taking blood tests and taking blood pressure. Non-consensual touching amounts to trespass to the person; to avoid an allegation of battery, professionals must disclose the broad nature of the procedure to be undertaken and certain risks arising from clinical procedures. Failure to do so might constitute negligence (*Chatterton* v *Gerson* [1981]).

Where service users are disabled, providing information in an accessible format may be necessary. A service user has no right to complete disclosure of all information about their treatment and any risks arising. The level of information disclosed should follow the Bolam standard (see Chapter 2) used to determine whether practice is negligent. Professional practice today supports enhanced disclosure of information. Where there is a significant risk which would affect the judgement of a reasonable patient, then a doctor should normally inform the patient of that risk (*Pearce* v *United Bristol Healthcare NHS Trust* [1999]).

When professionals encounter complex consent and confidentiality issues, they must consult their employer's policies, national guidance (DH, 2000c, 2003, 2006c) and their professional code, and take advice. For example, the Data Protection Act 1998 does not set a minimum age for a right of access. The test used is whether a child is sufficiently intelligent and mature to understand their records and the consequences of seeing them (*Gillick* v *West Norfolk and Wisbech Area Health Authority* [1985]). Children aged 16 or 17 are presumed to be competent to consent to treatment and are entitled to the same duty of confidentiality as adults. Children under the age of 16 may also make decisions about the use and disclosure of information they have provided if they have the capacity and understanding to take decisions about their own treatment (DH, 2003).

Where a patient is unconscious or unable to give consent or to communicate a decision because of a mental or physical condition, the professionals involved must take the patient's best interests and any previously expressed wishes into account as well as the views of relatives or carers as to the likely wishes of the patient. Where the patient is incapacitated and unable to consent, information should only be disclosed in the patient's best interests, and then only as much information as is needed to support their care.

CASE STUDY

Young people and access to records
A 14-year-old in hospital with a serious medical condition asks the ward sister to see her medical records.

How should the ward sister respond?

In the above case, an appropriate health professional should undertake an assessment of the child's mental capacity, having checked what the employer's policy says. The organisation's data protection officer would, together with the ward sister and other professionals, need to consider whether access to the records could cause serious mental or physical harm to the child (or others). Whilst the parents' views on the child's potential access would be sought, the parents would not be able to overrule the child's wishes unless the child was assessed as not being competent to see them, and no other reasons for refusing access existed. The age of the child will not in itself be a sufficient reason to refuse access, as some children show considerable maturity, especially when very ill.

If, in the case above, the view of the child's consultant paediatrician (after talking with her parents and other professionals) is that she should access her records, she should not need to formally apply using the statutory process. If access is provided, a healthcare professional involved in the child's treatment should probably be present. If access is refused by the paediatrician, then the 14-year-old would still be able to formally apply to see her records, using her statutory rights.

Confidentiality and record keeping

UK common law protects an individual's right to have personal information kept confidential when it is provided in circumstances where confidentiality can reasonably be assumed. Those circumstances include where information is given to a health or social care professional but do not include, for example, a casual conversation. A health or social care professional's duty of confidentiality derives from their:

- Professional registration.

- Contract of employment, which requires them to observe their professional code's confidentiality requirements and their employer's confidentiality policy.

- Statutory duties, notably the Data Protection Act 1998 and Article 8 of the European Convention as incorporated into UK law via the Human Rights Act 1998.

The courts can prevent the disclosure of confidential information and can protect the personal information of those to whom the duty of confidentiality is owed. The duty of confidentiality owed by professionals applies to information about the service user as well as that provided directly by the service user.

Information disclosed to someone's healthcare or social work professional is regarded as confidential to all staff, including support staff, except where the patient or service user agrees to disclosure to third parties or where information is shared on a need-to-know basis, such as with other members of the multidisciplinary team.

Relatives and carers (or friends) are not entitled to have service users' confidential information shared with them except with the agreement of the person who is the subject of that information. Neither are solicitors or insurance companies entitled to information.

Where the patient or service user is unconscious or is under age but seeking access to information, or is covered by the Mental Capacity Act 2005, especially careful attention must be given to the disclosure of information. The sharing of certain confidential information may be justified where, for example, volunteers are assisting in the recovery of a patient after an operation or are working with someone in the community and need to be aware of certain risk factors.

Both staff and service users also have rights to access certain other information which the employer may regard as confidential. The Data Protection Act 1998 entitles health and social care staff to access personal information held about them, whilst the Freedom of Information Act 2000 entitles anyone to obtain information held by public authorities on service provision or the organisation itself.

What is a health or social care record?

There may be information that should be kept confidential that is not recorded. However, it is the information contained in records that is the most likely source of dispute, both in terms of how useful and effective recording is in ensuring good practice, and whether the information's confidential status is respected and protected.

A health or social care record is any electronic or paper information recorded about a person for the purpose of managing their health or social care. It might include nursing records, social workers' records, doctors' records, x-rays, pathology reports, outpatients' reports, relevant police records (for instance around child protection) and the records of any other professional or person who has a duty of care towards a patient or service user. It should also include letters from service users or their carers.

Who owns records?

Legal ownership of health and social care records resides in the organisation, such as an NHS trust or a local authority, which owns the paper and equipment on which the information is stored. The employer generally owns occupational health records. The owner of the records also has a duty of confidentiality. The content of a record normally remains the property of the person who made it, in most cases the health or social care professional. The legal owner does not have an absolute right to deal with the record in any way they choose. The duty of confidentiality both at common law and under statute (the Data Protection Act 1998) binds the owner of the health or social care record, giving ultimate control over its content to the patient or service user who is the subject of the record.

To whom is there a duty of confidence?

Service users trust those providing services to collect and use sensitive information as part of the process of seeking and receiving treatment, support, care and advice. They have a right to assume that staff who collect or use such information will respect their privacy and use or disclose (or not disclose) such information appropriately. The framework of law and duty of care around the collecting, holding and use of information, including record keeping, must be met, and the trust of patients and service users must be preserved.

There may be some circumstances where those seeking or using services lack the competence to give such trust, or may even be unconscious, but even then the duty of confidentiality continues.

What information can be shared?

The duty of confidentiality is not absolute, because other duties such as safeguarding and protecting the welfare of children (Children Act 1989) may require disclosure of information (DH, 2000c; Braye and Preston-Shoot, 2009). Patients and service users must be told that their information might be shared and how widely it might be necessary to share that information, including with other organisations. Where information can identify individual patients or service users, it must not be used or disclosed unless:

• The individual concerned has given their explicit consent.

• There is a strong public interest or legal justification for so doing.

Those providing confidential information should be told that they have the right to object to its use and disclosure if it identifies them, even if that might mean that the care they can be provided with is limited or not possible. Where information is used on an anonymised basis (that is, the individual cannot be identified), then that information is not confidential and can be used much more easily with few constraints (Health and Social Care Act 2001, Section 60).

The law and confidentiality

Four main areas of law regulate the use and disclosure of confidential personal health and social care information.

Human Rights Act 1998

Article 8 of the European Convention establishes a right to respect for private and family life, and requires those who collect and process confidential information to maintain a duty to protect the privacy of individuals and preserve the confidentiality of their health and social care records. Any actions that interfere with the right to respect for private and family life, such as disclosing confidential information, must be justified as being necessary to support legitimate aims and be proportionate to the need.

Data Protection Act 1998

The Data Protection Act 1998 applies to confidential service user information and to personnel records. It covers all forms of media, including paper and images, and imposes limits on the processing of personal information about living individuals.

Other legislation

Health and social care professionals need to be aware of the impact of other legislation such as on fertilisation and embryos (Human Fertilisation and Embryology Act 1990), sexually transmitted diseases (the National Health Service Venereal Disease Regulations 1974) and protecting people who may lack capacity to make decisions themselves (Mental Capacity Act 2005).

Common law

Courts have made it clear that confidential information should not be used or disclosed, except as understood by the person providing that information. Common law confidentiality obligations require explicit prior patient and service consent before any disclosure, except where legislation explicitly provides otherwise. Staff may disclose confidential personal information to prevent and support the detection, investigation or punishment of serious crime. They may also disclose such information to prevent abuse or serious harm to others in cases such as rape, child abuse, murder, kidnapping, or knife or gunshot injuries.

There is no obligation on health and social care professionals to disclose confidential information in order to assist the police with the investigation of crimes (*Sykes* v *DPP* [1962]), but guidance clarifies when disclosure is permitted (DH, 2000c). Whether or not to disclose in the name of the public interest should be determined based on the facts of each individual case. Staff will not be obstructing police investigations by refusing to answer police questions, provided that they have 'lawful excuse' such as confidentiality, and provided there are no overriding obligations such as safeguarding (*Rice* v *Connelly* [1966]).

However, health and social care professionals must:

• Not withhold information relating to the commissioning of acts of terrorism contrary to the Terrorism Act 2000.

• Tell the police, when asked, the name and address of drivers if they are alleged to be guilty of road traffic offences.

• Report notifiable diseases in accordance with the Public Health (Control of Disease) Act 1984.

• Report relevant infectious diseases in accordance with the Public Health (Infectious Diseases) Regulations 1998.

Keeping records for a set period of time

There are varying periods for which records must be kept before they are disposed of. There are various statutory and recommended periods for health records (DH, 2006c). The good practice outlined therein is, however, applicable to all organisations, and social care organisations should adopt similar standards of practice.

The length of time for which records are kept is obviously especially significant where a patient or service user seeks to pursue a complaint or a claim of negligence, or where an employee wishes to make a personal injury claim following a workplace accident or illness.

Disclosing information

The Data Protection Act 1998 allows health and social care professionals to restrict access to information they hold on a person in their care, if that information is likely to cause serious harm to the individual or another person. However, a supplementary record should only be made in exceptional circumstances as it limits service user access to information held about them. All members of the care team should be aware that there is a supplementary record.

Common law and disclosure in the public interest

CASE STUDY

AIDS disclosure

Health authority employees gave the names of two practising doctors who had AIDS to a newspaper. The court concluded that the public interest in maintaining confidence in the doctors with AIDS was both significant and fundamental. The court accepted expert testimony that the prevention of the spread of the virus could be seriously hindered if those who might be infected did not disclose this to healthcare professionals because they felt disclosure would not remain confidential. The public interest in the freedom of the press was outweighed by the interests of public health.

(X v Y [1988])

Health and social care staff will be held to account when they release information, even if they believe it to be in the best interests of the public. They must always be able to justify their decision. The duty of confidence requires that information provided in confidence should not be used or disclosed further in an identifiable form, except as permitted by the person providing it and with the statutory exceptions discussed above. However, case law has established that a strong public interest will override a duty to maintain confidentiality (*W v Egdell* [1989]; *Re B (Children: Patient Confidentiality* [2003]).

Your own employer will have its own policies, which you must follow if your employer has faithfully translated the legal rules into local procedures on complex data issues such as safeguarding children, those convicted or suspected of sexual offences, or consent given by children.

If you are unclear or uncertain about whether to pass on or release information without consent, you must ask advice from other professional colleagues, from your professional body or your registration body. If you do disclose, you should record your reasons for doing so.

ACTIVITY *8.5*

Find out where your employer's policy for confidentiality on safeguarding children issues or consent given by children are to be found.

* *How does your employer's policy compare with the legal rules set out and the guidance referenced in this chapter?*

A health or social care professional summoned as a court witness must give evidence. If they refuse to disclose information when questioned, they may be in contempt of court and may risk prosecution themselves. Courts can summon professionals to give evidence under oath and be cross-examined. They can make orders for records to be disclosed. Under oath, a health or social care professional is not permitted to mislead the court or withhold information or records they may have (wrongly) promised patients and service users they would not disclose.

CASE STUDY

Duty to disclose?

Tom is an experienced social worker. On a home visit to a service user he is offered a new laptop at a ridiculously cheap price. When he queries the price, the service user shows him two other equally new and cheap laptops to choose from. The service user thinks he is doing Tom a favour.

Is Tom obliged to report the (almost certainly stolen) laptops to his manager or the police?

The Police and Criminal Evidence Act (1984) allows health and social care professionals to pass on information to the police if they believe that, unless the police are informed, someone may be seriously harmed or die. Put another way, disclosure might be allowed to assist with the prevention and detection of a crime. This should not be done lightly and, if possible, disclosure should be discussed with the individual concerned and prior consent sought; the professional's own manager, and if necessary the trade union or professional association should also be consulted first.

Confidentiality and cyberspace

Social networking guidance issued to nurses and midwives by the NMC (2011b) followed an increase in misconduct cases relating to online activities and ethical code breaches, including the case of a male psychiatric nurse struck off for an *inappropriate relationship with a patient*, after contacting a woman formerly in his care, through Facebook. The guidance also gives employers advice on how to deal with internal disciplinary issues arising from use of social media. The advice warns nurses to use such social media responsibly and to avoid unintentional breaches of patient confidently.

ACTIVITY 8.6

You want to say something about your workload via your Facebook or Twitter account.

* *What does your employer's policy on 'cyberspace' issues say, and is it unduly restrictive for you as a professional?*

* *Supposing you and your work colleagues set up a Facebook page to discuss those issues?*

Right of access to data

The Data Protection Act 1998 requires that patients be informed how their information may be used, who will have access to it, and the organisations it may be disclosed to. People must also be told who is responsible for their personal information – the 'data controller' – and how to contact this person. This should take place prior to the information being used, accessed or disclosed.

The Data Protection Act 1998 provides that, upon making a request in writing and payment of a small fee, an individual is entitled to be told by the data controller, within 40 days of a request, whether they or someone else on their behalf is processing their personal data and, if so, what information is held, and should be sent a copy of the information unless this would involve 'disproportionate effort'. There may be restrictions on disclosing such information if other people may be identified from these records. If you are an employee of the organisation holding the information on you, the information should be available free on request. The Information Commissioner's website includes a sample request letter (**www.ico.gov.uk/complaints/freedom_of_information.aspx**).

For certain types of request, for example on behalf of a child or an incapacitated adult, you will need to consult your employer's policy and may need to take advice. There will be a need to strike a balance between the rights of the carer to be able to exercise their responsibilities and the individual's right to confidentiality. Legal advice may be necessary, and possible reference to a family proceedings court (in respect of specific issues relating to young people) or the Court of Protection (for adults lacking capacity to make decisions) where what is in someone's best interests is disputed, prompted or amplified by safeguarding concerns.

Police access to medical records

CASE STUDY

A disturbance broke out following the death of a young man in police custody, in which a young man in a balaclava was alleged to have thrown a missile, injuring a policeman. The young man was chased and was caught by a police truncheon on his ribs, but escaped.

Later that day, a young man comes into casualty with suspected broken ribs. Whilst he is there, two police officers call asking if anyone with such injuries has been admitted.

What should the nurse or doctor in charge say?

The police have no automatic right to access someone's medical records. If, for example, the police wish to access medical records or obtain samples of human tissue, they normally need to obtain a warrant under the Police and Criminal Evidence Act 1984. The nurse or doctor should take advice and not automatically disclose to the police.

Health records and employment

In the case study below, Rodney's wife is required to comply with the NMC Code (NMC, 2008a). She must disclose information if she believes someone may be at risk of harm, in line with the law of the country in which she is practising. She must act without delay if she believes that she, a colleague or anyone else may be putting someone at risk. Clearly Rodney's wife will want to explain what she must do if he continues driving, and detail the risks to her registration if she stays silent.

Rodney is a bus driver who has been diagnosed with epilepsy. Since the epilepsy is not fully controlled by medication, Rodney's GP has asked him to inform his bus employer, but he does not want to do this for fear of losing his job or being demoted to non-driving duties at less pay. His wife is a nurse and realises the risk her husband could pose.

What should Rodney's wife do?

If the occupational health nurse at Rodney's workplace finds out, what should she do?

The same principles of the code apply to the occupational health nurse, who should immediately ask to meet Rodney, clarify the facts and then alert his management to the need for Rodney to stop driving pending clarification of the medical position. The employer should see if it is possible to find alternative work for Rodney within the company.

Employers process confidential health information about their employees or potential employees for occupational health purposes. Employees have the same rights to confidentiality and informed consent as the rest of the population. The same duty of confidentiality applies to those who provide health services (RCN, 2005). The Information Commissioner's guidance on Occupational Health (Information Commissioner, 2004) summarises how employers should process their workers' health data.

The Data Protection Act 1988 gives patients the right to access reports prepared for insurance or employment purposes. Anyone commissioning such a report must obtain the consent of the subject of the report, who also has the right to see it before it is sent to the employer or insurer, and who may veto its release and append comments where they believe there are inaccuracies.

One use of occupational health records is in compensation claims arising out of workplace accidents or illnesses. These sometimes take a long time to become evident, and it is therefore important that health records are not destroyed before the recommended archive time has elapsed.

Mental health confidentiality and employment

Susan is a speech and language therapist. She had declared on her confidential application prior to employment that she had previously had a short period of serious depression requiring her to leave her previous employer. Her previous work record was excellent and so was her current work record.

Susan applied for a promotion to a specialist post with additional demands, and was asked to complete another employment screening form. Following this the occupational health nurse sent a letter to the unit manager recommending that Susan might struggle in the new post in the light of her previous mental health condition. The manager informed Susan about the letter and put the promotion on hold pending discussions.

Was the occupational health nurse justified in disclosing the pre-employment screening information?

The case described above was a breach of confidentiality by the nurse, since no consent was sought or given for Susan's confidential medical details to be given to new manager. Susan might well have been able to sue for loss of earnings and distress caused if not employed because of the disclosure of the report, and the nurse is in breach of the NMC Code and could face disciplinary action from her employer, because she is in breach of her contract of employment.

Occupational health staff are sometimes treated with suspicion by other employees, and can sometimes come under pressure to disclose confidential information, especially where there is a grievance or a legal claim relating to health issues. Where an employee is taking legal action against the employer for personal injury allegedly caused during or arising out of the course of their employment, the employer cannot automatically access the employee's occupational health records. In the absence of occupational health records, the lawyers acting for the employer will need to seek from the court an order for disclosure unless the employee consents (*Dunn* v *British Coal Corporation* [1993]).

C H A P T E R S U M M A R Y

This chapter has explored the complex terrain of confidentiality and record keeping. You should now be aware of your rights as employees and your responsibilities towards service users as health or social care practitioners and managers. Detailed knowledge of the legal rules – including primary legislation, statutory guidance and case law – is necessary in this field of practice, together with openness with those with whom you are working about what you have a power and, in certain instances, a duty to do.

Chapter 9

Health and safety duties of health and social care employers

OBJECTIVES

By the end of this chapter, you should have an understanding of:

- The duties of employers to provide a safe working environment and the main health and safety hazards in health and social care.
- The health and safety responsibilities of managers.
- The link between staff health and safety and the well-being of patients and service users.
- The role of occupational health services.
- How to deal with accidents and incidents at work.
- How to raise health and safety concerns.

Introduction

More than 75% of nurses fear for their patients' safety due to inadequate staffing levels, poor ward layout and the bad attitudes of colleagues, a Nursing Times survey has found. Less than a quarter were confident their patients were safe on the ward or other care setting all of the time. Inadequate staffing levels some of the time was the top cause for concern, followed by poor attitude of colleagues, poor skill mix and bad ward layout.

A report by the Care Quality Commission published last week identified safety concerns with almost half of hospitals and care homes. Figures released by the National Patient Safety Agency showed an 8.5% increase in the number of incidents being reported between October 2010 and March 2011.

(Calkin, 2011)

Health and social care employers have a general duty to provide a safe working environment for:

- Their employees.
- Others working or training on their premises including students, trainees, contractors and agency staff.
- Members of the public including visitors to their premises.
- Anyone receiving services, treatment or advice.

The main (but not the only) hazards facing those working or training in health and social care, many of which impact on care provided, include:

- Musculoskeletal disorders, especially to the back and shoulders, particularly caused by lifting heavy or unsafe loads.
- Stress and other ill health resulting from excessive workloads and hours, and lack of control over work.
- Dangerous situations, including threats of violence, in residential or secure environments, in the community and on home visits, and elsewhere.
- Bullying and harassment by management and others.
- Poor working conditions in offices, including ventilation, lighting, space, equipment, furniture and floors.
- Hazardous substances, including infection-causing agents and latex gloves.

The harm caused is enormous. In the NHS alone, each year, 850,000 NHS patients are harmed by incidents, and each NHS hospital averages 40 patient deaths in which incidents played a part. In 2010–11, the NHS Litigation Authority received 8,655 claims of clinical negligence and 4,346 claims of non-clinical negligence against NHS bodies. During 2010–11, £863 million was paid in connection with clinical negligence claims (**www.nhsla.com**).

The duties of employers

Chapter 3 outlined the employer's health and safety duties towards staff, service users and the general public. Employers owe a general duty to have safe systems of work and a safe work environment. They must carry out a range of risk assessments of possible hazards, and they have specific legal duties regarding particular hazards. Employers must involve staff in their health and safety arrangements and, if asked, appoint health and safety representatives with legal rights and protection.

The Health and Safety at Work etc. Act 1974 (Section 2) sets out the legal framework requiring employers, so far as is reasonably practicable, to:

(a) *provide and maintain safe plant and systems of work;*

(b) *ensure the safe use, handling, storage and transport of articles and substances;*

(c) *provide such information, instruction, training and supervision as is necessary to ensure the health and safety at work of his employees;*

(d) *maintain any place of work, under the employer's control, and the means of entering and leaving it, in a safe condition without risks to health;*

(e) provide and maintain a working environment that is safe, without risks to health, and adequate as regards facilities and arrangements for their welfare at work.

Much health and safety legislation requires employers to take steps 'so far as is reasonably practicable'. That does not mean, as is sometimes suggested by employers, that they need not do something because it is expensive to do so. It means that the cost of controlling the risk must not be grossly disproportionate to the expected benefits. The onus is on employers to demonstrate that to go any further than they already have done would incur costs disproportionate to the amount of benefit provided (*Edwards* v *National Coal Board* [1949]).

Section 7 (a) of the Health and Safety at Work Act is important. It states (with our emphasis):

It shall be the **duty** of every employee while at work **to take reasonable care for the health and safety of himself and of other persons who may be affected by his acts or omissions at work.**

This means that, whilst it is the employer's duty that is most important, staff also have some personal responsibility for health and safety. A duty exists to raise health and safety concerns you may have with your employer, in a similar way that your professional code requires you to raise concerns.

ACTIVITY 9.1

Can you think of a situation where you might have needed to act in accordance with Section 7(a) of the Act?

Health and Safety Executive

The Health and Safety Executive (HSE) is responsible for enforcing UK health and safety law, including by prosecution and accident investigation. The HSE issues codes of practice and guidance to supplement statutory regulations. Anyone can contact the HSE. Workplace safety representatives have a right to contact HSE inspectors and see their reports. For many hazards there are specific regulations setting out what steps employers must take to prevent harm, supplemented by codes of practice or guidance.

ACTIVITY 9.2

*Look at the HSE website health service page (**www.hse.gov.uk**) and check how many of the hazards listed apply to your workplace. Do the same with the Trades Union Congress (TUC) website (**www.tuc.org.uk/healthandsafety**).*

Risk assessments

A hazard is something that can cause harm, for example electricity, chemicals, lifting, a keyboard, a bully at work, or stress. A risk is the chance, high or low, that any hazard will actually cause harm. At the heart of an employer's responsibilities is a duty to conduct assessments of the health and safety risks to employees and others (the Management of

Health and Safety at Work Regulations 1999). Risk assessments should be undertaken of the main work hazards. For example, where a member of staff lifts patients or moves heavy equipment, it is well known that injury can occur, so an employer is required to undertake an assessment of the risks involved. The courts have made it clear that employers must take the initiative to carry out risk assessments and take appropriate action. Employers must not wait until a health and safety concern is brought to their attention (*Wilson* v *London Underground Limited* [2008]). Any risk assessment should:

- Identify hazards that exist which may have the potential to cause harm.
- Evaluate the extent of the risks involved.
- Seek to eliminate the risk.
- Combat risks at source rather than relying on protective equipment.
- Adapt the work to the needs of the individual, not the other way around.
- Have a coherent proactive plan for preventing risk.

As far as is reasonably practicable, the risk should be eliminated, but where that cannot be done, risks should be identified and controlled. The assessment should cover all risks in the workplace for all groups of staff. The HSE states: *in all cases, you should make sure that you involve your staff or their representatives in the process.* The HSE provides guidance on risk assessments (HSE, 2006a). Once a risk assessment has been carried out, the staff concerned (and the health and safety representative) must be told what the risks are and what steps will be taken to enable them to work safely (the Management of Health and Safety at Work Regulations 1999). Regulations also require employers to survey their employees' health where there is an identifiable disease or adverse health condition related to the work concerned.

ACTIVITY **9.3**

Have you ever seen a risk assessment or been involved in helping to do one at work? Think of an element of your work that might require a risk assessment. Ask to see a copy.

The impact of health and safety on patients and service users

One-tenth (10 per cent) of NHS hospital patients suffer a clinical incident affecting their health and safety, such as a mistaken diagnosis, an error administering medicines, a failure to provide sufficient care, or an equipment failure. The NHS Litigation Authority believes that many adverse events and near-misses are not reported and lessons not learned in a 'non blame' environment. Obstacles to reporting include concerns about reprisals. Inadequate training, lack of experience, fatigue and workload pressures are key factors alongside poor systems of communication and a failure to learn from previous mistakes. Research suggests that it is 'normal' human error rather than poor judgement that is important (Weingart et al., 2000).

The National Patient Safety Agency (NPSA) was set up to address these concerns. The NPSA encourages the voluntary reporting of healthcare errors, and routinely requires confidential enquiries when maternal or infant deaths, childhood deaths to age 16, perioperative and unexpected medical deaths, and deaths involving patients with mental illness occur. The NPSA especially focuses on improving systems to prevent adverse events, notably those events related to poor diagnosis or tests, equipment or communication. Its excellent website (**www.npsa.nhs.uk**) has advice on measures to prevent harm to patients (and staff) on everything from cleanliness standards to reporting procedures. Every organisation should have approved risk assessment forms and a risk register. The NPSA and others collate incident reports from employers, but individuals (and indeed patients) can do so too.

ACTIVITY 9.4

Gemma is a nurse and discovers that a patient on her ward fell and hurt herself whilst being mobilised after an operation, because one rather than two people were supporting her. The member of staff concerned has recorded the bruises as being caused by the patient falling out of bed.

Gemma discovers from two other patients what actually happened. Should she tell the relatives?

If it is clear that two members of staff should have been assisting the patient, then one trying to mobilise this patient was an unsafe system of work. The staff member is also in breach of her duty to accurately record the incident, not least so that other staff know how the patient's bruises originated and what remedial action, if any, is needed.

The relatives must be told, but not necessarily by Gemma. Nor should Gemma simply accept the evidence from the other two patients, who may well genuinely believe they know what has happened, but matters may be more complicated. Gemma should take advice from her immediate manager, who in turn should interview the member of staff who made the report, and the two patients. If able to form a clear view of what happened, then the manager should consider what further investigation of the staff member is needed, and what the causes of the incident might have been (ranging from inadequate staffing to sloppy care).

The manager should also ensure that an appropriate professional (a doctor in this case) examines the patient to check for any other consequences. The relatives should be informed in a professional manner, in an appropriate location, probably in the company of the doctor, and should then be informed in writing of any consequences for the patient's health and assured that the incident and the associated record keeping is being investigated. If the reason for one staff member trying to mobilise the patient alone was a shortage of staff, then that should also be investigated. If the manager is reasonably clear what happened, she should take steps to prevent a repetition, including ensuring all staff are trained to lift safely, both in the interests of the person being lifted and themselves. The manager should then ensure that the patient's closest relative or carer knows what steps have been taken, and explain how the relative or carer may complain if they wish to. Those steps would include ensuring all staff are trained to lift safely, both in the interests of the person being lifted, and themselves.

Safety and complaints

There is a shared complaints procedure across health and adult social care in England (Local Authority Social Services and National Health Service Complaints (England) Regulations 2009), which should be an important part of assessing risks. Similar procedures exist in Scotland, Wales and Northern Ireland. Documents collated during the adverse incident procedure should be disclosed at the start of any investigation, along with standard medical records. (See more on complaints procedures in Chapter 6.)

CASE STUDY

The work environment and its impact in children's social work

Although social workers are often criticised for mistakes, investigation shows the employer's failure to provide a safe and supportive working environment is often a crucial factor. For example, consider the following text, quoted from a legal case:

For present purposes, what concerns me is not whether Ms Arthurworrey was capable of handling Victoria's case in a competent manner, but that no assessment of her capabilities would seem to have been made by her manager before allocating the case to her . . . nor would there seem to have been any consideration as to whether [her] work load at the time allowed her to devote enough time to Victoria's case.

We have formed the opinion that the office environment was chaotic, the reference tool was totally inadequate, and that mistakes made by Ms Arthurworrey in dealing with Victoria's case must be considered within that context as well as her inexperience, lack of training and lack of any effective supervision.

(LA v General Social Care Council *[2007]*)

As Chapter 4 highlighted, the case of Lisa Arthurworrey is not the first to have indicated that employers have yet to ensure that regular and quality supervision is embedded in departmental practice. It should be one aspect of an organisational health check (Social Work Task Force, 2009b), which employers are encouraged (but not obliged) to undertake annually.

The main risks to staff and service users

The most common health and safety hazards for health and social care staff and service users are considered below, together with how employers should prevent or minimise such hazards and promote good health.

Musculoskeletal disorders

Musculoskeletal disorders such as back pain, work-related neck and upper limb disorders, repetitive strain injuries, and lower limb disorders affect one million people in the UK. According to the HSE, more than a third of all musculoskeletal disorders lasting more than three days are caused by handling items wrongly at work. One in four nurses have had sick leave arising from a back injury sustained at work, as have many social workers and care staff.

Debbie was a social worker at a residential home for adults with learning disabilities. She was working alone, helping a resident with known mobility problems into bed. As the woman got out of her chair, she lunged forward to grab her Zimmer frame and fell onto Debbie, who injured her lower back.

During 12 years' employment, Debbie had only been on one manual handling course. There were substantial notes to show that this resident had poor mobility and a history of falls, but nevertheless Debbie was left to work with her alone.

(*www.thompsons.law.co.uk*)

What measures do you think the employer should have put in place to prevent Debbie's accident? Consult the HSE website on manual handling before answering.

The Manual Handling Regulations 1992 are intended to prevent injuries. They place a duty on employers to:

- As far as possible avoid the need for manual handling.
- Assess the risk of injury that cannot be eliminated.
- Reduce the risk of injury as far as possible.
- Train staff in safe handling practices.

The Manual Handling Regulations make clear that employers should take action to prevent or minimise risk, and may have to find another way of doing the job and provide training in any new methods. The regulations also require employees to make proper use of equipment provided by their employer, and to inform their employer if they identify hazardous handling activities.

The HSE reports that high job demands, time pressures and lack of control can make musculoskeletal disorders worse. The physical capability of individuals varies, so older workers and pregnant workers are at greater risk of injury, and, generally, women should carry lower weights (about two-thirds lower) than men.

Kathryn, a radiographer, was off work for four weeks after an accident when the wheels of an image intensifier screen she was pulling along a corridor hit her left ankle causing it to break. Kathryn had not received manual handling training, so had never been trained on how to move the heavy screens, which should have been pushed, not pulled. The NHS trust eventually offered compensation.

(Bradford Telegraph and Argus, 2009)

Employers have a duty of care to risk assess lifting, handling and moving tasks *before* their employees undertake them. Employees have a duty to comply with the outcome of risk assessments.

Suitable and safe equipment

Employers have an absolute duty under the Provision and Use of Work Equipment Regulations 1998 to ensure that work equipment provided is suitable and is used safely, kept in good working order and inspected regularly. If a piece of equipment causes an injury, the employer will generally be in breach of the regulation, regardless of the reason. Those using the equipment must be adequately trained.

There are specific regulations for particular hazards or types of equipment. For example, where staff regularly use display screen equipment in their normal work, specific protection is provided by the Health and Safety (Display Screen Equipment) Regulations 1992. If employers have done a general risk assessment and a hazard is identified that cannot be eliminated, then under the Personal Protective Equipment at Work Regulations 2002 employers have an absolute duty to provide suitable personal protective equipment for any employee at risk. Prior to obtaining such equipment, employers must do another assessment to ensure the equipment is suitable. Employees must be told the risks any piece of equipment is intended to avoid or limit, and how it should be used safely.

Needlestick injuries, which cause 100,000 injuries every year, are one common equipment hazard.

CASE STUDY

A trainee healthcare worker contracted the hepatitis C virus when she injured herself on a needle after being instructed to take blood from a patient known to be infected with the virus. After taking the sample, the trainee had difficulty reaching the sharps bin to dispose of the needle, because other equipment surrounding the patient prevented access for her trolley. Blood continued to seep through the patient's dressing, so the worker reached for a tissue to further dress the wound. The trainee placed the used needle on the nearest work surface but then caught her wrist on the needle.

The HSE investigation found that the employee was not made aware of the patient's infection status until after the injury occurred, and was not supervised during the procedure. Despite action to counter infection from the injury, the trainee was subsequently diagnosed with symptoms of the virus. The trust's system for taking blood samples from high-risk patients failed to include suitable risk assessments. The trust also failed to implement adequate controls or provide training around them, and lacked suitable arrangements for effective monitoring and review of safe working practices. The trust pleaded guilty to breaching Section 2(1) of the Health and Safety at Work etc. Act 1974 and Regulation 6 of the Control of Substances Hazardous to Health Regulations 2002, and was fined a total of £12,500 and ordered to pay £9,000 costs.

*(**www.hse.gov.uk/healthservices/needlesticks**)*

Employers should be using safer systems such as retractable needles, self-blunting devices or needles with protective shields, with a strict policy to ensure they are discarded appropriately. Only then will injuries decline.

ACTIVITY **9.5**

In the light of the case study above:

* *Do you know what steps your own employer has taken to prevent such incidents if they might occur? Do staff affected know?*

* *Who do you think is responsible for making sure that risk is minimised?*

Safe working environment, including floors

Unsafe workstations and dangerous floors are serious hazards to staff and service users. Fifty-four per cent of major injuries in healthcare come from slips or trips (HSE, 2003).

CASE STUDY

A care assistant in a home for older and mentally infirm residents was injured when slipping in a pool of urine left on the floor by one of the residents. Many of the residents of the home suffered from incontinence, and this was a regular occurrence. The smooth surface of the vinyl floor was slippery when wet.

The home rule was that if a member of staff came across urine on the floor, they must call for a cleaner to come immediately or, alternatively, clean it up themselves. The care assistant's unchallenged evidence was that notwithstanding the rule about immediate cleaning, a number of accidents had occurred due to the presence of urine on the floors.

(Ellis v Bristol City Council [2007])

The care assistant claimed that under Regulation 12(1) and (2) of the Workplace (Health, Safety and Welfare) Regulations 1992, the floor was not suitable for the purpose for which it was used, because it became slippery when wet, residents urinated on it frequently and a non-slip floor should have been installed. Further, under Regulation 12(3), the council had not, so far as was reasonably practicable, kept the floor free of a substance (urine) likely to cause people to slip. In addition, the care assistant claimed the council had failed to take adequate heed of previous accidents and to install a non-slip floor prior to her accident.

The Workplace (Health, Safety and Welfare) Regulations 1992 place a duty on employers to maintain their workplaces in good working order, and to keep them clean, ventilated, suitably lit, and at a reasonable temperature, with sufficient space to work in and welfare facilities such as suitable toilets and washing facilities. Floors should be kept free from holes, uneven or slippery surfaces, and obstructions, with a handrail by any slopes. Any holes should be repaired straight away; if this is not practicable, then the area should be protected by barriers and clearly marked. There are exceptions, notably building sites and domestic premises (HSE, 2003).

Hazardous substances

Employers have a duty to protect employees and others from exposure to hazardous substances, whether they are chemicals used at work or those, such as asbestos, in the work environment in buildings. The Control of Substances Hazardous to Health (COSHH) Regulations 2002 require employers to:

- Assess the risks.

- Decide what precautions are required.

- Prevent or adequately control any exposure.

- Ensure control measures are used and that safety procedures are followed.

- Monitor the exposure and carry out health surveillance.

- Prepare plans and procedures to deal with accidents and emergencies.

If employers cannot avoid using hazardous substances, then they must apply protective measures to prevent exposure, such as:

- Using appropriate processes, systems, controls and equipment; controlling exposure at source, for example by isolation and extraction.

- Limiting the number of employees exposed and the duration of the exposure.

- Providing protective equipment (for example face masks, respirators, protective clothing).

Employees must be provided with information about the hazards, appropriate instruction in the use of the hazardous substance and adequate training. There are specific regulations and detailed guidance for individual hazards such as asbestos, lead, ionising radiation and biological agents in the healthcare setting.

CASE STUDY

A dental nurse who worked for the NHS for over 30 years received damages of £200,000 after contracting occupational dermatitis, and had to be medically retired from work. Between 1980 and 2004 she was provided with powdered and non-powdered latex gloves to perform her dental duties. In 2003 she noticed that her wrists had become uncomfortably itchy. She was referred for tests and then told by a doctor that her condition was latex related and was so serious that she could no longer safely work in a dental surgery.

Her trade union branch secretary, Caroline Bedale, said: 'The trust ought to have known that the powdered latex gloves were a potential danger to users, yet it was not until [two years later] that a memo was issued for the gloves to be changed to a non-powdered alternative, and only then when existing stocks were exhausted. They could and should have been alert to the dangers and risks much earlier, and they should have provided a non-latex alternative.'

(www.thompsons.law.co.uk/ntext/damages-latex-allergy)

Allergies to latex gloves worn for protection against infections like hepatitis and HIV cost the NHS millions of pounds in sick pay, retraining and compensation costs, even though alternatives exist and replacing latex gloves can be cheaper (HSE, 2006b).

ACTIVITY 9.6

Your employer says that it would cost too much to eliminate a particular hazard in your workplace, so the main means of reducing the risk will be protective equipment.

Find the guidance on COSHH on the HSE website and think carefully about the balance between cost and prevention rather than control. How would you respond?

Stress at work

CASE STUDY

A successful landmark legal case on stress at work was taken by John Walker, a social worker manager who claimed that his managers knew that social work was particularly stressful, that such stress could give rise to mental illness, that his workload as an area officer was such as to impose increasing stress on him, and that his workload became so stressful that they ought reasonably to have foreseen that unless they took steps to alleviate the impact of that workload there was a real risk that the plaintiff would suffer mental illness.

The court agreed and concluded that:

. . . having regard to the reasonably foreseeable size of risk of repetition of the plaintiff's illness and the reasonably foreseeable gravity of the breakdown which could have resulted if nothing were done to assist him, the standard of care to be expected of a reasonable local authority required that in March 1987 such additional assistance should have been provided if not on a permanent basis at least until a restructuring of the social services had been effected and the workload on the plaintiff thereby permanently reduced.

(Walker v Northumberland County Council [1995])

If you and your colleagues found yourselves in a situation with any similarities to those of John Walker's, what do you think you should do, and what would you want your employer to do?

Stress is widely regarded as a modern workplace epidemic, but regrettably there are no regulations on stress at work. The HSE management standards for work-related stress (HSE, 2009a) do, however, define the six key areas of work design that, if not properly managed, are associated with poor health and well-being, lower productivity and increased sickness absence.

If stress is a significant issue in your workplace, then you should first raise your concerns informally with your manager and then set out those concerns in writing. It may be especially useful for a group or individual supervision meeting to discuss such concerns.

If your manager cannot (or will not) acknowledge and seek to address the concerns raised, you should contact your trade union safety representative, who should insist that, in line with the HSE stress management standards, a jointly planned risk assessment of stress in the department, locality or team should be carried out. Staff should tell their managers in writing that they are doing this to ensure that, in accordance with Section 7a of the Health and Safety at Work etc. Act 1974 and their professional code, they do not put themselves or other people at unnecessary risk. The safety representative is also entitled to obtain previous surveys or other evidence that management may have about stress levels, workloads, sickness absence and turnover (Safety Representatives and Safety Committees Regulations 1977).

Once the risk assessment is completed, management must respond with specific proposals to reduce any high staff stress levels. If management delay the assessment or the implementation of measures to reduce stress, then the safety representative should consider calling the HSE and obtain authoritative advice (TUC, 2010).

Working hours and excessive workloads

Key causes of stress include excessive hours or workloads. British workers work the longest hours in Western Europe. The Working Time Regulations 1998 set out maximum daily and weekly working hours for all workers, including junior doctors. Time spent on call by doctors is working time if they are required to be present at, for example, the health centre.

Your contract of employment should make clear what your working hours are, including any shifts and breaks. Your employer will know that you cannot be instructed to work more than 48 hours in any given week without your individual agreement. Such agreement cannot be given by trade union representatives in the context of a collective agreement. If you find yourself working such hours because of pressure of work, it is essential that you record them and talk to colleagues and then your safety representative. Long hours are bad for your health and bad for service users (TUC, 2010).

CASE STUDY

An early key legal challenge to excessive hours involved a junior doctor in the obstetric department at University College Hospital. His contract stated he was expected to be available on call for 48 hours a week on average, on top of his 40-hour contract. He claimed that it was a breach of the employer's duty of care to impose a contract which could cause foreseeable injury. The Court of Appeal held that Bloomsbury Health Authority had to pay damages for the harm to Dr Johnstone's health. This was some years before the Working Time Regulations applied to doctors.

(Johnstone v Bloomsbury Health Authority [1991])

Bullying and harassment

Bullying and harassment at work conflict with employers' duty of care to provide a safe working environment and their duty to provide a working environment free of discrimination (ACAS, 2010). Bullying and harassment are workplace hazards that harm staff, cost employers and undermine services. Bullying and harassment of staff is also unacceptable because it may prevent health and social care staff raising concerns, asking questions, challenging poor practice or working effectively in teams.

The HSE estimates that bullying is a key element in stress-related workplace illness and costs employers many millions of lost days a year. Although health and social care employers have policies to promote dignity at work, research shows that bullying is prevalent in the nursing, social care and teaching professions (Balloch et al., 1999; Carson, 2010).

CASE STUDY

NHS research has found that where there are 'clear, shared objectives amongst team members; high levels of participation including frequency of interaction . . . shared influence over decision making and a preparedness to encourage constructive controversy but to discourage interpersonal conflict', there are significant benefits for patient outcomes such that 'where more employees work in teams the death rate among patients is significantly lower (deaths within 30 days of emergency surgery and deaths after admission for hip fracture)'.

(Borrill et al., 2001)

These findings are of fundamental importance for all teams in health and social care. What do you think makes a good team? Why would bullying impede good team working? Does it affect any team you are in?

Your employer's dignity at work policy should make it clear that bullying and harassment are unacceptable for staff, unsafe for patients and service users, and are serious offences which can result in disciplinary action or dismissal. Bullying is a health and safety hazard, so it should be subject to a risk assessment.

Bullying is very common and is probably responsible for between one-third and half of all stress-related illnesses, with one in ten workers reporting being bullied in the preceding six months (TUC, 2007). The pressures in health and social care from reduced funding, less staffing, higher workloads, and pressures to hit targets make bullying more likely, as managers are bullied and in turn may regard coercing staff as an acceptable means of 'motivating' them.

CASE STUDY

Standing up to bullying

Susan is an experienced and competent manager with excellent appraisals. Her manager has changed and she found him very defensive when challenged politely and professionally over the first few weeks after his arrival. She finds that significant roles have been removed from her without discussion. She asks for a discussion to clarify what is happening, and the meeting ends when her manager shouts at her, bangs the table and warns her to 'fall into line'. Susan is very upset.

What should Susan do?

In the case study above, Susan should not ignore the bullying in the hope it will go away. It is bad for staff and bad for service users. She should talk about the problem with a friend, a colleague or a union representative, and ask whether anyone else is being treated similarly. She should collect evidence and keep a note of all relevant incidents, including dates, times, and places. At some point, Susan should place her concerns on the record by complaining. She should check whether a workplace survey has taken place to establish the scale of bullying and harassment, including 'hotspots'. Her representative should suggest one.

Violence at work, including in the community

Health and social care workers are more likely to experience work-related violence and aggression than other workers. In 2009–10 there were 56,718 assaults, up 3.5 per cent on the previous year, of which two-thirds were in the mental health and learning disability sector (House of Commons Committee of Public Accounts, 2003; HSE, 2011).

Employers must, as for other hazards, assess the risk of verbal and physical violence to their employees and take appropriate steps to deal with it (HSE, 2006c). That will include effective recording of incidents of verbal abuse and physical violence to help predict what type of incidents could occur and when or where. Inquiries into serious incidents in mental health settings have regularly identified the risks faced by health and social care staff and volunteers, and the importance of employers implementing safe systems of working (Sheppard, 1996).

For many health and social care staff, their workplace includes private homes, community centres and the streets. Whilst it would not be reasonable to expect an employer to risk assess every home visited, where a particular location might foreseeably be unsafe, employers should carry out a risk assessment and take all reasonably practicable measures

CASE STUDY

An NHS Trust was fined £28,000 and ordered to pay £14,000 in costs after Judge Gerald Gordon said the trust had fallen significantly below the standards required to ensure safety at the Springfield Hospital in south-west London.

He said: 'Bad practices grew up and nobody thought about them or to put them right. That was seriously unacceptable and incompetent, in my judgment. If the case serves no other purpose, I hope it will encourage those in charge of other establishments to urge a review of proceedings and keep them under review.'

Mamade Chattun, the lone nurse who was supervising the schizophrenic patient, had no walkie-talkie or personal alarm with him at the time, and the nearby wall alarm was broken. Jason Cann had been sectioned under the Mental Health Act earlier that day and had been both aggressive and potentially violent yet he was kept in a lobby under conditions which posed a serious risk to staff safety.

The employer admitted its neglect contributed to the death of Mr Chattun. The Health and Safety Executive, told the Old Bailey that the incident was a tragedy waiting to happen.

(The Times, 5 May 2005)

to protect employees and report incidents (HSE, 2009b). All employers must have employers' liability insurance, which covers compensation for employees' injuries at work whether they are caused on or off the employer's premises.

CASE STUDY

A family support worker feels threatened when making visits to two families with children in need. She has raised her concerns informally with her manager but was simply told to be careful and that no one else had reported feeling threatened at these two homes. However, last week, in a nearby home in the same street, a health visitor was bitten by a dog which she claims was deliberately allowed to bite her after her discussion with the parents became difficult. Judy is reluctant to visit the two homes alone as both of them have two fierce dogs.

What should Judy do?

If, as a health or social care worker, you visit a home, clinic or other premises not owned by the employer, then the occupier of those premises has a common law duty and a duty under the Occupiers Liability Act 1957 to ensure their premises are safe as long as they are entitled to be on those premises. Home visits must normally be by agreement. If there are warning signs (such as a dangerous dog) or if the occupants make it clear you are not welcome, then you must take heed of such warnings or risk being seen a trespasser to whom the same duty of care may not apply. Your employer cannot force you to enter dangerous premises. In some circumstances, if there is a threat of violence, it may be necessary to ask (or insist) that those using services attend clinics or community centres rather than have home visits, or it may be necessary to visit in pairs.

Your employer's duty of care to you applies as long as the duties you are undertaking are 'authorised'. If you decide to undertake unauthorised duties – for example to run an errand for a service user or change a light bulb – the employer's duty of care will cease.

Most managers take threats of violence or abuse seriously. Employers should have policies for minimising the risk of violence and managing violent incidents that make it clear to service users and carers that violence, threats or abuse to staff are unacceptable. On the other hand, the duty of care to vulnerable people remains, and the employer must ensure that where home visits are unsafe, other means of meeting the duty of care are considered (*R* v *Kensington and Chelsea RLBC, ex parte Kujtim* [1999]).

CASE STUDY

'On several occasions, the school, hospital, and ambulance staff expressed concerns about the neglect, the hygiene of the children, parental demeanour or behaviour. All three children had significant periods of absence from school', *the report said. There was evidence of escalating violence towards the children, and seven child protection conferences were held detailing concerns about physical abuse.*

But professionals had difficulty gaining access to the house, and some admitted being 'afraid' of the father.

(Cantrill, 2009, p. 9)

ACTIVITY **9.7**

If you were a social worker, health visitor or doctor in the situation described above, and were afraid of the father, what would you do?

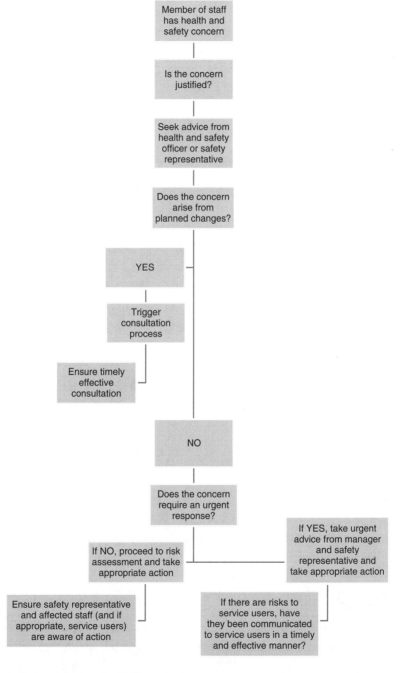

Figure 9.1 How a concern should be raised

Balancing the interests of service users and employees' safety

The courts have said that it will sometimes be necessary to strike a balance between the (possibly urgent and serious) interests of service users and staff health and safety.

CASE STUDY

Two women were wholly dependent on lifting for all personal care tasks related to their physical and social well-being. East Sussex County Council had a blanket ban on manual lifting, which was challenged. The court decided:

- *Health and safety law does not require a guarantee of absolute safety of employees – the employer's obligation is to avoid or minimise the risk to staff so far as is reasonably practicable.*

- *In the context of care arrangements for people with disabilities, their human right to dignity, independence and participation in the community must be taken into account when assessing risk.*

- *When assessing the impact on the disabled person, the physical and mental characteristics of the person, the nature and degree of disability, the wishes and feelings of the person, and negative reactions to proposals must be considered in a user-focused way. Prolonged resistance and obvious great distress may make it impracticable to avoid manual lifting.*

- *A balance must be struck between the needs and rights of service users and the needs and rights of carers, and in striking that balance matters of dignity and respect weigh heavily with people who are already shut out from so much of what makes life enjoyable and enriching for the majority of society.*

- *There will be situations in social care where manual lifting, even though it entails a real risk of injury to the care worker, is inherently necessary when providing an appropriate, adequate care package which takes accounts of the needs and human rights of service users.*

(R (A & B and X & Y) v East Sussex County Council [2003])

The judge did, however, expressly reject any suggestion that those who choose to take employment in high-risk jobs (for example, firemen, ambulance staff, nurses and others in the caring professions) were presumably content to accept those risks.

ACTIVITY 9.8

What do you think of the decision described above? Can you think of other examples in your own work where the interests of service users have to be balanced against the safety of employees?

Occupational health and sickness absence

Sickness absenteeism levels in health and social care are higher than in many other occupations, costing the NHS alone £1 billion a year. Whilst that may partly be due to higher exposure to ill service users, much is due to the absence of a safe and healthy work environment.

Medical certificates, now called fit notes rather than sick notes, mean your GP can indicate whether a flexible return to work is possible, not just whether you are too ill to be at work at all. However, this scheme could risk some staff being forced back to work before they are ready (see **www.tuc.org.uk/extras/fitnote.pdf**).

Although sickness absence is experienced individually, there are often patterns of absence, such as high levels of absence linked to stress or back injuries, which good occupational health services will investigate to improve the work environment. Unfortunately, too many occupational health services are of uneven quality, consisting of little more than access to a nurse or doctor when you return to work after sick leave. Occupational health referrals are often seen as part of absence management procedures and a potential disciplinary tool. If you think that you are being forced back to work too soon, or without appropriate adjustments and assistance, you should speak to your manager and/or your trade union representative. If your sickness absence was part of a wider pattern which could be prevented through improved health and safety, you should talk to your health and safety representative.

Employers must record all accidents at work, however minor, in an accident book. More serious injuries must be reported through RIDDOR (the Reporting of Injuries, Diseases and Dangerous Occurrences Regulations 1995). Regulation 6 of the Management of Health and Safety at Work Regulations 1999, and also COSHH and some other regulations, require employers to undertake health surveillance of the workforce where necessary. You should be given information about your employer's occupational health services when you start work (HSE, 1993).

Injuries and ill health at work

ACTIVITY 9.9

John is asked to help a colleague lift a heavy box blocking a corridor where a patient trolley needs to move. In doing so he hurts his back.

What should John do immediately and then over the next few days?

In the situation described in the activity above, John should:

- Contact his manager and ask his safety representative to conduct an inspection.
- Only agree to be interviewed by management when he feels well enough and has a safety representative present. At this stage John should describe what happened but not attribute blame (including to himself).
- Keep careful records of the injury and resultant health problems, and medical reports.

- Check the accident was recorded properly in the work accident book and elsewhere.

- Not be rushed back to work after the accident until he is ready to return according to his GP or consultant.

If you have experienced a personal injury or have suffered an illness arising from your work, you may be able to make a personal injury claim. Your trade union or professional body will be able to advise you how to do this. The HSE has useful guidance on incidents at work (HSE, 2007).

What should you do if you have health and safety concerns for staff or patients and service users?

Your contract of employment requires you to follow reasonable and lawful management instructions. Management instructions may sometimes conflict with your duty of care to service users or even with your statutory rights. However, you cannot be instructed to work in a way that is unsafe to service users, yourself or colleagues, since that would not be a reasonable and lawful instruction (Preston-Shoot, 2000). If the working environment poses a risk to service users, the employees' duty of care also requires them to draw management's attention to such risks, and managers may need to alert service users.

Staff should, therefore, question any requirement to work in circumstances where dangerous substances are present, manual handling arrangements are unsafe, or where staff are being asked to take on additional work of such amount and complexity that it is reasonably foreseeable that they will become ill. In serious, urgent circumstances safety representatives have legal protection to stop work taking place or ask staff to leave an area (Employment Rights Act 1996, Section 44 (1) (e) and Section 100 (1) (e)), but such steps should normally only be taken after taking careful advice.

In order to meet your contractual health and safety duties, you must:

- Be made aware at induction of the main health and safety aspects of your job and working environment, including relevant risk assessments and measures taken to eliminate or reduce risks.

- Understand your manager's responsibilities for health and safety.

- Adhere to any health and safety training provided.

- Ensure any concerns you have with health and safety and the environment of care are drawn to the attention of appropriate people.

- Ensure any accidents, however minor, are recorded in the workplace accident book.

- Question and, where necessary, challenge acts, omissions, or systems and procedures that might be unsafe to you, colleagues, service users or the wider public.

- Know who your workplace health and safety representative is.

Whilst most concerns can be raised at any time or in supervision, urgent concerns should be acted upon at once. Remember your professional code requires you to raise concerns about the working environment.

Access to reliable health and safety information is essential and should include access to:

- The employer's health and safety policies and procedures.
- Risk assessments and procedures relevant to your work and working environment.
- The accident book to make sure any incidents are recorded.
- Details of your health and safety representative.

If you have difficulty obtaining essential information, you should speak with your safety representative.

Students and trainees

Employers' health and safety duties towards students and trainees are similar to those towards employees. Students and trainees should take special care to ensure they are aware of relevant policies and procedures, and are appropriately supervised and trained. If students and trainees do not get the support and advice they need, they should raise their concerns with their college tutor or workplace supervisor.

Raising staff concerns as an individual or as a team?

It can be difficult for a lone individual to raise a concern. An employee may be worried about the consequences or of being labelled as a troublemaker, even though failure to raise concerns may be a breach of the employee's statutory duty, employment contract and professional code. However, most health and safety concerns are not individual issues but affect other staff in the team or department. Dangerous floors, unsafe equipment, hazardous substances and a stressful working environment rarely affect only one person. It is always more effective for the team or department to raise concerns collectively. This stops any individual being singled out, and is much more difficult to ignore.

Sometimes there may be no opportunity to raise matters as a group, because an individual is faced with an immediate unsafe situation and may need to decide there and then whether to question or refuse to undertake a task. However, working together as a team to raise concerns is preferable, using the health and safety representative.

Health and safety representatives

There are 150,000 safety representatives in the UK with legal rights and protection to help them prevent accidents and ill health. Research has shown that workplaces with union recognition and safety representatives experience around half the number of serious injuries of those without such representatives. This is because trade union safety representatives know the workplace, are supported by their union and are trained to help promote a good safety culture and allow employees to raise issues that concern them (TUC, 2011).

Local authorities, NHS employers and many voluntary and private sector health and social care employers recognise trade unions. Where a union is recognised, that union has the right to appoint safety representatives, and it is up to the union (through its members) to decide who should be a safety representative. Being a safety representative can be a very rewarding experience, with training and support provided by the union. Staff elect such representatives and hold them to account, but the representatives rely on staff support. A safety representative listens to members' concerns and uses the staff's legal rights to resolve them. If you are a trade union safety representative then you are legally entitled (Safety Representatives and Safety Committees Regulations 1977) to (amongst other functions):

- Investigate potential hazards and dangerous occurrences in the workplace, and the causes of accidents in the workplace.
- Investigate complaints by any employee relating to health, safety or welfare at work.
- Take up health, safety or welfare issues with the employer.
- Carry out inspections at least four times a year or following any substantial change.
- Form a health and safety committee with which the employer must consult.

The employer must:

- Consult safety representatives in good time on any health and safety matters, including any changes to the workplace or work organisation.
- Give representatives the information necessary to enable them to fulfil their functions.
- Give health and safety representatives the paid time and facilities they need to carry out their functions and to undergo training in those functions.

The employer must not subject safety representatives to any detriment for undertaking these functions.

What responsibilities do managers have?

Employers have a responsibility to ensure the health and safety of both service users and staff. Employers must:

- Publish a written health and safety policy setting out who is responsible for which aspects of health and safety.
- Assess the risks to employees and others who could be affected by their activities.
- Arrange for the effective planning, organisation, control, monitoring and review of preventive and protective measures.
- Ensure that employees' managers have access to competent health and safety training and advice.
- Consult employees about risks at work and preventative measures.
- Make service users and visitors to premises, as well as employees, aware of health and safety risks and hazards.
- Have a named lead employee for health and safety.

Each manager is responsible for understanding the hazards of the work and premises they manage and must know where to get advice about relevant health and safety risks. Areas are likely to include:

- Risk assessment (including COSHH assessments where applicable).

- Emergency and evacuation procedures.

- Accident and clinical incident reporting.

- Use of work equipment.

- Manual handling.

- Assessing contractors' competence.

Managers must proactively check for health and safety risks and seek to prevent accidents and ill health, not just react to incidents or concerns. Managers should ensure that staff report and record incidents, and should monitor, evaluate and review practices and procedures on a regular basis, including, where appropriate, during supervision. They have immediate responsibility for the duty of care of their staff and those they serve (*Wilson* v *London Underground Limited* [2008]).

If any new equipment, chemical, working area, working practice (including work patterns or skill mix), means of transport or lifting is introduced, then each manager should consider the possible health and safety implications, and also consider training. Contractors must have their own arrangements in place.

> Clients, contractors and sub-contractors must consult their employees on health and safety matters. Where there are recognised trade unions, consultation should be through safety representatives appointed by the unions.
>
> (HSE, 2002, p. 10)

If an employer recognises trade unions, then trade union safety representatives must be consulted on health and safety matters affecting the employees they represent (HSE, 2008). Employers have a duty of care towards managers. If managers are to discharge their duties effectively they need proper training, sufficient time and resources. Managers must draw attention to any concerns about their ability to undertake their health and safety duties effectively and also draw to the attention of their line managers and to the employer's health and safety specialist any concerns they have about health and safety that they are not able to address.

CHAPTER SUMMARY

After reading this chapter, you should be clear about your employer's health and safety duties as well as your own, and be able to understand:

- Why good and safe working conditions are important for those using health and social care services, as well as for the staff providing them.

- Why, as well as being potentially harmful to staff, workplace hazards can affect the provision of services and help cause clinical incidents and staff sickness absence.

- Where you can find out more information and advice about specific hazards.

- The key steps that you need to take to prevent hazards at work.

Further guidance may be found on the HSE website at **www.hse.gov.uk** which has detailed advice on each of the hazards discussed in this chapter.

The TUC Hazards at Work manual explains an employer's duties and workers' rights in some detail. This can be found at: **https://www.tuc.org.uk/workplace/index.cfm?mins= 124&minors=4&majorsubjectID=2**

Finally, Hazards magazine mixes opinion with advice and is especially useful for health and safety representatives: **hazards.org**

Chapter 10
What to do if . . .

O B J E C T I V E S

By the end of this chapter, you should understand what to do if:

- You have concerns about the environment of care, the rights of service users and carers, or the safety of yourself or your colleagues.

- The normal means by which your employer expects you to raise concerns are not available, are ineffective or are not speedy enough.

- Your own practice or that of your colleagues falls below the standards it is reasonable for a competent professional to meet.

- Poor practice is identified and individuals are blamed, rather than systemic problems tackled.

- You are subjected to a detriment as a result of raising concerns or assisting others to do so.

Introduction

We will all be hospital patients at some time in our lives, and so will our loved ones. Many of us will need social care. At Mid Staffordshire Hospital, staff failed to raise concerns effectively, or in many cases failed to raise concerns at all (Francis, 2010).

> The Inquiry found that a chronic shortage of staff, particularly nursing staff, was largely responsible for the substandard care. Morale at the Trust was low, and while many staff did their best in difficult circumstances, others showed a disturbing lack of compassion towards their patients. Staff who spoke out felt ignored and there is strong evidence that many were deterred from doing so through fear and bullying. It is now clear that some staff did express concern about the standard of care being provided to patients. The tragedy was that they were ignored and worse still others were discouraged from speaking out.
>
> (Robert Francis QC, statement at the publication of his final report into care provided by Mid Staffordshire NHS Foundation Trust, **www.midstaffsinquiry.com/pressrelease.html**)

Are you confident you would raise concerns until you got answers? Only a few years before the Mid Staffordshire inquiry, an independent inquiry into another institutional failure – one involving baby deaths at Bristol Royal Infirmary – concluded:

Currently, there continues to be a sense among the workforce that they cannot discuss openly matters of concern relating to the care of patients and the conduct of fellow workers. There is a real fear among junior staff (particularly amongst junior doctors and nurses) that to comment on colleagues, particularly consultants, is to endanger their future work prospects. The junior needs a reference and a recommendation; nurses want to keep their jobs. This is a powerful motive for keeping quiet.

(Kennedy, 2001, Chapter 22, para 28)

Not one regulator, trade union or professional body managed to effectively highlight and halt the poor practice at these two hospitals. Perhaps these are examples of the hidden or silent curriculum, referred to in Chapter 3 (Preston-Shoot, 2012).

ACTIVITY 10.1

In small groups, discuss why you think that even when some staff did raise concerns they were so unsuccessful.

Have you ever been in a position when you ought to have raised concerns? If so what happened?

Why you need to raise concerns when necessary

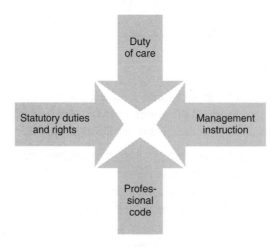

Figure 10.1 *The three duties that interface with management and seek to impact on poor practice*

Qualified professionals must raise concerns and challenge poor practice for three reasons:

1. Your status as a registered professional requires you to comply with your professional code and protect the rights and promote the interests of patients and service users (and in the case of social workers, patients' and service users' carers too). For social workers, for example, compliance with their code requires:

Bringing to the attention of your employer or the appropriate authority resource or operational difficulties that might get in the way of the delivery of safe care.

(General Social Care Council (GSCC), 2002, para 3.4)

2. Your contract of employment requires you to exercise your duty of care and to comply with the relevant code, which will be explicitly referred to in your job description.

3. Statutory duties, some professional and some derived from equality and health and safety legislation, may conflict with management instructions.

You cannot be instructed to breach a statutory duty, your professional code or your contract of employment (Preston-Shoot, 2000; Kline, 2003, 2009). Such an instruction would itself be a breach of your contract of employment, and might lead to the person issuing such an instruction being held to account by their own professional regulator or by a court for causing you to breach your duty of care.

Students and trainees

Students and trainees also have a duty of care, but the standard is different to that of a qualified practitioner. This was discussed in Chapter 2. Trainees and students are not professionally accountable to the extent that qualified professionals are. They are not expected to reach the standards of a fully qualified practitioner.

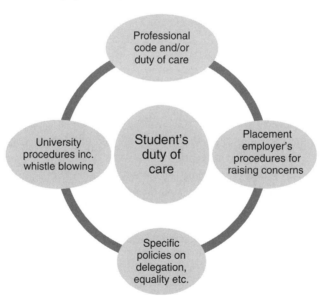

Figure 10.2 Factors influencing how students comply with their duty of care

When undertaking work as a student or trainee, you must always:

- Be clear what you can and cannot do.

- Not undertake any role or task for which you have not been properly prepared.

- Be supervised by an appropriately qualified member of staff.

- Raise concerns about yourself, colleagues or service users.

If students or trainees are asked to undertake tasks or roles which they believe they are not competent to undertake, they must draw this to the attention of their supervisor and, if necessary, to their college tutor or a more senior manager. The supervisor (and the organisation providing a work placement) and the tutor (and the education institution) are required to ensure that students or trainees do not undertake tasks or responsibilities they are not qualified or competent to undertake.

Students must also receive clear guidance and support to ensure they can still raise concerns. For nurses, for example, the Nursing and Midwifery Council (NMC) guidance on professional conduct for nursing and midwifery students requires students to:

> 27 Inform your mentor or tutor immediately if you believe that you, a colleague or anyone else may be putting someone at risk of harm.

> (NMC, 2010c, p. 15)

Raising concerns effectively

There is no 'one size fits all' approach to raising concerns effectively, but this chapter draws on the experience of those who have raised concerns.

CASE STUDY

Panorama care home abuse investigation prompts government review

A nurse blew the whistle on systematic abuse that left vulnerable people to face months of physical and verbal abuse at a Bristol care home. Staff pinned residents to the floor and forced one into the shower fully dressed and then outside until she shook from cold. Residents were slapped and taunted, and one was teased about a suicide attempt. Experts told the programme what they had seen amounted to 'torture'. Immediately after the broadcast, four of the staff were arrested.

(The Guardian, 1 June 2011, p. 8)

ACTIVITY 10.2

In the case study above, the former nurse employee whistle blew to the BBC after the Care Quality Commission (CQC) and his employer ignored his claims.

* *What would you have done if you had been a student nurse, health professional or social worker on work placement?*

* *What does your professional regulator suggest?*

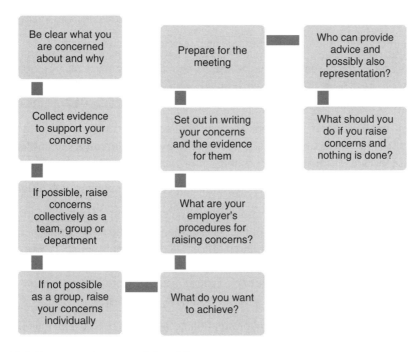

Figure 10.3 Ten steps to successfully raising concerns

Before raising your concerns with management, you need evidence to underpin your concerns

ACTIVITY **10.3**

You work as an agency nurse in a residential nursing home. You become appalled at the standard of care by two members of staff, and the failure of the manager to act, apparently because all three of them are good friends.

What sort of evidence might help you to raise a concern?

Without evidence, you will not be taken seriously. If it is your word against someone else's, you are unlikely to be successful. Documentary evidence is best, particularly if there is a discrepancy between your employer's policies and procedures, established good practice, or legal requirements and what has happened or is likely to. Emails, letters or notes of meetings form an audit trail, especially if you have previously raised concerns in writing. Other evidence might include witness statements from colleagues, service users or carers to corroborate your claims, but make sure such statements are dated and signed and that there is little chance they might be withdrawn.

Other sources of evidence might include:

- Your employer's risk register possibly showing your concerns are held by others.

- Records of previous adverse incidents.

- Health and safety data on employees' accidents and illness, and risk assessments.

- Survey information and data on staffing levels, caseloads and workloads.

- Discrimination data (see Chapters 3 and 7) showing how particular groups of staff or service users have been treated (Equality and Human Rights Commission (EHRC), 2011c).

- Data on the health and social care needs of the local population, often in the form of reports to NHS trust boards and local authority overview and scrutiny committees, which may also include information on cuts and future plans for services.

- Information on how your local authority or health provider compares with others.

There are two ways of seeking this information. You can submit a freedom of information claim for almost any information a public sector organisation holds by sending an email to the organisation's freedom of information officer, who must reply within 20 working days. Don't make a request too large or it can be refused or charged for. The website **www.what-dotheyknow.com** has model letters, or check the Freedom of Information website at **www.ico.gov.uk/for_the_public/official_information/how_access.aspx**

Trade unions have statutory rights to information necessary for collective bargaining (negotiating) (The Trade Union and Labour Relations (Consolidation Act 1992 (TULRCA)) in areas such as staffing, workloads, absenteeism and use of agency staff. If the concerns arise from a restructuring involving redundancies or a transfer to another organisation (such as a contractor), then recognised trade unions must be consulted with details of such proposals. A model letter requesting such information is available on the website. Health and safety representatives also have information rights (see Chapter 9).

Raise concerns collectively as a team, group or department, rather than individually, if possible

---

CASE STUDY

A group of health visitors in Southern England had serious concerns about the risks heavy workloads created for safe working, but only two were prepared to raise concerns in writing. Eventually, with support from their local trade union official, they all agreed to write a letter to management. Their manager responded by stating that there was no additional funding for posts and refused to consider taking the matter further. Two weeks later, there was a child death in the area, precisely the risk the manager was warned about. The health visitors were able to demonstrate they had raised concerns, and none were disciplined. The manager never returned to work.

Your duty of care, like professional accountability, is a personal one. You are personally responsible for your acts and omissions. So, when necessary, you must stand up to be counted as an individual. However, individuals can be isolated and scapegoated. Individuals are easier to intimidate than a group. Individuals are more likely to feel the pressure if they are alone than if they are part of a group.

Moreover, the concerns that one individual in a team has are often shared by, or affect, others in the team. If the rest of the team allow the first person who raises concerns to be isolated and picked off, then it will be much easier for the same to happen to them. Indeed, it's even easier for the employer to claim that the member of staff raising concerns is the real problem. A group working together can be much more powerful than an individual. The group will draw strength from each other. The group might be a team in a base, ward, laboratory or service.

One good way of helping a group of staff to stand together and raise concerns collectively is to conduct a staff survey, which can show that issues reflect wider concerns. Tips on successful surveys are available on the website.[1]

If necessary, raise concerns individually

ACTIVITY **10.4**

You work in a team of five staff who all believe that current workloads are potentially unsafe, but you are the only one who wants to raise these with your manager.

What should you do?

Raising concerns arising from your duty of care or your code of professional conduct is not an optional extra that you can choose to do if you feel strongly enough or are brave enough. It is something you are contractually and professionally obliged to do so. Doing so does not make you a troublemaker; it makes you a responsible professional.

It can sometimes, indeed often, be difficult to raise concerns, especially if informal low-key attempts to raise them through supervision fail. However, whilst not raising them may make your life easier in the short term, that would be indefensible if it risked unsafe practice, harm, or essential needs not being met.

When raising concerns does not happen, harm may result. Moreover, staff who fail to record concerns and do not draw them to the attention of appropriate people may face disciplinary action, charges of professional misconduct, public opprobrium and the knowledge that they did not do what they should have done to protect those who put their trust in them and needed their care.

In the case above, you might consider inviting a union or professional association representative to come and discuss with the team why and how they can raise their concerns in the most effective way. Collectively raising those concerns would be the best way forward. However, if colleagues really will not raise those concerns, you must personally place them on the record. Following the Mid Staffordshire Hospital tragedy, both the General Medical Council (GMC) and NMC sought to hold to account those whose practice was poor or who failed to raise concerns. Fifty-seven doctors and nurses faced investigation and the director of nursing was suspended from the register.[1]

> **CASE STUDY**
>
> ## The price of not raising concerns
> *A new set of baby-weighing scales arrived at a GP practice. The assembly instructions were in German, and Helen the health visitor struggled to assemble the scales. The GP, who was a very strong character, instructed her to 'do her best' and get on with it, since there was a baby clinic that afternoon. Helen reluctantly agreed to do so. When the first baby was placed on the scales that afternoon, they collapsed and the baby received a serious fracture of the skull. Helen explained she had acted under instruction from the doctor, but she had no evidence that she was unhappy assembling the scales or had advised against it. The doctor denied the conversation had taken place and accepted no responsibility.*

> **ACTIVITY 10.5**
>
> *In the case study above, what should Helen have done when she first thought there was a problem with the scales?*

It helps to have some idea of what you want

Sometimes your goal is straightforward, for example that a piece of equipment is unsafe and should be replaced, or that staff need additional training, or that you want a risk assessment of an aspect of your work, such as certain home visits. Other issues, however, may be more complex or difficult to resolve, but if you or your colleagues have constructive ideas, then you should put them forward.

Understand the procedures your employer has for raising concerns

> **ACTIVITY 10.6**
>
> *Fatima has just started work as a new member of staff and discovers everyone in her team is complaining privately but no one seems clear how to raise their concerns. They eventually lodge a grievance as follows:*
>
> *'We the undersigned wish to lodge a grievance that workloads are too high to be able to work safely. We request that urgent action be taken to prevent a serious incident.'*
>
> *If you were in their situation, could you have raised this issue more effectively?*

In every employer providing health and social care services, and indeed in every university or college providing training, there are procedures you must follow to raise concerns if they can't be resolved informally.

Supervision is a means of raising concerns during which they can be discussed fairly informally, but where the outcomes should be recorded. Professional staff should have supervi-

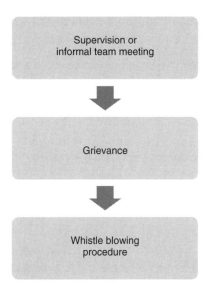

Figure 10.4 The hierarchy of procedures

sion regularly, and there should be a formal policy setting out who should have sessions, who convenes them and how often, and how they should be prepared for and followed up. Pressure of work or poor management may mean that sessions are less frequent and well organised than they should be; however, supervision should normally be the first place to raise concerns unless they are very urgent. Individual professions have their own guidance on professional supervision. Setting out your concerns ahead of the meeting ensures discussion and enables the manager to consider a response (Children's Workforce Development Council, 2007).

Grievances are a more formal means of raising concerns when informal means have failed. Your employer's grievance procedure will explain:

- Who should use it, when, and any time limits.

- How grievance hearings are organised, when any written statement of concerns and evidence must be submitted, and the need to state a desired outcome.

- How to appeal if your grievance is rejected.

- If there is a 'status quo' clause which stops management implementing the change you are concerned about – a potentially important safeguard.

Grievances may be on behalf of an individual or a group of staff, and can help highlight issues and support for your case.

Set out in writing your concerns, the evidence for them, and link them to your professional, contractual or statutory duties

Once you have evidence of a genuine concern, you must raise it in writing to an appropriate person such as your manager. If you don't place your concerns on the record in writing, there is no evidence you ever had them. If the concerns affect a whole team, then a team letter will be more appropriate. If the concerns affect staff across a wider area or across different teams, then take advice from your trade union or professional body.

Letters have advantages over phone calls or conversations since they can:

- Clarify issues.
- Create an audit trail confirming you did raise issues and the response (or lack of it) you got.
- Let other affected staff know concerns have been raised.

Detailed advice on letters and some model examples of letters are available on the website.

ACTIVITY 10.7

You and your team have raised concerns in supervision and in a team discussion about the role of a new support worker, but nothing seems to have happened as a result.

With a colleague, write a letter to your manager setting out your concerns. Compare the letters and then check them against the model letter on the website.

Try to anticipate what your manager might say or do in response to your raising these concerns

Try to get the moral high ground. You will feel much more comfortable if you can demonstrate your concerns are well founded and they have been raised in a professional way. The manager may privately (or not so privately) agree with what you are saying but, either way, she will be under pressure to keep to her budget, not upset her own managers, and be seen to be firm. So try to anticipate claims such as:

- I'm not clear what you are seeking.
- I'll need more evidence than that.
- Why are you the only one(s) with this problem?
- There are five names on this letter, but I understand one of them has already said they don't want to continue with the concerns.
- I'm sorry, there is simply no money.
- The situation may not be ideal, but it is not unsafe.
- Is this about your own situation or that of the patients or service users?
- I'm not clear what procedure or policy you're following here.

Some of those may be reasonable questions, but some will be attempts to sidetrack you or prevent the matter going any further. Depending on how claims are expressed, managers may also misunderstand the requirements of the legal rules, for example concerning when resources may and may not be taken into account in decision-making about what services to provide or what standards of care are required. This illustrates the importance of one of this book's themes, namely legal literacy.

ACTIVITY 10.8

A group of you have raised concerns in writing about the role of a new support worker and your manager invites you to a meeting to discuss them.

If your manager makes the points listed above, how would you respond?

The manager's responsibility

When concerns are raised about the duty of care, managers may respond in one of three ways:

- Reject the concerns as not being well founded or impossible to meet for budgetary or policy reasons.

- Acknowledge the concerns and respond appropriately so that work can be done safely.

- Refer to their own managers for advice, setting out their recommendations or the options.

If the manager decides to address the concern or agrees that there may be an issue but more evidence is needed, then you will need to decide how urgent the matter is, agree a deadline for the response, or get confirmation in writing as to what the manager is going to do. Some managers will share the concerns raised and encourage a written record that they can, in turn, forward to their own manager. Others may try to persuade staff to not raise concerns, potentially in breach of their duty of care.

Employers operate within a framework of vicarious liability whereby they would almost certainly be held responsible for negligence by their employees. Employers have a duty to:

- Ensure that what is actually done is done safely and appropriately.

- Make clear what cannot be done, or at least what cannot be done safely.

- Ensure that patients and service users are treated with appropriate urgency.

- Prioritise statutory duties over other responsibilities.

- Ensure staff can meet their duty of care and comply with their code.

Chapter 4 sets out in more detail what a good manager is expected to do.

You need to know how to prepare for and follow up any meeting

Be prepared! You need to be clear about the following:

- What is to be discussed at the meeting? Are you clear what you want from the meeting? Do you know what management want? What procedure, if any, is the meeting part of?

- Who is attending the meeting with you? Except in supervision, do not normally attend a meeting on your own. Ask a colleague or a trade union representative to accompany you. If you are part of a team concern, who is putting your case?

- What is the agenda and what are you going to say? What do you think you might be asked? Setting out your concerns in writing as 'I thought it would be helpful if you knew what I/we wanted to discuss in advance' can helpfully focus the meeting.

- Be prepared for management to make an offer during the meeting. If they say 'We will investigate this and get back in a month' or 'I can't offer you any more staff but we could get some agency support', are you ready to call a quick adjournment to discuss the offer with your colleagues or representative in private? Alternatively, you could offer to respond once you have the proposal in writing.

- If management agree to all or most of what you seek, don't rush away. Write it down, read it back to the manager, and then confirm it in an email with your response.

- If you are in the meeting on behalf of colleagues, make it clear that whatever is offered will need to be agreed by your team or department – another reason to confirm it in writing before you do anything.

There is a myth that what is achieved in meetings and negotiations is due to some special negotiator's skill. This is simply not true. Negotiating skills are very useful, but more important is whether there is a good case, support for the case from other staff or service users, and any pressure on management to reach agreement such as fear of the matter becoming more public. Nonetheless, how the case is presented certainly makes a difference, but without evidence or support you won't win. You can't build a house without good bricks!

On the website you will find additional tips for meetings, explaining what to look out for when:

- Setting the agenda and preparing evidence.

- Running the meeting.

- Reaching agreement (or not).

ACTIVITY 10.9

From your own experience, list what made a meeting useful (or not) by checking against the tips on the website. Then stage a mock meeting with colleagues in which two of you role-play managers and two of you role-play staff who wish to raise concerns that management do not acknowledge and respond to. Make notes of what happened and reflect on how the staff might have been more effective.

What advice and possible representation can you expect your union or professional body to give?

Professional bodies can provide advice, information, and occasionally representation. They also set standards. Trade unions can provide you with advice and representation. If you are a student or trainee, you may be a member of a trade union and professional body, but you should also be able to get advice and support from your tutor or students union if your concerns arise out of a work placement. Specific advice on how students can access advice and support can be found on the website.

Trade unions usually have two sorts of people who can give advice and representation.

- Local representatives are fellow workers, normally also doing a full job, who have volunteered. They get some training from their union and should usually be your first 'port of call'. There may be a local representative for your own department or profession, and your union's head office can help you find one. Some local representatives are very experienced, but many will also seek support from paid officials.

- Paid officials are employed by the union and have more knowledge and expertise, but normally only get directly involved if there is a serious grievance or disciplinary matter, or a matter (such as whistle blowing) where specific expertise is required.

Both representatives and paid officials are busy people, but you will need to work together with them (and they with you) if informal attempts to resolve concerns about the duty of care do not succeed. It is important to know what you can expect from them and what they will expect from you. A checklist you should refer to prior to contacting your union is available on the website. It is important that you agree and confirm by email, if possible, what you and your representative will do, and when.

Joining a union and/or professional association is your decision. You can be accompanied by a friend at any meetings. You can also get advice (at a price) from lawyers if you are not in a union, or possibly even via your home insurance. But not being in a union or professional association is a bit like leaving yourself without insurance when a fire breaks out. Belonging to such organisations may also give you a chance to proactively influence what happens in your workplace before the fire breaks out, to try to prevent it, because your union will have consultation rights.

ACTIVITY **10.10**

How would you find out where you can get further advice and possible representation from? Research by asking what you can expect the trade union or professional body to do when you first make contact. Would it make any difference if you were a student on placement?

You need to know what to do next if you raise concerns and nothing is done

---

ACTIVITY **10.11**

Melody and a group of nursing staff have raised concerns in a team meeting and then in writing about a senior member of staff's contemptuous attitude to patient complaints. Nothing has happened. They are concerned about taking matters further because the manager is a bully.

What else, if anything, should they do?

If, having raised concerns, you meet a brick wall, you have two choices: place your concerns on the record, or use your employer's whistle blowing procedure.

Your professional code requires you to draw your concerns to the attention of an appropriate person in authority. Doing so in writing is essential since it leaves an audit trail that is much harder to ignore. Moreover, such an audit trail largely protects your own position, so if something goes wrong there is a record that you recognised risks and alerted management.

So, even if Melody does nothing else, she must place her concerns on the record. Once such concerns have been raised, it is a very foolish manager who does not respond at all, and at the very least explain why they are not going to act on her concern. However, some concerns will be so serious that you will want to take matters further for your own sake or for that of those receiving services.

If your concerns have either been raised (unsuccessfully) through supervision and then a grievance, or are urgent or serious, then you should consider using your employer's whistle blowing procedure. Chapter 3 discussed the legal framework. Such procedures are important and can be very helpful. They can be a way of bypassing local management and laying responsibility at a senior level. In a responsible organisation, whistle blowing is welcomed and encouraged, but in too many organisations whistle blowers are ignored, resented and victimised. As discussed in Chapter 3, despite the legal protection of the Public Interest Disclosure Act 1998, whistle blowing can be a hazardous step.

If you need to consider using the whistle blowing procedure, you should do the following:

- Obtain and read your employer's whistle blowing procedure.

- Take advice from your trade union, professional organisation or from Public Concern at Work, an independent whistle blowing charity. Send the statement to the person identified by your employer's whistle blowing procedure and be prepared to be asked to attend a meeting. It will normally be important to take a colleague with you to witness any discussion.

- Be clear what your concerns are and try to ensure you have as much documentary evidence as possible to support your claims.

- Be sure you have explored all the informal ways of raising your concerns.

- Set out a clear statement of your concerns and supporting evidence in professional language, emphasising the risks to service users, staff or the organisation if your concerns are not properly and promptly investigated.

- Ensure you are clear what will happen once you have made your disclosure – and in particular when it is likely to be acted upon, whether there will be any immediate action, and what steps the employer will make to protect you from any attempts at victimisation.

Social worker Nevres Kemal raised concerns, well before the death of Baby P, that vulnerable children in the borough were not being adequately protected. Kemal first raised concerns in 2004. The council said that it investigated and that it had not put children at risk. It subsequently suspended her and eventually had to pay substantial compensation after she claimed victimisation for whistleblowing and race discrimination. Six months later the Baby Peter scandal became public yet Haringey denied Kemal had ever raised concerns four years previously that its child protection practice was seriously flawed.

(The Times, 14 November 2008, p. 6)

Although the Public Interest Disclosure Act provides for unlimited compensation if whistle blowers are victimised, gaining legal redress can be complex. Staff should never seek to use an internal whistle blowing procedure or whistle blow externally without taking advice from their professional body, trade union or Public Concern at Work (**www.pcaw.co.uk**).

NHS and local government employers must have whistle blowing policies, whilst for NHS employees it is a contractual duty to report genuine concerns about malpractice, patient safety or other serious risks (The Social Partnership Forum, 2010).

An NHS worker with an unblemished 27-year career was sacked after she blew the whistle on senior doctors who were moonlighting at a private hospital while being paid to diagnose NHS patients. Sharmila Chowdhury, 51, the radiology service manager at Ealing Hospital NHS Trust, repeatedly warned the hospital's most senior managers that doctors were dishonestly claiming thousands of pounds every month.

A Watford employment tribunal judge took the unusual step last week of ordering the trust to reinstate Ms Chowdhury's full salary and said: 'I have no hesitation in saying that you are probably going to win.' Ms Chowdhury was suspended after a counter-allegation of fraud made against her by a junior whom she had reported for breaching patient safety. Ms Chowdhury was sacked for gross misconduct in June, eight months after her suspension. The judge awarded her full pay until the hearing begins in February, including pay for the work which the trust claims was fraudulently completed.

(The Independent, 11 July 2010, p. 6)

Find and read your own employer's or university's whistle blowing policy.

Why is it important to try to raise issues with your own manager, if possible, before taking the matter further?

Linking up with service user groups, patients' organisations and community groups

As citizens and future patients and service users, you are entitled to make common ground with service user groups, patient organisations and community groups to share concerns and uphold safe and effective services. If, as a result of reductions in funding or restructuring, services may be cut or quality compromised, then you are entitled to explain to service users their rights to be consulted and the implications of such changes. As a citizen you may support local campaigns, and as a member of a trade union you may take collective action to question and challenge such changes.

You must be careful that no service user confidentiality is breached, and must make it clear that you are speaking as a trade union or professional association member and not on behalf of your employer. Local campaigns, which staff may support, can organise petitions and lobbies, and contact local councillors, MPs, service regulators such as Ofsted and the CQC, and the media.

ACTIVITY 10.13

Imagine that your team has serious concerns about the impact of cuts and service changes on a particular service.

- *Consider who you might approach and how to gain support.*

- *Think about whether and how you might persuade other staff to join in, and what you must be really careful of.*

The local media and MPs can be invaluable, but you must take advice on how to use them. Get it wrong, and you will be accused of breaching confidentiality and local procedures. Get it right, and you may have a powerful ally. You are legally entitled to explain your concerns to your own MP (contact your MP at **findyourmp.parliament.uk**).

Local media may well be sympathetic to concerns about standards of care and service users' rights, but be careful and get some advice from your union or a supportive journalist before speaking with them.[2]

CASE STUDY

Health visitors in South London became concerned about workloads and vacant posts and the impact on children and their families following a high profile child death in a neighbouring borough. The health visitors undertook a staff survey and then collectively took out a grievance against their NHS employer, which some senior nurse managers were sympathetic to, explaining why caseloads were unsafe and seeking additional staff.

The Health Authority refused to recruit saying it had no money. Staff then launched a local petition, got local media publicity and the support of a prominent local vicar. The senior managers decided (correctly) that faced with staff shortages, most caseloads and many

---

clinics should be closed, so that staff could concentrate on the high risk child protection cases and wrote to local GPs and social services to explain this. The resultant uproar led to lobbying of the Health Authority by health visitors and local parents, some of whom brought babies in prams with placards saying 'I want my health visitor back'.

The next day a meeting with the Minister of Health was held at which union representatives and the vicar obtained a funded commitment to fill all vacancies and increase staffing levels.

Sometimes a member of staff has no choice but to go to the media. This was done very effectively when social worker Liz Davies and former care home resident Demetrious Panton blew the whistle to stop serious abuse in children's homes in Islington (Shifrin, 2003).

It is essential, whatever concerns you may have about jobs, terms and conditions and the treatment of staff, that the interests of service users are always paramount, giving you the moral high ground. After all, insufficient staff, unsafe practice and a bullying culture are bad for the service as well as for staff. Staff should be custodians of the interests of service users and carers.

Raising concerns about the poor practice of other staff

Adverse incident procedures (and indeed disciplinary procedures) should enable staff and their employer to learn from mistakes and poor practice. That does not mean disciplinary action might not be appropriate on occasion. However, it is crucial that an environment exists where staff feel able to raise concerns about their own practice without fear that doing so will automatically trigger disciplinary action.

*ACTIVITY **10.14***

Harinder is a newly qualified nurse working on a medical ward. He is concerned at the poor standard of hygiene of nurses and healthcare assistants, who are not washing their hands between patients even after a hospital report showing a rise in MRSA cases. Harinder then witnesses a carer challenging this poor practice but staff claim it is almost impossible to meet hygiene standards and do all the work required. The unsafe practice continues.

* *What should he do?*

* *What should the ward sister do?*

* *What should relatives be told in future if they complain?*

In the situation outlined in the activity above, Harinder's NMC Code (NMC, 2008a) states he must act without delay if he believes that he, a colleague or anyone else may be putting someone at risk, and he must report his concerns in writing if problems in the environment of care are putting people at risk. Harinder should try to speak informally with his colleagues, explaining that under-staffing should be raised with the ward sister. If that has no effect, Harinder should raise the matter with the ward sister himself, probably as a general concern without naming individual staff members, especially if the poor practice is widespread.

The ward sister should then tell all staff, both in writing and personally, the standards expected, notably the hospital's infection control standards. If that does not lead to compliance with the policy, then the hospital's infection control officer must be alerted. However, if there really is a staffing shortage, then the ward sister must also draw her own manager's attention to it – she must report her concerns in writing if problems in the environment of care are putting people at risk (NMC, 2008a). If the issue caused by the staffing shortage is made worse by cleaning standards not being met, then that must also be formally raised with the appropriate manager.

If patients or their relatives raise concerns, then they should be directed to the ward sister. The ward sister, in line with the hospital policy and with her own NMC code (NMC, 2008a, para 52), must: 'give a constructive and honest response to anyone who complains about the care they have received'.

Your professional responsibilities are clear. You must: 'act without delay if you believe that you, a colleague or anyone else may be putting someone at risk' (NMC, 2008a, para 32).

What if your own practice falls below an acceptable standard?

Poor practice may involve relatively straightforward concerns such as poor record keeping, mistaken administration of medicines or a breach of confidentiality, or involve a less tangible lack of care and respect towards service users or carers.

If your own practice is not of an acceptable standard, you need to urgently reflect why this is. You might want to talk to a trusted colleague. The cause might be excessive workloads, being asked to undertake roles you do not feel competent to perform, as a result of a flawed instruction from another member of staff, or it may be your ill health and stress caused by work or other pressures.

If you make a mistake that could have caused harm to yourself, colleagues or a patient or service user, then you must record it at once and tell your line manager. If there is a reason you believe caused the mistake, then you should provide that reason. The most important outcome is that you and the organisation learn from your mistake. That may mean taking time in supervision to consider what happened, taking additional training or support, or considering whether systems or other staff were at fault.

What if the practice of a colleague falls below an acceptable standard?

If you are concerned about the practice of a colleague, your first loyalty is to the service user. Professional codes (for example, NMC, 2008a) are clear on this point. If possible, you should speak directly and informally to the person whose practice you are concerned about. You should seek to encourage them to reflect on their poor practice, and suggest they draw it to the attention of their line manager before someone else does it for them or before there is an avoidable adverse incident.

If that does not have the desired effect, then you should report your concerns to your manager. If you are aware of underlying causes, then you should mention those as well, especially as they may discourage attempts to blame the practitioner rather than considering first how the person's practice might improve. You may also want to alert your trade union representative, especially if you are concerned that the cause of the poor practice is excessive workload, inappropriate delegation, unsupportive colleagues, a bullying manager or stress.

If the practice causing concern might constitute a serious risk, then disciplinary action might result. The interests of patients and service users come first, but the employer also has a duty of care to the member of staff. Unfortunately, disciplinary action is often the knee-jerk reaction to poor practice, especially where the alternative is a more profound examination of underlying systemic organisational problems behind poor practice.

> *A review of studies and fitness to practise cases did find evidence that 'inexperienced, poorly trained, or poorly supported managers use suspension inappropriately' and concluded 'managers should refrain from adopting punitive forms of performance management.'*
>
> (Stone et al., 2011, p. 803)

Sometimes, when a member of staff is dismissed, a subsequent court hearing highlights the wider management responsibility for poor systems of work, as when a social worker's removal from the GSCC register was overturned when the Care Standards Tribunal considered that the chaotic context in which she was working was crucial (*Forbes* v *General Social Care Council* [2008]).

When disciplinary action is considered, there should be a thorough investigation prior to any proceedings commencing. The person facing allegations must have the opportunity to examine the allegations, see the evidence, be accompanied at all meetings where the allegations are discussed, and be properly represented at any hearing (Healthcare Commission, 2009).

Employers are sometimes (often) keener to rush to disciplinary action than to consider whether systemic failure rather than individual human mistakes was at fault. In doing so, they risk not learning the lessons that would help prevent future similar events. There is unfortunately some evidence that whether disciplinary proceedings are commenced, and what outcomes they produce are discriminatory. As one major NHS report put it:

> *Staff from minority ethnic groups are disproportionally involved in bullying and harassment cases, and are over-represented in disciplinary and grievance procedures.*
>
> (Healthcare Commission, 2009, p. 6)

There is also evidence from cases, discussed earlier in this book, in both health (Sharmila Chowdhury) and social care (Nevres Kemal) that when staff raise concerns they may be subject to a range of victimisation, which can include unfounded allegations resulting in disciplinary action.

Protection from victimisation when raising concerns

A member of staff, having raised concerns, may then find promotion blocked, face trumped-up allegations about poor practice, or be harassed. There is statutory protection from victimisation for staff who formally raise concerns or assist others in raising concerns that employers may be at risk of breaching their common law duty of care or statutory duties. In the wake of tragedies such as Mid Staffordshire Hospital Trust and Baby Peter, public opinion is becoming increasingly supportive of those professionals such as Margaret Haywood and Terry Bryan who raise concerns in the public domain.

CASE STUDY

Terry has reluctantly blown the whistle on abusive practice in a learning disability institution. His allegations are partly upheld but no action is taken against those responsible. One month later, Terry is called in by the manager he accused and suspended because it is wrongly alleged he has defrauded the trust on his expenses.

What should Terry do?

In the case study above, Terry should immediately seek advice and support from his trade union, contacting the regional office, because expert external support is needed. Advice on what support he should expect is available on the website. Terry should check what his employer's disciplinary policy says should happen next. He should make a careful note of what has happened and collate all relevant documents on both his whistle blowing and his travel claims. If he can, he should copy relevant documents and emails, and keep a diary of his treatment during the investigation or disciplinary process, including any impact on his health. He should request equality monitoring information on employee disciplinary action and the treatment of service users.

His trade union official should clarify what Terry is supposed to have done, ensure he does not attend any meetings without being accompanied, and insist that notes of any meetings are agreed.

Terry must ensure he is accompanied by a competent trade union representative at any hearing, as he is entitled to be (ACAS, 2009). Terry should be aware of the deadlines for lodging employment tribunal claims to protect his position or seek redress.

A complex issue?

Some 40 per cent of referrals to the GSCC involve allegations of inappropriate relations, with social workers accused of crossing professional boundaries in their work with service users. This can be a complex area. For example, hugging a service user may be appropriate in one context (say, when a new resident arrives in a residential home), but completely inappropriate in another. A good test might be whether you as a social worker (or indeed as a nurse or doctor) would be comfortable talking about your actions in supervision.

(Doel et al., 2009; GSCC guidance (GSCC, 2011b) comprehensively addresses such issues)

Regulators and poor practice

If your alleged misconduct or poor practice is serious, then your employer will report you to the appropriate regulator. Unfortunately, this sanction is sometimes misused by employers, and regulators themselves have been criticised for their own governance and practices (see Chapter 1) (Healthcare Commission, 2007a; Council for Healthcare Regulatory Excellence, 2008, 2009; Francis, 2010). Professional regulation exists to protect the interests of the public. Regulators require you to be fit to practise, such that you have the skills, knowledge, good health and good character to do your job safely and effectively. Referrals to regulators such as the GMC, NMC and Health Professions Council may be made by employers, employees or the public. The precise processes differ between regulators, but there are some common strands.

Should you face that sanction, it is essential you urgently take advice. You may also wish to refer to professional regulators those senior staff who have failed to comply with their own code in the practices which they may have permitted, encouraged or ignored.

C H A P T E R   S U M M A R Y

After reading this chapter, you should understand how to raise concerns effectively, either individually or collectively, about the environment of care, including standards of care and the rights of patients and service users, the safety of yourself and those you work with, including students and trainees, illegal activities or other matters of public interest.

You should also understand how to assist patients and service users or their carers and relatives to raise concerns about the environment of care, including standards of care and the rights of patients and service users, illegal activities or other matters of public interest.

You should also know what to do if your own practice or that of your colleagues falls below the standards it is reasonable to expect a competent professional to meet.

You should know what to do if you or others raising concerns are subjected to less favourable treatment as result of raising concerns or assisting others to do so, or if the management response to your raising concerns is to make allegations about you or discipline you.

Notes

1 You can find useful practical materials linked to this book on the Sage/Learning Matters website. Point your browser to **www.uk.sagepub.com/books/Book238690** (please note that this is case sensitive), and click on the 'sample materials' tab. Available on the site are:

- further advice on writing effective letters;

- some model letters you can download;

- further advice on getting the most out of meetings;

- advice on making the most of your trade union membership;

- advice on conducting a staff survey;

- advice on how to raise concerns as a student.

2 Useful examples of successful campaigns online are:

- **www.endchildpoverty.org.uk/london/campaigns/campaigners-toolkits-69**

- **www.peopleandplanet.org.uk/unis/gg/campaignskills**

Bibliography

ACAS (2009) *Disciplinary and Grievance Procedures*. London: The Stationery Office.

ACAS (2010) *Bullying and Harassment at Work: Guidance for Employees*. London: The Stationery Office.

Ackerman, B (2011) Statutory framework for practice. In Macdonald, S and Magill-Cuerden, J (eds) *Mayes' Midwifery*, 14th edition. Edinburgh: Baillière Tindall Elsevier.

Action on Elder Abuse (2006) *Adult Protection Data Collection and Reporting Requirements: Conclusions and Recommendations from a Two Year Study into Adult Protection Recording Systems in England*. London: Action on Elder Abuse.

Adams, G and Balfour, D (1998) *Unmasking Administrative Evil*. London: Sage.

Age UK (2011) *A Snapshot of Ageism in the UK and Across Europe*. London: Age UK.

Audit Commission (1999) *Setting the Record Straight. A Study of Hospital Medical Records*. London: Audit Commission.

Audit Commission (2005) *Governing Partnerships: Bridging the Accountability Gap*. London: Audit Commission.

Audit Commission (2008) *Are We Getting There? Improving Governance and Resource Management in Children's Trusts*. London: Audit Commission.

Ayre, P and Preston-Shoot, M (eds) (2010) *Children's Services at the Crossroads: A Critical Evaluation of Contemporary Policy for Practice*. Lyme Regis: Russell House Publishing.

Baginsky, M, Moriarty, J, Manthorpe, J, Stevens, M, MacInnes, T and Nagendran, T (2010) *Social Workers' Workload Survey – Messages from the Frontline. Findings from the 2009 Survey and Interviews with Senior Managers*. London: Department for Children, Schools and Families.

Balloch, S, McLean, J and Fisher, M (1999) *Social Services: Working under Pressure*. Bristol: Policy Press.

Banks, S (2005) The ethical practitioner in formation: issues of courage, competence and commitment. *Social Work Education*, 24(7): 737–753.

Banks, S (2010) Integrity in professional life: issues of conduct, commitment and capacity. *British Journal of Social Work*, 40(7): 2168–2184.

Bates, N, Immins, T, Parker, J, Keen, S, Rutter, L, Brown, K and Zsiog, S (2010) 'Baptism of fire': the first year in the life of a newly qualified social worker. *Social Work Education*, 29(2): 152–170.

Bichard, M (2004) *The Bichard Inquiry Report*. London: The Stationery Office.

Bilson, A (2007) Promoting compassionate concern in social work: reflections on ethics, biology and love. *British Journal of Social Work*, 37(8): 1371–1386.

Blom-Cooper, L (1985) *A Child in Trust* (Beckford Report). London Borough of Brent.

Boorman, S (2009) *NHS Health and Well-Being. Final Report*. London: Department of Health.

Borrill, C, Carletta, J, Carter, A, Dawson, J, Garrod, S, Rees, A, Richards, A, Shapiro, D and West, M (2001) *The Effectiveness of Health Care Teams in the NHS*. Aston Centre for Health Service Organisational Research, University of Aston; Human Communications Research Centre, Universities of Glasgow and Edinburgh; Psychological Therapies Research Centre, University of Leeds.

Boylan, J and Dalrymple, J (2011) Advocacy, social justice and children's rights. *Practice*, 23(1): 19–30.

Branch, W (2000) Supporting the moral development of medical students. *Journal of General Internal Medicine*, 15(7): 503–508.

Braye, S and Preston-Shoot, M (1999) Accountability, administrative law and social work practice: redressing or reinforcing the power imbalance? *Journal of Social Welfare and Family Law*, 21(3): 235–256.

Braye, S and Preston-Shoot, M (2006) *Teaching, Learning and Assessment of Law in Social Work Education: Resource Guide*. London: Social Care Institute for Excellence.

Braye, S and Preston-Shoot, M (2007) *Law and Social Work E-Learning Resources*. London: Social Care Institute for Excellence. **www.scie.org.uk/publications/elearning**

Braye, S and Preston-Shoot, M (2009) *Practising Social Work Law*. 3rd edition. Basingstoke: Palgrave Macmillan.

Braye, S, Orr, D and Preston-Shoot, M (2011) *The Governance of Adult Safeguarding: Findings from Research into Adult Safeguarding Boards*. London: SCIE.

Braye, S, Preston-Shoot, M and Thorpe, A (2007) Beyond the classroom: learning social work law in practice. *Journal of Social Work*, 7(3): 322–340.

British Association of Social Workers (2011) *BASW Survey Reveals 'Extreme Abuse' in Care Homes*. Birmingham: British Association of Social Workers. Media Release, 11 August.

British Institute of Human Rights and the Department of Health (2007) *Human Rights in Health Care – A Framework for Local Action*. London: Department of Health.

Broad, B (2005) Young people leaving care: implementing the Children (leaving Care) Act 2000? *Children and Society*, 19, 371–384.

Brooker, C (2001) A decade of evidence-based training for work with people with serious mental health problems: progress in the development of psychosocial interventions. *Journal of Mental Health*, 10(1): 17–31.

Butler-Sloss, E (1988) *Report of the Inquiry into Child Abuse in Cleveland*. London: HMSO.

Calkin, S (2011) Three quarters of nurses fear for their patients' safety. *Nursing Times*, 19 September.

Cantrill, P (2009) *Serious Case Review in Respect of Q Family*. Sheffield Safeguarding Children Board and Lincolnshire Safeguarding Children Board.

Cantrill, P, Foster, E, Lane, P and Pate, R (2010) *Report of the Independent Inquiry into the Colin Norris Incidents at Leeds Teaching Hospitals NHS Trust in 2002*. Leeds: Yorkshire and the Humber SHA.

Care Council for Wales (2002) *Codes of Practice for Social Care Workers and Employers of Social Care Workers*. Cardiff: Care Council for Wales.

Care Council for Wales (2011) *Annual Report and Accounts 2010–11*. Cardiff: Care Council for Wales.

Care Quality Commission (CQC) (2009a) *Investigation into West London Mental Health NHS Trust*. London: Care Quality Commission.

CQC (2009b) *Safeguarding Children: A Review of Arrangements in the NHS for Safeguarding Children*. London: Care Quality Commission.

CQC (2010) *Essential Standards of Quality and Safety*. London: Care Quality Commission.

CQC (2011a) *CQC Publish First of Detailed Reports into Dignity and Nutrition for Older People*. London: Care Quality Commission. Media release, 26 May.

CQC (2011b) *Whistleblowing: Guidance for Providers Who are Registered with the Care Quality Commission*. CQC: London.

Care Quality Commission and Equality and Human Rights Commission (CQC and EHRC) (2011) *Equality and Human Rights in the Essential Standards of Quality and Safety: Equality and Human Rights in Outcomes.* London and Manchester: Care Quality Commission and Equality and Human Rights Commission.

Carson, G (2010) Bullying in the workplace. *Community Care*, 18 March.

Changing Lives Practice Governance Group (2011) *Practice Governance Framework: Responsibility and Accountability in Social Work Practice.* Edinburgh: The Scottish Government.

Chief Inspectors (2008) *Safeguarding Children: The Third Joint Chief Inspectors' Report on Arrangements to Safeguard Children.* London: The Stationery Office.

Children's Commissioner for Wales (2003) *Telling Concerns. Report of the Children's Commissioner for Wales' Review of the Operation of Complaints and Representations and Whistleblowing Procedures and Arrangements for the Provision of Children's Advocacy Services.* Swansea: Children's Commissioner for Wales.

Children's Workforce Development Council (2007) *Providing Effective Supervision. A Workforce Development Tool including a Unit of Competence and Supporting Guidance.* Leeds: Children's Workforce Development Council and Skills for Care.

Coffey, M, Dughill, L and Tattersall, A (2009) Working in the public sector: a case study of social services. *Journal of Social Work*, 9(4): 420–442.

Commission for Social Care Inspection (CSCI) (2007) *Inspection of Services for People with Learning Disabilities: Cornwall County Council.* London: Commission for Social Care Inspection.

CSCI (2008a) *Putting People First: Equality and Diversity Matters 1. Providing Appropriate Services for Lesbian, Gay and Bisexual and Transgender People.* London: Commission for Social Care Inspection.

CSCI (2008b) *Putting People First: Equality and Diversity Matters 2. Providing Appropriate Services for Black and Minority Ethnic People.* London: Commission for Social Care Inspection.

CSCI (2008c) *Experts by Experience. The Benefit of Experience: Involving People who Use Services in Inspections.* London: Commission for Social Care Inspection.

CSCI (2009) *Putting People First: Equality and Diversity Matters 3. Achieving Disability Equality in Social Care Services.* London: Commission for Social Care Inspection.

Commission for Social Care Inspection (CSCI) and Healthcare Commission (2006) *Joint Investigation into the Provision of Services for People with Learning Disabilities at Cornwall Partnership NHS Trust.* London: Commission for Healthcare Audit and Inspection.

Cordingley, L, Hyde, C, Peters, S, Vernon, B and Bundy, C (2007) Undergraduate medical students' exposure to clinical ethics: a challenge to the development of professional behaviours? *Medical Education*, 41(12): 1202–1209.

Council for Healthcare Regulatory Excellence (2008) *Special Report to the Minister of State for Health Services on the Nursing and Midwifery Council.* London: CHRE.

Council for Healthcare Regulatory Excellence (2009) *Report and Recommendations to the Secretary of State for Health on the Conduct Function of the General Social Care Council.* London: CHRE.

Cousins, C (2010) 'Treat me don't beat me' … exploring supervisory games and their effect on poor performance management. *Practice*, 22(5): 281–292.

Critical Care Programme Modernisation Agency (2003) *Allied Health Professionals and Healthcare Scientists Critical Care Staffing Guidance. A Guideline for AHP and HCS Staffing Levels.* London: Intensive Care Society Standards Committee.

Department for Constitutional Affairs (2007) *Mental Capacity Act 2005: Code of Practice.* London: Department for Constitutional Affairs/The Stationery Office.

Department for Education (2010) *Working Together to Safeguard Children: A Guide to Inter-Agency Working to Safeguard and Promote the Welfare of Children.* London: The Stationery Office.

Department for Education and Skills (DfES) (2005) *Statutory Guidance on the Roles and Responsibilities of the Lead Member for Children's Services and the Director of Children's Services.* London: DfES.

Department of Health (DH) (1990) *Community Care in the Next Decade and Beyond: Policy Guidance.* London: HMSO.

DH (1999) *Caldicott Guardians. HSC 1999/012.* London: DH.

DH (2000a) *No Secrets. Guidance on Developing and Implementing Multi-Agency Policies and Procedures to Protect Vulnerable Adults from Abuse.* London: The Stationery Office.

DH (2000b) *Framework for the Assessment of Children in Need and their Families.* London: HMSO.

DH (2000c) *Data Protection Act: Guidance to Social Services.* London: DH.

DH (2002a) *Children's Homes. National Minimum Standards. Children's Homes Regulations.* London: The Stationery Office.

DH (2002b) *Fair Access to Care Services. Guidance on Eligibility Criteria for Adult Social Care.* London: DH.

DH (2003) *Confidentiality: NHS Code of Practice.* London: DH.

DH (2006a) *Our Health, Our Care, Our Say.* London: The Stationery Office.

DH (2006b) *Statutory Guidance on the Strategic Chief Officer Post of Director of Adult Social Services.* London: DH.

DH (2006c). *Best Practice Guidance on the Role of the Director of Adult Social Services.* London: DH.

DH (2006d) *Records Management: NHS Code of Practice.* London: DH.

DH (2007) *Duty to Involve Patients Strengthened. Briefing on Section 242 of NHS Act 2006.* London: DH.

DH (2008) *Code of Practice: Mental Health Act 1983.* London: The Stationery Office.

DH (2009a) *Listening, Responding, Improving. A Guide to Better Customer Care.* London: DH.

DH (2009b) *Making Decisions: The Independent Mental Capacity Advocate (IMCA) Service.* London: Office of the Public Guardian.

DH (2010) *Handbook to the NHS Constitution.* London: DH.

DH (2011a) *The Government's Response to the Recommendations in Front Line Care: The Report of the Prime Minister's Commission on the Future of Nursing and Midwifery in England.* London: DH.

DH (2011b) *Enabling Excellence. Autonomy and Accountability for Healthcare Workers, Social Workers and Social Care Workers.* London: The Stationery Office.

DH (2011c) *Implementing a 'Duty of Candour'; A New Contractual Requirement on Providers. Proposals for Consultation.* London: DH.

Department of Health, Social Services and Public Safety (2004) *Good Management, Good Records. Guidelines for Managing Records in Health and Personal Social Services Organisations in Northern Ireland.* Belfast: Department of Health, Social Services and Public Safety.

Department of Health, Social Services and Public Safety (2008) *Caseload Management Model. Proposed Guidance for Implementing the Model across Family and Child Care Services within the Northern Ireland Health and Social Care Trusts.* Belfast: Department of Health, Social Services and Public Safety.

Dimond, B (2011) Law and the midwife. In Macdonald, S and Magill-Cuerden, J (eds), *Mayes' Midwifery,* 14th edition. Edinburgh: Baillière Tindall Elsevier.

Disability Rights Commission (2006) *Equal Treatment: Closing the Gap. A Formal Investigation into Physical Health Inequalities Experienced by People with Learning Disabilities and/or Mental Health Problems.* London: Disability Rights Commission.

Doel, M, Allmark, P, Conway, P, Cowburn, M, Flynn, M, Nelson, P and Tod, A (2009) *Professional Boundaries: Research Report.* London: General Social Care Council.

Dombeck, M and Olsan, T (2007) Ethics and the social responsibility of institutions regarding resource allocation in health and social care: a US perspective. In Leathard, A and McLaren, S (eds), *Ethics: Contemporary Challenges in Health and Social Care.* Bristol: Policy Press.

Drakeford, M (1996) Education for culturally sensitive practice. In Jackson, S and Preston-Shoot, M (eds), *Educating Social Workers in a Changing Policy Context.* London: Whiting and Birch.

Drury-Hudson, J (1999) Decision-making in child protection: the use of theoretical, empirical and procedural knowledge by novices and experts and implications for fieldwork placement. *British Journal of Social Work*, 29(1): 147–169.

Duffy, J and Collins, M (2010) Macro impacts on caseworker decision-making in child welfare: a cross-national comparison. *European Journal of Social Work*, 13(1): 35–54.

Dunning, J (2011) Home care staff face worsening pay and reduced safety. *Community Care*, 6 September.

Dunworth, M and Kirwan, P (2009) Ethical decision-making in two care homes. *Practice*, 21(4): 241–258.

Dwyer, S (2009) The good news and the bad news for frail older people. *Practice*, 21(4): 273–289.

Ellis, P (2004) Have changes in the context of doctors' work altered the concept of the professional in medicine? *Medical Teacher*, 26(6): 529–533.

Equality and Human Rights Commission (EHRC) (2011a) *Inquiry Reveals Failure to Protect the Rights of Older People Receiving Care at Home.* London: Equality and Human Rights Commission.

EHRC (2011b) *Making Fair Financial Decisions.* London: Equality and Human Rights Commission.

EHRC (2011c) *The Essential Guide to the Public Sector Equality Duty. Equality Act 2010 Guidance for English Public Bodies (and Non Devolved Bodies in Scotland and Wales).* London: Equality and Human Rights Commission.

EHRC Scotland (2011) *Meeting the Public Sector Equality Duty in Scotland: Interim Guidance for Scottish Public Authorities on Meeting the General Duty.* Glasgow: Equality and Human Rights Commission Scotland.

Estyn and Care and Social Services Inspectorate Wales (CSSIW) (2011) *Joint Investigation into the Handling and Management of Allegations of Professional Abuse and the Arrangements for Safeguarding and Protecting Children in Education Services in PembrokeshireCounty Council.* Cardiff: The Stationery Office.

Flynn, M (2004) Challenging poor practice, abusive practice and inadequate complaints procedures: a personal narrative. *Journal of Adult Protection*, 6(3): 34–44.

Flynn, M (2006) Joint investigation into the provision of services for people with learning disabilities at Cornwall Partnership NHS Trust. *Journal of Adult Protection*, 8(3): 28–32.

Flynn, M (2011)*Executive Summary: Serious Case Review re 'Ann'.* Sheffield: Sheffield Adults Safeguarding Partnership Board.

Ford, S (2011) Lansley unveils plan for voluntary registration of HCAs. *Nursing Times*, 15 November.

Francis, R (2010) *Independent Inquiry into Care Provided by Mid Staffordshire NHS Foundation Trust January 2005 – March 2009.* London: The Stationery Office.

Furness, S (2006) Recognising and addressing elder abuse in care homes: views from residents and managers. *Journal of Adult Protection*, 8(1): 33–49.

Fyson, R and Kitson, D (2010) Human rights and social wrongs: issues in safeguarding adults with learning disabilities. *Practice*, 22(5): 309–320.

Galpin, D (2010) Policy and the protection of older people from abuse. *Journal of Social Welfare and Family Law*, 32(3): 247–255.

General Medical Council (GMC) (2008) *Good Practice in Prescribing Medicines – Guidance for Doctors*. London: General Medical Council.

GMC (2009) *Tomorrow's Doctors. Outcomes and Standards for Undergraduate Medical Education*. London: General Medical Council.

General Social Care Council (GSCC) (2002) *Codes of Practice for Social Care Workers and Employers*. London: General Social Care Council.

GSCC (2009) *Social Worker Whistle Blowing Goes Unheard*. London: General Social Care Council. Media Release, 9 September.

GSCC (2011a) *Annual Report 2010–11*. London: General Social Care Council.

GSCC (2011b) *Professional Boundaries: Guidance for social workers*. London: General Social Care Council

General Teaching Council (GTC), GSCC and NMC (2007) *Values for Integrated Working with Children and Young People*. London: General Teaching Council.

Giordano, A and Street, D (2009) Challenging provider performance: developing policy to improve the quality of care to protect vulnerable adults. *Journal of Adult Protection*, 11(2):5–12.

Goldie, J, Schwartz, L, McConnachie, A and Morrison, J (2003) Students' attitudes and potential behaviour with regard to whistle blowing as they pass through a modern medical curriculum. *Medical Education*, 37, 368–375.

Goldie, J, Schwartz, L, McConnachie, A and Morrison, J (2004) The impact of a modern medical curriculum on students' proposed behaviour on meeting ethical dilemmas. *Medical Education*, 38(9): 942–949.

Gordon, J and Cooper, B (2010) Talking knowledge – practising knowledge: a critical best practice approach to how social workers understand and use knowledge in practice. *Practice*, 22(4): 245–257.

Green, J (2009) The deformation of professional formation: managerial targets and the undermining of professional judgement. *Ethics and Social Welfare*, 3(2): 115–130.

Gulland, J (2009) Independence in complaints procedures: lessons from community care. *Journal of Social Welfare and Family Law*, 31(1): 59–72.

Health and Safety Executive (HSE) (1993) *The Management of Occupational Health Services for Healthcare Staff*. Bootle: HSE.

HSE (2002) *Use of Contractors: A Joint Responsibility*. Bootle: HSE.

HSE (2003) *Slips and Trips in the Health Services*. Information sheet no. 2. Bootle: HSE.

HSE (2006a) *Five Steps to Risk Assessment*. Bootle: HSE.

HSE (2006b) *Latex and You*. Bootle: HSE.

HSE (2006c) *Violence at Work. A Guide for Employers*. Bootle: HSE.

HSE (2007) *Incident at Work?* Bootle: HSE.

HSE (2008) *Consulting Employees on Health and Safety. A Brief Guide to the Law*. Bootle: HSE.

HSE (2009a) *How to Tackle Work-Related Stress. A Guide for Employers on Making the Management Standards Work*. Bootle: HSE.

HSE (2009b) *Working Alone. Health and Safety Guidance on the Risks of Lone Working*. Bootle: HSE.

HSE (2011) *Violence in Health and Social Care*. Bootle: HSE.

Health Professions Council (HPC) (2008) *Standards of Conduct, Performance and Ethics*. London: Health Professions Council.

HPC (2011) *How to Raise and Escalate a Concern*. London: Health Professions Council. **www.hpc-uk.org/registrants/ raisingconcerns/howto**

Health Service Ombudsman (2003) *NHS Funding for Long-Term Care*. London: The Stationery Office.

Healthcare Commission (2007a) *Investigation into Outbreaks of Clostridium Difficile at Maidstone and Tunbridge Wells NHS Trust*. London: Commission for Healthcare Audit and Inspection.

Healthcare Commission (2007b) *Investigation into the Service for People with Learning Disabilities Provided by Sutton and Merton PCT*. London: Commission for Healthcare Audit and Inspection.

Healthcare Commission (2007c) *Safeguarding Children and Young People: A Shared Responsibility*. London: Commission for Healthcare Audit and Inspection.

Healthcare Commission (2007d) *A Life Like No Other. A National Audit of Specialist Inpatient Healthcare Services for People with Learning Difficulties in England*. London: Commission for Healthcare Audit and Inspection.

Healthcare Commission (2008) *Towards Better Births: A Review of Maternity Services in England*. London: Commission for Healthcare Audit and Inspection.

Healthcare Commission (2009) *Tackling the Challenge: Promoting Race Equality in the NHS in England*. London: Commission for Healthcare Audit and Inspection.

HM Government (2010) *Building a Safe and Confident Future: Implementing the Recommendations of the Social Work Task Force*. London: Department for Children, Schools and Families.

Holt, J (2006) *Exploring Learning and Teaching Ethics in the Nursing Curriculum*. York: Higher Education Academy, Health Sciences and Practice.

Horwath, J (2000) Child care with gloves on: protecting children and young people in residential care. *British Journal of Social Work*, 30(2): 179–191.

Horwath, J (2010) Rearing a toothless tiger? From area child protection committee to local safeguarding children board. *Journal of Children's Services*, 5(3): 37–47.

House of Commons Committee of Public Accounts (2003) *A Safer Place to Work – Protecting the NHSHospital and Ambulance Staff from Violence and Aggression*. London: HMSO.

House of Commons Health Committee (2004) *Elder Abuse. Session 2003–4: Volume 1*. London: The Stationery Office.

House of Commons Health Committee (2009a) *Patient Safety. Sixth Report of Session 2008–9: Volume 1*. London: The Stationery Office.

House of Commons Health Committee (2009b) *Health Inequalities. Third Report of Session 2008–9: Volume 1*. London: The Stationery Office.

Hussein, S, Martineau, S, Stevens, M, Manthorpe, J, Rapaport, J and Harris, J (2009a) Accusations of misconduct among staff working with vulnerable adults in England and Wales: their claims of mitigation to the barring authority. *Journal of Social Welfare and Family Law*, 31(1): 17–32.

Hussein, S, Moriarty, J and Manthorpe, J (2009b) *Variations in Progression of Social Work Students in England. Using Student Data to Help Promote Achievement: Undergraduate Full-Time Students' Progression on the Social Work Degree*. London: Kings College, Social Care Workforce Research Unit.

Information Commissioner (2004) *Employment Practices Data Protection Code. Part 4: Information about a Worker's Health.* Wilmslow: Information Commissioner's Office.

Institute of Biomedical Science and the Royal College of Pathologists (n.d.) *Principles of Good Practice for Biomedical Scientist Involvement in Histopathological Dissection.*

Institute of Medical Ethics (2009) *Draft Revised Core Curriculum for Medical Ethics and Law.* London: Institute of Medical Ethics.

Jack, G and Donnellan, H (2010) Recognising the person within the developing professional: tracking the early careers of newly qualified child care social workers in three local authorities in England. *Social Work Education*, 29(3): 305–318.

Jenness, V and Grattet, R (2005) The law-in-between: the effects of organizational perviousness on the policing of hate crime. *Social Problems*, 52(3): 337–359.

Jones, S (2011) Ethics and midwifery practice. In Macdonald, S and Magill-Cuerden, J (eds), *Mayes' Midwifery*, 14th edition. Edinburgh: Baillière Tindall Elsevier.

Karban, K and Frost, N (1998) Training for residential care: assessing the impact of the Residential Child Care Initiative. *Social Work Education*, 17(3): 287–300.

Kennedy, I (2001) *Learning from Bristol. The Report of the Public Inquiry into Children's Heart Surgery at the Bristol Royal Infirmary 1984–1995.* London: The Stationery Office.

Kinman, G and Grant, L (2011) Exploring stress resilience in trainee social workers: the role of emotional and social competencies. *British Journal of Social Work*, 41(2): 261–275.

Kline, R (2003) *The Duty of Care. A Handbook to Assist Health Care Staff Carrying Out their Duty of Care to Patients, Colleagues and Themselves.* London: Unison.

Kline, R (2009) *What If? Social Care Professionals and the Duty of Care. A Practical Guide to Staff Duties and Rights.* Wakefield: Association of Professionals in Education and Children's Trusts.

Kline, R (2011) *The Social Work Reform Board Recommendations and an Equality Impact Assessment.* (Unpublished.)

Kroll, L, Singleton, A, Collier, J and Rees Jones, I (2008) Learning not to take it seriously: junior doctors' accounts of error. *Medical Education*, 42, 982–990.

Laming, H (2003) *The Victoria Climbié Inquiry: Report of an Inquiry by Lord Laming.* London: HMSO.

Laming, H (2009) *The Protection of Children in England: A Progress Report.* London: HMSO.

Leslie, A (1997) *Practice, Planning and Partnership. The Lessons to be Learned from the Case of Susan Patricia Joughlin.* Isle of Man Government.

Local Government Association (2010) *Workforce Survey England.* London: LGA.

Local Government Group, Association of Directors of Children's Services and Society of Local Authority Chief Executives (2011) *Towards Excellence for Children: Sector-led Improvement and Support in Children's Services.* London: LGG.

Local Government Ombudsman (LGO) (2002) *Report Summaries: Social Services.* London: Local Government Ombudsman.

LGO (2007) *Report Summaries: Social Services.* London: Local Government Ombudsman.

LGO (2008) *Injustice in Residential Care: A Joint Report by the Local Government Ombudsman and the Health Service Ombudsman for England. Investigations into Complaints Against Buckinghamshire County Council and Oxfordshire and Buckinghamshire Mental Health Partnership.* London: HMSO.

LGO and PHSO (2009) *Six Lives: The Provision of Public Services to People with Learning Disability.* London: The Stationery Office.

Maben, J (2010) Long days come with a high price for staff and patients. *Nursing Times*, 15 January.

Machin, S (1998) Swimming against the tide: a social worker's experience of a secure hospital. In G Hunt (ed.), *Whistleblowing in the Social Services. Public Accountability and Professional Practice*. London: Arnold.

Macpherson, W (1999) *The Stephen Lawrence Enquiry: Report of an Enquiry by Sir William MacPherson of Cluny*. London: The Stationery Office.

Mansell, J, Beadle-Brown, J, Cambridge, P, Milne, A and Whelton, B (2009) Adult protection: incidence of referrals, nature and risk factors in two English local authorities. *Journal of Social Work*, 9(1): 23–38.

Manthorpe, J and Martineau, S (2011) Serious Case Reviews in adult safeguarding in England: an analysis of a sample of reports. *British Journal of Social Work*, 41(2): 224–241.

Manthorpe, J, Cornes, M, Moriarty, J, Rapaport, J, Iliffe, S, Wilcock, J, Clough, R, Bright, L and OPRSI (2007) An inspector calls: adult protection in the context of the NSFOP review. *Journal of Adult Protection*, 9(1):4–14.

Manthorpe, J, Rapaport, J and Stanley, N (2009) Expertise and experience: people with experiences of using services and carers' views of the Mental Capacity Act 2005. *British Journal of Social Work*, 39(5): 884–900.

Marsden, E and Mechen, D (2008) *An Independent Review into the Board Leadership of Maidstone and Tunbridge Wells NHS Trust*. London: Verita.

Marsh, P and Triseliotis, J (1996) *Ready to Practise? Social Workers and Probation Officers: Their Training and First Year in Work*. Aldershot: Avebury.

Marsland, D, Oakes, P and White, C (2007) Abuse in care? The identification of early indicators of the abuse of people with learning disabilities in residential settings. *Journal of Adult Protection*, 9(4):6–20.

McDonald, A, Postle, K and Dawson, C (2008) Barriers to retaining and using professional knowledge in local authority social work practice with adults in the UK. *British Journal of Social Work*, 38(7): 1370–1387.

Ministry of Justice (2006) *Human Rights: Human Lives: A Handbook for Public Authorities*. London: Ministry of Justice.

Morris, S (2011) Winterbourne View staff charged with neglect and ill-treatment. *The Guardian*, 28 November.

Morrison, T (2007) Emotional intelligence, emotion and social work: context, characteristics, complications and contribution. *British Journal of Social Work*, 37(2): 245–263.

Munro, E (2011) *The Munro Review of Child Protection: Final Report, A Child-Centred System*. London: The Stationery Office.

National Leadership Council (2010) *Clinical Leadership Competency Framework Project. Report on Findings*. London: NHS Institute for Innovation and Improvement.

National Patient Safety Agency (2005) *Annual Report and Accounts 2004–2005*. London: HMSO.

National Youth Agency (NYA) (2004) *Ethical Conduct in Youth Work. A Statement of Values and Principles from the National Youth Agency*. Leicester: National Youth Agency.

Newton, J and Browne, L (2008) How fair is fair access to care? *Practice*, 20(4): 235–249.

NHS Constitution State of Readiness Group (2009) *Final Report*. London: Department of Health.

NHS Future Forum (2011) *Summary Report on Proposed Changes to the NHS*. London: Department of Health.

Northern Ireland Social Care Council (2002) *Codes of Practice for Social Care Workers and Employers of Social Care Workers*. Belfast: Northern Ireland Social Care Council.

Nursing and Midwifery Council (NMC) (2006) *An NMC Guide for Students of Nursing and Midwifery*. London: NMC.

NMC (2007) *Standards for Medicines Management*. London: NMC.

NMC (2008a) *The Code: Standards of Conduct, Performance and Ethics for Nurses and Midwives*. London: NMC.

NMC (2008b) *Delegation*. London: NMC.

NMC (2010a) *Raising and Escalating Concerns: Guidance for Nurses and Midwives*. London: NMC.

NMC (2010b) *Standards for Pre-Registration Nursing Education*. London: NMC.

NMC (2010c) *Guidance on Professional Conduct for Nursing and Midwifery Students*. London: NMC.

NMC (2010d) *Record Keeping: Guidance for Nurses and Midwives*. London: NMC.

NMC (2011a) *Annual Report and Accounts 2010–2011*. London: The Stationery Office.

NMC (2011b) *Social Networking Sites. Advice Sheet*. London: NMC.

O'Rourke, L (2009) Practitioners demand more guidance and training in record-keeping. *Community Care*, 16 April.

Office for Public Management, and Chartered Institute of Public Finance and Accountancy (OPM and CIPFA) (2004) *The Good Governance Standard for Public Services*. London: Independent Commission on Good Governance in Public Services (Office for Public Management/Chartered Institute of Public Finance and Accountancy/Joseph Rowntree Foundation).

Office of Public Sector Information (OPSI) (2010) *Safeguarding the Future: A Review of the Youth Justice Board's Governance and Operating Arrangements*. London: Office of Public Sector Information.

Ofsted (2009) *Learning Lessons from Serious Case Reviews: Year 2*. Manchester: Ofsted.

Orme, J and Rennie, G (2006) The role of registration in ensuring ethical practice. *International Social Work*, 49(3): 333–344.

Parliamentary and Health Service Ombudsman (PHSO) (2010) *Listening and Learning: The Ombudsman's Review of Complaint Handling by the NHS in England*. London: The Stationery Office.

PHSO (2011) *Care and Compassion? Report of the Health Services Ombudsman on Ten Investigations into NHS Care of Older People*. London: The Stationery Office.

Patients Association (2011) *We've Been Listening, Have You Been Learning*? London: The Patients Association.

Payne, M (2006) *What is Professional Social Work?* Bristol: Policy Press.

Payne, M (2007) Performing as a 'wise person' in social work practice. *Practice*, 19(2): 85–96.

Pemberton, S and Tombs, S (2008) *Whistleblowing and the Social Control of Organisational Harm*. London: British Academy.

Penhale, B (2002) Ethical dilemmas in charging for care: contrasting the views of social work and legal professionals. *Journal of Interprofessional Care*, 16(3): 235–247.

Perkins, N, Penhale, B, Reid, D, Pinkney, L, Hussein, S and Manthorpe, J (2007) Partnership means protection? Perceptions of the effectiveness of multi-agency working and the regulatory framework within adult protection in England and Wales. *Journal of Adult Protection*, 9(3): 9–23.

Peters, K, Luck, L, Hutchinson, M, Wilkes, L, Andrew, S and Jackson, D (2011) The emotional sequelae of whistleblowing: findings from a qualitative study. *Journal of Clinical Nursing*, 20(19/20): 2907–2914.

Phair, L and Heath, H (2010) Neglect of older people in formal care settings part one: new perspectives on definition and the nursing contribution to multi-agency safeguarding work. *Journal of Adult Protection*, 12(3): 5–13.

Pinkney, L, Penhale, B, Manthorpe, J, Perkins, N, Reid, D and Hussein, S (2008) Voices from the frontline: social work practitioners' perceptions of multi-agency working in adult protection in England and Wales. *Journal of Adult Protection*,10(4): 12–24.

Preston-Shoot, M (2000) What if? Using the law to uphold practice values and standards. *Practice*, 12(4): 49–63.

Preston-Shoot, M (2001) Regulating the road of good intentions. Observations on the relationship between policy, regulations and practice in social work. *Practice*, 13(4):5–20.

Preston-Shoot, M (2010a) Looking after social work practice in its organisational context: neglected and disconcerting questions. In Ayre, P and Preston-Shoot, M (eds), *Children's Services at the Crossroads: A Critical Evaluation of Contemporary Policy for Practice*. Lyne Regis: Russell House Publishing.

Preston-Shoot, M (2010b) On the evidence for viruses in social work systems: law, ethics and practice. *European Journal of Social Work*, 13(4): 465–482.

Preston-Shoot, M (2012) The secret curriculum. *Ethics and Social Welfare*, 6(1): 18–36.

Preston-Shoot, M and Kline, R (2009) *Memorandum of Written Evidence in House of Commons Children, Schools and Families Committee Training of Children and Families Social Workers. Seventh Report of Session 2008–09*. Volume II. London: The Stationery Office.

Preston-Shoot, M and McKimm, J (2010) Prepared for practice? Law teaching and assessment in UK medical schools. *Journal of Medical Ethics*, 36(11): 694–699.

Preston-Shoot, M and McKimm, J (2011) Towards effective outcomes in teaching, learning and assessment of law in medical education. *Medical Education*, 45, 339–346.

Preston-Shoot, M and McKimm, J (2011a) Tutor and student experiences of teaching and learning law in UK social work education. *Social Work Education* (advanced publication online).

Preston-Shoot, M and McKimm, J (2011b) Perceptions of readiness for legally literate practice: a longitudinal study of social work student views. *Social Work Education* (advanced publication online).

Preston-Shoot, M, McKimm, J, Kong, W M and Smith, S (2011) Readiness for legally literate medical practice? Student perceptions of their undergraduate medico-legal education. *Journal of Medical Ethics*, 37(10): 616–622.

Public Concern at Work (PCaW) (2008) *Public Concern at Work/Nursing Standard Whistleblowing Survey*. London: PCaW.

PCaW (2011) *Speaking Up for Vulnerable Adults: What the Whistleblowers Say*. London: PCaW.

Quality Assurance Agency (QAA) (2001) *Subject Benchmark Statement: Health Care Programmes*. Gloucester: QAA.

QAA (2002) *Subject Benchmark Statement: Medicine*. Gloucester: Quality Assurance Agency.

QAA (2008) *Subject Benchmark Statement: Social Work*. 2nd edition. Gloucester: QAA.

QAA (2009) *Subject Benchmark Statement: Youth and Community Work*. Gloucester: QAA.

Reder, P and Duncan, S (2003) Understanding communication in child protection networks. *Child Abuse Review*, 12, 82–100.

Richardson, B, Kitchen, G and Livingston, G (2002) The effect of education on knowledge and management of elder abuse: a randomized controlled trial. *Age and Ageing*, 31, 335–341.

Rodie, S (2008) Whistleblowing by students in practice learning settings: the student perspective. *Ethics and Social Welfare*, 2(1): 95–99.

Royal College of Nursing (RCN) (2003/2007) *Safeguarding Children and Young People – Every Nurse's Responsibility. Guidance for Nursing Staff*. London: RCN.

RCN (2005) *Confidentiality: Guidance for Occupational Health Nurses*. London: RCN.

RCN (2010) *RCN Policy Position: Evidence-Based Nurse Staffing Levels*. London: RCN.

Royal College of Nursing (RCN), Royal College of Speech and Language Therapists, the British Dietetic Association and the Chartered Society of Physiotherapy (2006) *Supervision, Accountability and Delegation of Activities to Support Workers. A Guide for Registered Practitioners and Support Workers*. London: RCN.

Santry, C (2009) Bullying: the 'corrosive' problem the NHS must address. *Health Service Journal*, 23 April.

Santry, C (2011) Protection for whistleblowers to become a contractual right. *Health Service Journal*, 18 October.

Scott, J and Hill, M (2006) *The Health of Looked After and Accommodated Children and Young People in Scotland. Messages from Research*. Edinburgh: Scottish Government.

Scottish Executive (2006) *Changing Lives. Report of the Recommendations made by the 21st Century Social Work Review Group for the Future of Social Services in Scotland*. Edinburgh: Scottish Executive.

Scottish Government (2008) *Records Management: NHS Code of Practice (Scotland)*. Edinburgh: Scottish Government.

Scottish Social Services Council (SSSC) (2009) *Codes of Practice for Social Services Workers and Employers*. Dundee: Scottish Social Services Council.

SSSC (2010) *Annual Report and Accounts 2009–2010*. Dundee: Scottish Social Services Council.

Sercombe, H (2010) *Youth Work Ethics*. London: Sage.

Sharpe, E, Moriarty, J, Stevens, M, Manthorpe, J and Hussein, S (2011) *Into the Workforce. Report from a Study of New Social Work Graduates Funded under the Department of Health Social Care Workforce Research Initiative*. London: Kings College London Social Care Workforce Research Unit.

Sheather, M (2011) *Serious Case Review concerning Parkfields Care Home*. Taunton: Somerset Safeguarding Adults Board.

Sheppard, D (1996) *Learning the Lessons*. 2nd edition. London: Zito Trust.

Shifrin, T (2003) Timeline: Margaret Hodge row. *The Guardian*, 19 November.

Skinner, K and Whyte, B (2004) Going beyond training: theory and practice in managing learning. *Social Work Education*, 23(4): 365–381.

Social Work Reform Board (2010) *Building a Safe and Confident Future: One Year On*. London: Department for Education.

Social Work Task Force (2009a) *First Report of the Social Work Task Force*. London: Department of Children, Schools and Families.

Social Work Task Force (2009b) *Building a Safe, Confident Future. The Final Report of the Social Work Task Force*. London: Department of Children, Schools and Families.

Spratt, T (2001) The influence of child protection orientation on child welfare practice. *British Journal of Social Work*, 31(6): 933–954.

Stevens, M and Manthorpe, J (2007) Barring 'inappropriate people'? The operation of a barring list of social care workers: an analysis of the first referrals to the Protection of Vulnerable Adults list. *Health and Social Care in the Community*, 15(4): 285–294.

Stevenson, O (1974) *Minority Report in DHSS Report of the Committee of Inquiry into the Care and Supervision Provided in relation to Maria Colwell*. London: HMSO.

Stirrat, G, Johnson, C, Gillon, R and Boyd, K (2010) Medical ethics and law for doctors of tomorrow: the 1998 Consensus Statement updated. *Journal of Medical Ethics*, 36, 55–60.

Stone, K, Traynor, M, Gould, D and Maben, J (2011) The management of poor performance in nursing and midwifery: a case for concern. *Journal of Nursing Management*, 19(6): 803–809.

Sullivan, M (2009) Social workers in community care: ideologies and interactions with older people. *British Journal of Social Work*, 39(7): 1306–1325.

Sykes, W and Groom, C (2011) *Older People's Experiences of Home Care in England*. Manchester: Equality and Human Rights Commission.

Taylor, N (2008) Obstacles and dilemmas in the delivery of direct payments to service users with poor mental health. *Practice*, 20(1): 43–55.

The Social Partnership Forum (2010) *Speaking up for a Healthy NHS*. London: Department of Health.

Trade Union Congress (TUC) (2007) *Bullying at Work. Guidance for Safety Representatives*. London: Trade Union Congress.

TUC (2010) *Hazards at Work. Organising for Safe and Healthy Workplaces*. London: Trade Union Congress.

TUC (2011) *The Union Effect. How Unions Make a Difference to Health and Safety*. London: Trade Union Congress.

UK Foundation Office (2007) *The Foundation Programme: Curriculum*. Cardiff: UK Foundation Office.

van Heugten, K (2011) Registration and social work education: a golden opportunity or a Trojan horse? *Journal of Social Work*, 11(2): 174–190.

Wardhaugh, J and Wilding, P (1993) Towards an explanation of the corruption of care. *Critical Social Policy*, 37, 4–31.

Waterhouse, R (2000) *Lost in Care: Report of the Tribunal of Inquiry into the Abuse of Children in Care in the Former County Areas of Gwynedd and Clwyd*. London: The Stationery Office.

Weingart, S, Wilson, R, Gibberd, R and Harrison, B (2000) Epidemiology of medical error. *BMJ*, 320 (7237): 774.

Welbourne, P (2010) Accountability. In Long, L-A, Roche, J and Stringer, D (eds), *The Law and Social Work: Contemporary Issues for Practice*, 2nd edition. Basingstoke: Palgrave Macmillan.

Welsh Assembly Government (2005) *Confidentiality: Code of Practice for Health and Social Care in Wales*. Cardiff: Welsh Assembly Government.

Welsh Assembly Government (2011a) *Sustainable Social Services for Wales: A Framework for Action*. Cardiff: Welsh Assembly Government.

Welsh Assembly Government (2011b) *Guidance on the Equality Duty for the Welsh Public Sector*. Cardiff: Welsh Assembly Government.

White, C, Holland, E, Marsland, D and Oakes, P (2003) The identification of environments and cultures that promote the abuse of people with intellectual disabilities: a review of the literature. *Journal of Applied Research in Intellectual Disabilities*, 16, 1–9.

Woods, M (2011) An ethic of care in nursing: past, present and future considerations. *Ethics and Social Welfare*, 5(3): 266–276.

Worsley, A, Richardson-Foster, H, Spandler, H and Pilgrim, D (2010) *We're Helping to Support Newly Qualified Social Workers. Research Report Examining Activity Supporting Newly Qualified Social Workers in the North West*. Preston: Skills for Care North West.

Index